Advances in Understanding Multilingualism: A Global Perspective

WARSCHAUER STUDIEN ZUR GERMANISTIK
UND ZUR ANGEWANDTEN LINGUISTIK

Herausgegeben von Sambor Grucza und Lech Kolago

BAND 24

Sambor Grucza / Magdalena Olpińska-Szkiełko / Piotr Romanowski (eds.)

Advances in Understanding Multilingualism: A Global Perspective

PETER LANG
EDITION

Bibliographic Information published by the Deutsche Nationalbibliothek
The Deutsche Nationalbibliothek lists this publication in the
Deutsche Nationalbibliografie; detailed bibliographic data is available in the
internet at http://dnb.d-nb.de.

This publication was financially supported by the University of Warsaw.

ISSN 2192-7820
ISBN 978-3-631-66761-3 (Print)
E-ISBN 978-3-653-06389-9 (E-Book)
DOI 10.3726/978-3-653-06389-9
© Peter Lang GmbH
Internationaler Verlag der Wissenschaften
Frankfurt am Main 2016
All rights reserved.
Peter Lang Edition is an Imprint of Peter Lang GmbH.

Peter Lang – Frankfurt am Main · Bern · Bruxelles · New York ·
Oxford · Warszawa · Wien

This publication has been peer reviewed.

www.peterlang.com

Contents

6   Contents

Editorial Note

Multilingualism, broadly understood as the knowledge and use of two or more languages by individuals or groups of individuals in their everyday lives, both private and professional, is increasingly acknowledged as an important issue of the contemporary world. Interest in the matters of multilingualism is growing rapidly in many areas such as research, politics, or education.

Typical questions asked in these areas include:

- the role of English and other (national) languages in the globalized context;
- the impact of bi- and multilingualism on the educational and social success of concerned individuals, especially immigrants;
- the increasing value of the "linguistic capital";
- the "destiny" of minority and heritage languages in the context of increasing mobility of the population and massive emigration;
- the best strategies of raising children in multilingual families and environments;
- the different ways people deal with language diversity in their environments;
- the best policies for promoting language diversity and lifelong (language) learning around the world.

In this book we combine some of the questions in a truly interdisciplinary perspective in order to try to provide an insight into the variety and diversity of research problems of multilingualism. This collection is divided into 10 chapters considering the selected matters from different points of view and gathering together empirical research from various fields. The authors of this volume represent universities and research centres from all over the world. Their scientific interests and experience, as well as their position in the scientific community, guarantee a highly informative and satisfying lecture.

In Chapter 1, Katja Andersen concentrates on multilingual practices in both formal and non-formal sectors of Luxembourgish early childhood education (i.e. up to 6 years of age). The author ascertains that there is no focus on multilingualism in the early childhood education in Luxembourg, which is rather surprising in a country with three official languages and where almost every second inhabitant has a nationality other than Luxembourgish. She also states that in a multilingual environment children do not automatically develop multilingualism and reflects what could be done to implement multilingual pedagogies in the daily practices of early childhood education.

Chapter 2, by Wai Meng Chan, focuses on the dynamic changes of the linguistic situation in Singapore that have taken place in the last 50 years (since the gaining of independence in 1965) as the results of the consequent and long-sighted language policy of the Singaporean government. The author proposes that Singapore's economic and social success can be attributed, at least in part, to the adoption of English "as the cornerstone of its national language planning". What consequences the English-knowing-bilingual educational policy has had for the other native languages of Singapore's inhabitants is one of the most interesting issues presented in this chapter.

The role of formal language instruction and education in language learning and its maintenance among its heritage speakers is the main issue of Lidija Cvikić, Jasna Novak Milić and Katarina Aladrović Slovaček's chapter, Chapter 3. In order to answer this question the authors examine the general language proficiency, attitudes towards language and culture and usage of language skills in daily life (e.g. listening to Croatian radio or music, reading on the Internet etc.) of Croatian emigrants and their descendants in 1st, 2nd, 3rd or even 4th generation around the word.

Kyria Finardi and Virag Csillagh in Chapter 4 analyze, referring to the theoretical framework of language economics – a relatively new branch of economics that examines the interrelationship between economic and linguistic phenomena – the linguistic diversity and changes of the national linguistic and cultural landscape in Switzerland under the influence of English as a lingua franca of the modern world. By focusing on the linguistic practices of the second largest Swiss University of Geneva and language skills among students at its four selected faculties the authors show that there are some significant and surprising developments in student's attitudes toward English in comparison with the official/national languages of Switzerland.

To what extent speakers of minority languages in New Zealand are passing their language on to their children is the main theme of Jeanette King and Una Cunningham's chapter, Chapter 5. The authors address the question of the circumstances under which intergenerational transmission of languages other than the three official languages in New Zealand might be successful with the aim of ascertaining how families who are raising or intend to raise the children as speakers of their heritage language can be supported.

Ana Cristina Neves's study, Chapter 6, investigates the linguistic landscape of Macau as a community that is not only multilingual but is also employing more than one writing system. In order to demonstrate the kinds of coexistence of different languages, especially the three main languages in Macau, i.e. Cantonese, English and Portuguese, and different writing systems (e.g. the Arabic and Chinese numbers, the romanized Cantonese etc.) she analyses a considerable number of signs displayed in shopping areas in Macau, such as advertising slogans, shop sign-boards or announcements. The main subjects of the analysis are the contents of the messages and their communication functions and the processes of trans-languaging, such as transliteration and translation.

The contribution of Michał B. Paradowski, Aleksandra Bator and Monika Michałowska, Chapter 7, centres on strategies applied by multilingual families in the process of raising the children. The authors introduce the theoretical back-ground and state of affairs in the field of bi- and multilingualism's research before proceeding with the presentation and discussion of the main results of their study into the effectiveness of selected methods parents of different nationalities employ if they wish to raise their children multilingually.

Stefania Scaglione and Sandro Caruana in Chapter 8 demonstrate a thorough review of data gathered through the MERIDIUM Project, an EU-founded Life Long Learning project, conducted from 2009 to 2011. In the focus of the investiga-tion stood five Southern European countries, i.e. Portugal, Spain, Italy, Slovenia and Malta, which have recently become popular immigration destination, and thus have experienced a significant and sudden increase of linguistic diversity. The authors discuss whether both educational policies and practices in these countries promote multilingualism (plurilingualism) and linguistic diversity efficiently. The study takes into account traditional minority languages spoken on their territory as well as foreign languages taught as compulsory subjects in general education and "new" minority languages of migrant groups and families.

Kutlay Yagmur in Chapter 9 examines how compatible are the language poli-cies of the European Union with actual institutional and educational practices in the EU member States. On the basis of the data collected through Language Rich Europe Project (2012) the author tries to establish whether the European policy to maintain and enhance linguistic diversity and multilingualism in Europe has been successfully implemented in the EU countries and regions. The outcomes of the LRE Project reviewed in this chapter excellently complement the findings discussed in Chapter 8.

The study presented in the final Chapter 10 by Eugen Zaretsky and Benjamin P. Lange aim at an identification of the geographical distribution of verbal skills of German preschoolers in Frankfurt/Main, as well as their error patterns and their language(-related) disorders and impairments. Statistical analyses of the col-lected data allowed the authors to identify the linguistically weakest and strongest districts of the city. The authors propose that there are statistically significant as-sociations between the scores of the language tests by children and variables that indicate lower or higher income of their families (e.g. size of the flats, number of family members, percentage of unemployed people and lone parents etc.).

Although some of the results can be accurately anticipated by the readers, there will be also same baffling conclusions of the study.

This cross-disciplinary volume will appeal to researchers, students and professionals engaged in the developing and shaping of language policies as well as educational policies on the local or even international level (EU). The editors sincerely hope that the findings of research presented in this collection might contribute to the better understanding of "multilingual matters" occurring in our contemporary, globalized, yet still very differentiated and diverse world.

Warsaw, January 2016   *Sambor Grucza*
                                          Magdalena Olpińska-Szkiełko
                                                  Piotr Romanowski

Katja Andersen
(University of Luxembourg)

Multilingualism and Multimodality in Luxembourgish Early Childhood Education

1. Research background

This pilot-study is placed in Luxembourg, the country with 549,700 inhabitants, of whom 45.3% are foreign nationals (status as of 2014, STATEC 2014: 9). The highest percentage of non-Luxembourgish inhabitants is from Portugal (16.5%), France (6.7%), Italy (3.4%), Belgium (3.3%) and Germany (2.3%) (STATEC 2014: 9). More than one third of the foreign nationals come from Portugal. In absolute numbers, there are 90,800 Portuguese inhabitants living in Luxembourg, which is approximately every sixth inhabitant. Almost every second inhabitant in Luxembourg has a nationality other than Luxembourgish. When compared to all the countries in the EU, Luxembourg is the second least populated country after Malta. At the same time, the percentage of foreign nationals in Luxembourg is the highest of all the EU countries (Eurostat 2015).

1.1 Language situation in the Luxembourgish educational system

The language situation in Luxembourg is diverse (MENJE 2014: 100). Next to the three official languages Luxembourgish, French and German, there are multiple languages used in daily life in Luxembourg, whether in the private, professional or educational sector. At the Luxembourgish *école fondamentale*, which is attended by 3- to 11-year-olds, there are children of 123 different nationalities (MENJE 2015: 8). In the school year 2013/2014, 55% of all the school children did not speak Luxembourgish as their first home language (MENJE and Université du Luxembourg 2015: 21). This percentage is even higher if you exclusively look at the language situation in early childhood education. Among 3- to 6-year-olds, 64.9% of the children speak languages other than Luxembourgish as the first language (MENJE and Université du Luxembourg 2015: 21). Of all the children at the elementary and primary school age, 28.2% speak Portuguese as their first home language (S. Ugen, R. Martin, B. Böhm *et al.* 2014: 101). Nevertheless, children do not automatically develop multilingualism in early childhood education. The studies conducted by S. Neumann (2015) and C. Seele (2014) have empirically

shown that there is a focus on Luxembourgish in language practices in the early
childhood education and on the separation of languages.

1.2 Formal and non-formal education in Luxembourg

The formal sector of Luxembourgish early childhood education starts with *Education Précoce* (3- to 4-year-olds), followed by preschool (4- to 6-year-olds, compulsory), which are, as well as the following school years (6- to 12-year-olds), part of
the *école fondamentale*. For the entire elementary and primary level, there exists one
common curriculum, which was established in 2011, following the PISA debate.
The non-formal education system also went through a reform in 2005, under which
different institutions for the non-formal sector were constituted. For the care of 0- to
4 year-olds, there are the *Crèche* and the *Maison Relais pour Enfants*, of which the
latter continues in the care of children until the age of 12. The Ministry of Education is in charge of both parts, the formal and the non-formal sector of education
in Luxembourg. Concerning the language situation, the focus in the formal and
non-formal early childhood education (3- to 6-year-olds) is on Luxembourgish,
whereas the primary school education (6- to 12-year-olds) in the formal sector
builds on the three official languages Luxembourgish, German (6-year-olds), and
French (7-year-olds).

2. Theoretical implications and state of the art

For this research, there are two scientific discourses of relevance. First, the discourse on multilingualism in early childhood education and its pedagogies, which
focuses on the question of what types of multilingual pedagogies can be differentiated and how these pedagogies are implemented in classes. Secondly, the discourse
on pedagogic dimensions of multimodality, which asks what factors activate a
multimodal communication.

2.1 Multilingualism in early childhood education

Studies on multilingual pedagogies have rapidly increased in recent years (*cf.*
M. Achugarand, B. D. Carpenter 2012; M. Farr and J. Song 2011). However, most
of them focus on multilingual practices in primary or secondary school education, whereas empirical research on multilingual pedagogies in early childhood
education is rare and is almost entirely missing in the non-formal early years of
education and childcare (*cf.* O. Garcia and W. Li 2014). At the same time, commercial programmes for multilingualism in early childhood education have been
recently published (K. Jampert, V. Thanner, D. Schattel *et al.* 2011), which focus

on the development of vocabulary and the learning of an additional language. As mentioned earlier, for Luxembourg it has been shown that the language practices in early childhood education concentrate on Luxembourgish and on a separation of languages (S. Neumann 2015, C. Seele 2014). The country does not follow the language ideology and policy of multilingual pedagogies in the early childhood education as required, for instance, by O. Garcia and N. Flores (2012) or M. Farr and J. Song (2011), but, if at all, rather the "second language pedagogies" (O. Garcia and N. Flores 2012: 233).

O. Garcia and N. Flores (2012) provide four types of multilingual pedagogies by differentiation in language use, orientation, views, and arrangements. The multilingual pedagogies are the most complex and dynamic ones next to the foreign language pedagogies, the second language pedagogies and the bilingual pedagogies. When compared, foreign as well as second language instruction focus on adding a language to the existing one. Especially in foreign language instruction, the emphasis is on reading and not on communicating with speakers of the foreign language (O. Garcia and N. Flores 2012: 233). In contrast, plurilingual instruction focuses on the communicative aspects of languages. It builds on the different linguistic profiles that children have in kindergarten (O. Garcia and N. Flores 2012: 233). Language learning in that perspective is not about adding one foreign or second language, but it forms a dynamic shift of different languages.

2.2 Pedagogic dimensions of multimodality

The dimensions of multimodality go beyond linguistic aspects and include social as well as material-based components. Following G. Kress (2013), the multimodal social semiotic theory of education combines social and semiotic practices. It frames pedagogic as well as psychological classifications with "larger-level social categories" (G. Kress 2013: 121), such as gender, ethnicity or class. The communication that happens lies in focus, for instance, when children visit an exhibition in a museum. In the multimodal social semiotic theory communication is described as interaction, which implies processes of knowledge construction and meaning-making. This means that communication, and furthermore learning, occur while learners interact with the world, either as members of a social group or to analyze the cultural, natural or technical environment. In this sense, the multimodality of communication appears through speech, gaze, actions, and touch (G. Kress 2013: 123) as a prompt response that occurs when there has been an interpretation or transformation.

The discourse on multimodality explores the question of which multimodal aspects affect children's constructions. L. D. Buchholz (2014) emphasizes the importance of visual images for the reader's construction of interior spaces within a story world. G. A. Hull and M. E. Nelson (2005) have empirically shown that visual representations are parts of multimodal narratives and that the combination of visual images and oral language is semiotically richer than the written word by itself. Whereas Hull and Nelson's study focuses on visual representations as a stimulation of oral language, P. Duncum (2004) claims that visual images are something more than a "communicative mode". He combines images, words, and sound as an "interaction of music, the spoken voice, sound effects, language, and pictures" (P. Duncum 2004: 252). Similarly, in what G. Kress (2013: 121) calls the "interaction-as-communication", P. Duncum (2004) found the interaction to have a high impact on multimodality that does not limit itself to literacy as it helps children to form their own opinions.

3. Research approach and design

The present pilot-study entitled MultOra (multilingual oracies in early childhood education; C. Kirsch and K. Andersen) focuses on the language use among children and practitioners in the field of formal and non-formal education in Luxembourg through professional development. The research project follows the professional development course "Mit Versen in die Welt" (Rhymes as a stepping stone into the world; C. Kirsch, in press), which was financed by the ministry. The professional development included a 10-hour course, in which 16 teachers and educators were involved, and two follow-up mentoring sessions with 7 selected teachers and educators out of the group of 16.

3.1 Research question

In the above described research context, there are two aspects particularly relevant for the project MultOra. First of all, since multilingualism is a part of daily life in Luxembourg and is of high relevance for learning in Luxembourgish schools, where children are alphabetized in German, while they communicate in Luxembourgish and French at the same time, a question arises why there is no focus on multilingualism in the early childhood education. Secondly, teachers and educators are concurrently involved in the Luxembourgish early childhood education. Nevertheless, there existed no professional development training course before "Mit Versen in die Welt", which comprised teachers and educators in a common pool of experience.

Based on this, the research question of the pilot-project MultOra is: What kind of multilingual practices occur in the early years of formal and non-formal educational settings during the activities with posters and rhymes, and what components of multilingual pedagogies do teachers and educators identify?

3.2 Sample and methodology of research

The 16 participants in the professional development course comprised four edu-cators from two different *Crèches*, six educators from three *Maisons Relais pour Enfants*, two educators from a *Précoce* and four teachers from two pre-schools. The criterion for the selection was based on the representation of all four institu-tions of the Luxembourgish early childhood education system and contrasting intake, which was provided by including the institutions from different regions of Luxembourg (central, southern and northern). Before a professional develop-ment course, a survey focusing on the previous knowledge and experience of the educators' and teachers' multilingual practices was conducted. Based on its results and with the aim of selecting practitioners from the formal as well as non-formal sector, a sample of six educators and one teacher was created for the two follow-up mentoring sessions. This sample involved one educator from a *Crèche*, five educators from three different *Maison Relais pour Enfants*, and one pre-school teacher. The children in these settings speak 17 different first languages, such as, but not only: Luxembourgish, Portuguese, Italian, Spanish, French and German.

The methods used in the present research are qualitative and based on the grounded theory (K. Charmaz 2006). They draw on video-recordings of multilin-gual pedagogical practices. The practitioners self-recorded their own pedagogical practices in class, using posters and German rhymes that were introduced in the professional development course. The originality of this method is that the practi-tioners reflect on their practices based on self-recorded videos. Each educator and each teacher chose one video-recorded multilingual practice to be discussed in the mentoring sessions within the group of selected practitioners. In these sessions, the practitioners systemized their own videos by means of the repertory grid technique (*cf.* for mathematics: R. Bruder, K. Lengnink and S. Prediger 2003), which was adapted to the field of early childhood education. The task was to categorize photos, which were taken by screenshot of their self-recorded videos, to group them on a poster and to create titles for each group of photos. In addition, the discussions of the follow-up mentoring sessions were video-recorded and transcribed.

4. Findings and discussion

The analysis of the data corpus has led to five central findings. First, the data generated by recording the educators' practices has shown that a multimodal and multilingual communication is activated through the use of posters and rhymes. It became visible that the children, while sharing their ideas about the posters, switched in single moments from one language to another. It showed that these language shifts involved mostly two languages, and that the shifts occurred in almost all the cases of sentences spoken in Luxembourgish, and involved adding a word from another language (German, English, French, and a self- constructed language). Rarely the children included more than one word in a row of another language, and it never occurred that a child spoke several sentences in a different language than Luxembourgish. Neither did a single child speak one language and another in a second language. One of the examples of particular interest from the group (four children, 3- to 4-year-olds) did not only include single German words, but the children also used two Luxembourgish synonyms for the word dog ("Hond" and "Mupp"). In this case, three children (Luxembourgish as a home language) used both synonyms alternately, whereas one child (Spanish as a home language, a 4-year-old) insisted on the correctness of using "Hond", and the incorrectness of "Mupp". This became visible when the child, while touching the dog on the poster, repeated the word "Hond" several times and denied the accuracy of "Mupp": "Nee, Mupp, end'ass net Hond" (No, Mupp, he, this is not dog). Another child from this group (Italian and Luxembourgish as home languages, a 3-year-old) added to this, while touching the visual representation: "Mupp ass wéi Hond" (Mupp is as dog). In this situation, it becomes obvious that the communication about pictures in smaller groups of multilingual children activates the children's language reflection in a multimodal way as the children connected permanent physical contact (tactile stimulation) and language reflection (verbal expression). This instance shows that language reflection through the use of pictures can already be activated in three-year olds. In addition, this case shows that repetition is of importance for a multimodal and multilingual communication in a sense that it comprises the children's reflection on synonyms and transformation of words.

Secondly, the data corpus collected in the video-recordings of the practices showed a more complex form of multimodality in synergy with multilingualism when the children used gestures, facial expressions and narrative elements. It showed that in almost all the cases they did not communicate only linguistically, but they additionally used their body language. This became especially visible as the children underlined single words or contexts by illustrating them with the movement of their hands. It is particularly striking that this only occurred when the children stood right in front of the poster and along with their gestures they enthusiastically touched the illustrated elements on the poster. In addition, it proved that in many cases these multimodal moments happened in relation to the switch of languages. You could almost say that multilingual practices occurred especially when the communication involved the children's body language that was in a close contact with the poster. Such multimodal and multilingual moments appeared as well on the children's and practitioners' sides during the activities with the posters and German rhymes.

Third, the data sources generated by recording the educators' practices showed the relevance of a combined use of posters and German rhymes for the activation of multilingual language practices in early childhood education. It occurred that on many occasions the children switched their languages when posters were used along with German rhymes and that the switch of languages was especially activated in an exchange where the practitioner encouraged the children to use a language other than Luxembourgish. This became visible when the practitioner answered a child's question in another language than Luxembourgish, which in turn encouraged the group of children to use that language as well. As mentioned earlier, these language shifts were in almost all the cases limited to adding single words in another language.

Fourth, the data collected in the mentoring sessions showed predominantly that the practitioners often did not perceive the multimodal and multilingual moments when watching their own video-recordings. Indeed, they noticed in many cases the switch from Luxembourgish to another language, though in some situations, the practitioners did not observe the multilingual switches or at least they did not communicate them within their mentoring group. This occurred especially when the multilingual practices were limited to one-word-switches. In addition, the practitioners in their reflection on multilingual moments in the videos, did not pay attention to either of the children's or their own multimodal practices. It showed that situations of multimodal communication, including gestures, facial expressions and/or gaze at the poster, were not seen in relation with the activation of multilingualism, at least this was not discussed within the group of practitioners. However, it can be noted that the exchange among the participants in the mentoring group helped them to view their own practices from a new perspective and that the input of the other educators and the teacher helped them to re-evaluate certain aspects of their own multilingual practices in relation to the needs of early childhood education in a broader context.

Fifth, the data sources collected in the mentoring sessions showed that systemizing by means of the repertory grid technique helped the practitioners to reflect on their own practices. It showed that the question of how to categorize the self-recorded videos of multilingual pedagogical practices activated an in-depth discussion that embraced the teacher and the educators in a common pool of experience. For instance, the practitioners discussed in many details what the self-grouped photos of their own practices should be called. They suggested the following titles: "relaxed listening", "relaxed questioning", "relaxed listening and suggestion", "active telling along", "participatory telling", which shows that the

titling itself activated a reflection on the essential pedagogical elements of stimulating multilingual practices in the early childhood education. This especially
occurred when the practitioners discussed their own practices in a mixed group
of teachers and educators.

4.1 Outlook: Possibilities and borders

The findings show that there is still great potential for increased reflection on multilingual pedagogies in the early childhood education and for the development of a
more intense exchange among educators and teachers. Following the discussion on
the implementation of multilingual pedagogies in daily practices of early childhood
education (*cf.* O. Garcia and W. Li 2014, O. Garcia and N. Flores 2012), this pilot-
study strengthens the view of the importance of developing appropriate visual material for the activation of multilingual moments in class. The findings show that the
combination of pictures and German rhymes helps children in the Luxembourgish
early childhood education to activate their multilingual use of languages, by which
the discourse on "plurilingual scaffolding" (O. Garcia and N. Flores 2012: 243) is
strengthened. According to J. Cummins (2000: 71), contextual or linguistic scaffolds
are central for successful task completion. O. Garcia and N. Flores (2012: 244.) claim
that for bilingual children the scaffolding strategies must build on the children's
dynamic plurilingualism in interaction with the practitioner. This comprises,

- firstly establishing instructional routines and language patterns by means of
  varying languages according to the interests of the children and the context
  of the class,
- secondly contextualizing through the practitioners' use of the children's home
  languages as well as other paralinguistic strategies (e.g. gestures, visuals),
- thirdly modelling the language use in think-aloud situations by using all language practices of the children,
- fourthly bridging and building schema through the practitioner's previewing
  the material that will be taught in another language than the one in class, and
- fifthly allowing multiple entry points by means of children's demonstration of
  their understanding in different languages.

The findings of the pilot-study MultOra strengthen the discourse insofar as they
show empirically that the activation of the practitioners' use of another language
than the one in class is of relevance for a dynamic multilingualism of the children.
In addition, the findings show that a multimodal communication, comprising gestures, facial expressions and/or gaze at the poster, leads to multilingual moments
of the children in interaction with the practitioner. The results give rise to the

assumption that the practitioners benefit from each other's different experiences in multilingual language use and that it is of importance for them to reflect in a mixed group of teachers and educators on their prior knowledge on how to apply multilingual practices in the early childhood education.

Another research has shown that the initial deficiency to supersede involves the lack of proficiency level of languages (cf. C. Pérez-Cañado 2014; F. Lorenzo, S. Casal and P. Moore 2009). In these researches, it has been proven that a low level of foreign language proficiency caused practitioners to feel insecure about their fluency. For the pilot-project MultOra, the practitioners' foreign language proficiencies were not evaluated. Further studies will need to implement the data on the language proficiencies of the practitioners (e.g. as part of a survey done at the beginning of the professional development training) to question in how the proficiency correlates with the practitioners' flexible code switching in the practical application of multilingual language use in the early childhood education. However, the discussion of the results must take into account that the professional development training "Mit Versen in die Welt" comprised no exercises for the practitioners to try out by themselves within the training course of how to implement a flexible language use in their practices. In further professional development courses, it would be of relevance to develop such types of exercises where educators practise by themselves (e.g. in smaller groups of the professional development training course) the dynamic code switching in the use of posters and German rhymes. In follow-up studies, it could then be evaluated how different types of exercises in professional development training influence the practical application of flexible language use in daily practices of early childhood education.

Finally, it is to state that the findings of the pilot-study MultOra give rise to the assumption that the peer-mentoring in a mixed group of practitioners from formal and non-formal educational institutions take an important role in reflecting and comparing different types of multilingual practices. In further studies, it might be worth evaluating how the peer-mentoring of teachers and educators contributes to re-evaluating the practitioners' beliefs about developing multilingual practices. Furthermore, in future studies a sample needs to be enlarged, by means of which the above mentioned findings of the pilot-study MultOra, can be exhaustively validated empirically to guarantee their representative status. Of interest it might seem to know whether in a bigger sample, comprising more teachers, the practitioners will reflect the multimodal and multilingual practices of the children differently in the group of teachers and in the group of educators, and in what types of differences will occur. Even though the sample of the project MultOra was not representative, it could be shown that there is a great potential for increased reflection on the interaction of multimodality and multilingualism in the early childhood education.

References

Bruder, R., Lengnink, K. and Prediger, S. 2003. *Ein Instrumentarium zur Erfassung subjektiver Theorien über Mathematikaufgaben.* Darmstadt: TU Darmstadt. Available at: <http://wwwbib.mathematik.tu-darmstadt.de/MathNet/Preprints/Listen/shadow/pp2265.html>.

Buchholz, L. D. 2014. Illustrations and Text: Storyworld Space and the Multimodality of Serialized Narrative. In: *Style* 48(4). 593–611.

Charmaz, K. 2006. *Constructing Grounded Theory: A Practical Guide through Qualitative Analysis.* London: Sage.

Cummins, J. 2000. *Language, Power and Pedagogy: Bilingual Children in the Crossfire.* Clevedon: Multilingual Matters.

Duncum, P. 2004. Visual Culture Isn't Just Visual: Multiliteracy, Multimodality and Meaning. In: *Studies in Art Education* 45(3). 252–264.

Eurostat. 2015. *European Social Statistics. Population on 1 January by five year age group, sex and citizenship.* Luxembourg: Publications Office of the European Union. Available at: <http://appsso.eurostat.ec.europa.eu/nui/show.do?dataset=migr_pop1ctzandlang=en>.

Farr, M. and Song, J. 2011. Language Ideologies and Policies: Multilingualism and Education. In: *Language and Linguistics Compass* 5(9). 650–665.

Garcia, O. and Li, W. 2014. *Translanguaging: Language, Bilingualism and Education.* New York: Palgrave Macmillan.

Garcia, O. and Flores, N. 2012. Multilingual Pedagogies. In: Martin-Jones, M., A. Blackledge and A. Creese (Eds.), *The Routledge Handbook of Multilingualism.* New York: Routledge. 232–246.

Hull, G. A. and Nelson, M. E. 2005. Locating the semiotic power of multimodality. In: *Written Communication* 22(5). 224–261.

Jampert, K., Thanner, V., Schattel, D. *et al.* 2011. *Die Sprache der Jüngsten entdecken und begleiten: Sprachliche Bildung und Förderung für Kinder unter Drei.* Berlin: Netz.

Kirsch, C. in press. Multilingual Oracies: Ein Bericht einer Weiterbildung zur Förderung der Mündlichkeit anhand von Versen und Bilderbüchern. In: MENJE (Ministère de l'Éducation nationale, de l'Enfance et de la Jeunesse) (Eds.), *Beiträge zur Plurilingualen Bildung: Non-formale Bildung und Betreuung in früher Kindheit und im Schulalter.* Bd. 3. Dudelange. 73–100.

Kress, G. 2013. Recognizing Learning: A Perspective from a Social Semiotic Theory of Multimodality. In: De Saint-Georges, I. and J. J. Weber (Eds.), *Multilingualism and Multimodality: Current Challenges for Educational Studies*. Rotterdam: Sense Publishers. 119–140.

Lorenzo, F., Casal, S. and Moore, P. 2009. The Effects of Content and Language Integrated Learning in European Education: Key Findings from the Andalusian Bilingual Sections Evaluation Project. In: *Applied Linguistics* 31(3). 418–442.

MENJE (Ministère de l'Éducation nationale, de l'Enfance et de la Jeunesse). 2015. *Enseignement fondamental: Cycles 1 à 4. Éducation différenciée. Année scolaire 2013/2014*. Luxembourg. Available at: <http://www.men.public.lu/catalogue-publications/fondamental/statistiques-analyses/statistiques-globales/2013-2014/fr.pdf>.

MENJE (Ministère de l'Éducation nationale, de l'Enfance et de la Jeunesse) and Université du Luxembourg. 2015. *Bildungsbericht Luxemburg 2015. Bd 1: Sonderausgabe der Chiffres Clés de L'Éducation Nationale 2013/2014*. Luxembourg.

MENJE (Ministère de l'Éducation nationale, de l'Enfance et de la Jeunesse). 2014. *Les chiffres clés de l'éducation nationale. Statistiques et indicateurs*. Luxembourg: Service des Statistiques et Analyses.

Neumann, S. 2010. Lost in Translanguaging? Practices of Language Promotion in Luxembourgish Early Childhood Education. In: *Global Education Review* 2(1). 23–39.

Pérez-Cañado, M. 2015. Teacher Training Needs for Bilingual Education: In-Service Teacher Perceptions. In: *International Journal of Bilingual Education and Bilingualism*. Available at: <http://dx.doi.org/10.1080/13670050.2014.980778>.

Seele, C. 2014. Differenzproduktion durch sprachliche Praktiken. Ethnographische Beobachtungen zum Umgang mit Mehrsprachigkeit in luxemburgischen Kinderbetreuungseinrichtungen. In: Schnitzer, A. and R. Mörgen (Eds.), *Mehrsprachigkeit und Ungesagtes*. Weinheim: Beltz Juventa.

STATEC (Institut national de la statistique et des études économiques). 2014. *Luxemburg in Zahlen: 2014*. Luxembourg.

Ugen, S., Martin, R., Böhm, B. et al. 2014. Einfluss des Sprachhintergrundes auf Schülerkompetenzen. In: MENPF (Ministère de l'Éducation nationale et de la Formation professionnelle) and Université du Luxembourg (Eds.), *PISA 2012: Nationaler Bildungsbericht Luxemburg*. Luxemburg. Available at: <http://www.men.public.lu/>.

Wai Meng Chan
(National University of Singapore)

From Multilingualism to Bilingualism – and Back? Charting the Impact of Language Planning in Singapore

Introduction

Since its independence in 1965, Singapore has witnessed phenomenal economic growth on the basis of political stability and social harmony. Most would agree that Singapore's success can be attributed, at least in part, to the adoption of English as the cornerstone of its national language planning. Its English-knowing bilingual educational policy was largely motivated by the government's anticipation that English would become the world's *lingua franca* and the main language of trade, business and technology. First language proficiency in English was thus viewed as a means to plug into the international network and to acquire Western technology and expertise to fuel Singapore's growth and development (S. K. C. Chua 2011, L. Q. Dixon 2009; S. Gopinathan 1998). Moreover, it was intended to act as an important link language for inter-ethnic communication (K. Y. Lee 2012).

The post-independence government's language planning has had an immense impact on the language situation in Singapore, causing language shifts among the population, especially those generations of Singaporeans who were educated after 1965. From a British colony, where ironically less than 2% of the resident population spoke English as mother tongue and most inhabitants were multilingual in several vernacular languages (such as Malay, Chinese languages like Hokkien and Teochew, Tamil and other South Asian languages; see K. Bolton and B. C. Ng 2014), Singapore has evolved today into a nation whose citizens are essentially bilingual with English as first language and second language proficiency in their respective mother tongue languages. As A. Pakir (1993) ascertains, within the space of just ten years, from 1980 to 1990, the percentage of Singaporeans speaking English as the predominant home language had almost doubled – a trend which has continued into this millennium. At the same time, there has also been a significant shift among the ethnic Chinese away from the Chinese vernaculars (or 'dialects', the term used by the Singapore government) to Mandarin, designated as the mother tongue language for ethnic Chinese students in schools.

Despite these major language shifts towards the English-knowing bilingualism promoted by the government, Singapore's language planning cannot be described as a complete success, for the implemented policies did not always lead to the intended outcomes. Indeed, the government had on some occasions admitted to mistakes in its policy decisions, which had to be ameliorated through subsequent policy adjustments (see e.g. K. Y. Lee 2012, L. Wee 2011). Furthermore, top-down policy efforts often interface with bottom-up forces – responses from sectors of the population which may resist these efforts, or have a bearing on their eventual outcomes. A. Pakir (1994) points to the role of 'invisible' language planners in Singapore – parents, children and teachers – who may have interfered with state policy processes, albeit non-intentionally. In anticipation of the socio-economic benefits of English language competence, Singapore parents were instrumental in the adoption of English as the predominant home language.

In the subsequent sections, I will first selectively discuss some key concepts of bilingualism and multilingualism. Thereafter, I will chart the socio-historical development of the language situation in Singapore, focusing mainly on the government's major policy decisions from independence to the new millennium. I will also discuss emerging trends, especially among the better educated, towards the learning of third and foreign languages, which could restore multilingualism to Singapore's population of the future, although this is expected to be a form of 'prestigious' multilingualism, elitist in nature and promising cultural and economic benefits to those endowed with knowledge of multiple languages.

1. Key concepts and definitions

Bilingualism and *multilingualism* are highly complex concepts that involve more than the ability to use two or more languages (C. Baker and S. P. Jones 1998, O. Garcia 2009, C. Baker 2011). For W. Li (2013: 26), bilingualism and multilingualism "refer to the coexistence, contact, and interaction of different languages." He distinguishes between bilingualism and multilingualism at the societal and individual level. While many different languages may be spoken in a society, its individual members may not be bilingual or multilingual. This distinction is fundamental for the understanding and discussion of bilingual/multilingual communities, such as in Singapore where four languages are officially recognized by the state, although the population is essentially literate in only two languages.

At the individual level, there has been much debate about the kind and level of language proficiency that has to be reached for a person to be classified as bilingual. For a long time, it was argued that a true bilingual is a *balanced bilingual* who is more or less equally proficient in two languages (C. Baker and S. P. Jones

1998, O. Garcia 2009). An early and highly restrictive perspective to bilingualism takes the view that native-like competence (i.e. proficiency equivalent to that of a monolingual native speaker) in both languages is a necessary criterion for bilingualism (L. Bloomfield 1933), although this has since been dispelled as non-representative of the realities of actual bilingual people and communities. Most scholars (e.g. H. Baetens Beardsmore 1986, C. Baker 2011, C. Baker and S. P. Jones 1998, O. Garcia 2009) are now quick to point out that we cannot expect a bilingual to be the addition of two equally proficient monolinguals, as bilinguals tend to acquire and use their languages in different contexts, for different purposes and with different interlocutors. C. Baker (2011: 9) criticizes the prejudicial judgement of bilinguals through this double-monolingual view as unfair, and reminds us that "bilinguals may be stronger in each language in different domains." The extent of a bilingual's linguistic competence, or his/her discursive practices, is dependent on a multitude of factors in the social environment such as the roles and functions ascribed to the languages, including their relative socio-political power, as well as the kind and level of input available for language acquisition, just to name a few possible constraints (see also C. Baker and S. P. Jones 1998, O. Garcia 2009, S. Romaine 1994). Scholars (e.g. O. Garcia 2009, W. Li 2013) thus argue that the languages available to a bilingual, regardless of the level of competence, represent important resources for one's discursive practices and should not be dismissed as deficient.

The literature on bilingualism distinguishes between several models of bilingualism. For instance, scholars (e.g. J. Edwards 2013, O. Garcia 2009) distinguish between *additive* and *subtractive* bilingualism, depending on whether the second language acquired extends the individual's linguistic and discursive repertoire or (eventually) replaces the first language. O. Garcia (2009) cites as an example of subtractive bilingualism the case of immigrants to the United States, who acquire English, the majority language, and typically become bilingual by the second generation, only to lose their original language by the third generation, reverting to monolingualism. In additive bilingualism, another language is added to the individual's repertoire and both languages are maintained.

J. Edwards (2013) discusses the concept of *elite* bilingualism which typically involves the acquisition of two (or more) languages of prestige that not only satisfies one's thirst for knowledge and cross-cultural exploration, but also serves to enhance one's status. English was (and still is) viewed in Singapore as a socially powerful – and thus prestigious – language. In the present day, foreign languages such as Japanese, French, German and Korean are also increasingly gaining in status as languages of prestige, for they allow learners to connect with an increasingly globalised and multilingual world, and also provide access to high-status Asian and European countries, often admired for their advanced economies, technologies, media and cultures.

Globalization and the proliferation of technology-enabled communication have led to a surge in language contact among people of different cultures, and the nature of such intercultural discourse is becoming increasingly complex. As people interact for more diverse purposes and with a wider target audience, they may find it necessary to add new languages to their current repertoires to meet their expanded communicative needs. The bilingual and, indeed, multilingual discursive practices resulting from this trend are best described as *dynamic* (O. Garcia 2009), as opposed to the more static and linear models of bilingualism described above. Language repertoires are acquired and developed to varying extents in response to new and ever-changing interactional opportunities and needs, or to satisfy personal interests stimulated by the increased language and intercultural contact.

2. Language planning in Singapore and its impact

2.1 The linguistic situation in pre-independence Singapore

Singapore's society has always been characterized by the multi-ethnic, multicultural and multilingual mix of its population. Even before the arrival of the British in 1819, the island of Singapore had served as "the nexus of the trade routes in Southeast Asia" (P. G.-L. Chew 2013: xi). As early as in the 14th century, it was already the site of a cosmopolitan community, consisting mainly of Arab, Chinese, Malay and other traders from the Southeast Asian region (P. G.-L. Chew 2013). After the island was ceded by the Johor Sultanate to the British in 1824, the subsequent establishment of a free port brought the first major wave of migrants to Singapore, comprising labourers, craftsmen and merchants, mainly from Asia (P. G.-L. Chew 2013, S.-H. Saw 2012). Inevitably, the linguistic landscape was highly diverse, as the migrants had brought their respective vernacular languages to the British colony. The *lingua franca* of pre-independence Singapore until the 1950s and 1960s was not English, but Bazaar Malay, a colloquial, non-standard variety of Malay heavily influenced by Hokkien, the language of the largest and most influential Chinese community group from Fujian province (P. G.-L. Chew 2013). Even though English was the administrative language, only a small proportion of the residents, besides the British themselves, were able to speak English and served in various positions in the civil service. Census data from 1957 reveal that only 22% of the population spoke English, while 48% spoke Malay, including 32.5% of the Chinese and 88.3% of the Indians (K. Bolton and B. C. Ng 2014, E. C. Y. Kuo 1980).

The Chinese in Singapore had hailed from many different regions of China, and Mandarin was by no means the main or a common language among them.

Apparently, only 0.1% of the total population spoke Mandarin as their mother tongue (E. C. Y. Kuo 1980). The diversity of their origins is reflected in the many vernaculars spoken by the various regional groups, such as Hokkien, Cantonese, Teochew, Hainanese and Hakka. Similarly, the Indians represented a mixed group in terms of ethnicity and languages spoken (including Malayalam, Telugu, Punjabi, Hindi, Bengali and Gujarati), although the majority were Tamil-speaking Southern Indians (A. Pakir 1994, M. H. Shi 1991). Pre-independence Singapore was thus characterized by multilingualism at the individual level. J. Platt (1980) reasons that Chinese Singaporeans, the largest community, would command linguistic repertoires of four to possibly eight languages. It was not uncommon for a Chinese Singaporean to speak several Chinese vernaculars, in addition to his/her own mother tongue, and to also communicate with other communities in Bazaar Malay. The Malays would generally be proficient in more than one variety of Malay and speak some English, while the Indians could call upon a repertoire comprising one or more related Indian languages, as well as some English and Bazaar Malay.

2.2 Singapore's multilingual language policy

When Singapore became a fully independent nation in 1965, it introduced legislation to preserve its societal multilingualism from pre-independence times. The government decreed that Malay, Mandarin, Tamil and English would be the country's four official languages, with Malay being the national language. This multilingual policy had its roots in the 1950s, when the All-Party Committee on Chinese Education (APC) recommended that the afore-mentioned four languages be recognized as Singapore's official languages and that these languages be accorded equal status in public life and education (APC 1956). Decades later, Singapore's first prime minister, Lee Kuan Yew, explains the decision to make English an official language:

> Trade and industry were our only hope. But to attract investors here to set up their manufacturing plants, our people had to speak a language they could understand. That language had to be English – since World War II ended, the English language had spread. It was the language of international diplomacy, the language of science and technology, and the language of international finance and commerce. Singaporeans would have increased opportunities if they had a strong mastery of English. For political and economic reasons, English had to be our working language. This would give all races in Singapore a common language to communicate and work in (K. Y. Lee 2012: 59).

Despite the decision to recognize four official languages, English was chosen as the main administrative language because of its utilitarian value as the language of international trade and business, and as a vehicle to access western science and the technology (S. Gopinathan 1998). In addition, it was to assume the role of a link language and aid in the integration of the country's multi-ethnic society. Like in many modern states, the principle of rationalization (see D. D. Laitin 1992) was applied by newly independent Singapore in managing racial and cultural issues. As P. G.-L. Chew (2013: 172) elaborates, "an overarching quadratomy known popularly as the 'CMIO' model, that is, 'Chinese', 'Indian', 'Malay' and 'Others' ('Others' referring to the Eurasians, Jews, Armenians, Sikhs and other minorities) was created as a means of governance." The same principle of rationalization was also extended to the official language policy, with the government exercising a radical reduction of the large number of languages spoken in the city state to just four official languages, one each for the major ethnic groups – Mandarin for the Chinese, Malay for the Malays and Tamil for the Indians – in addition to English.

2.3 Singapore's bilingual language-in-education policy

While Singapore has adopted a policy of societal multilingualism, the individual Singaporean is not expected to be multilingual. Singapore has crafted and implemented an educational language policy that is aimed at individual bilingualism, with proficiency in English and their respective mother tongues. The origins of this policy date back to 1956, when the APC recommended that: 1) education be offered in any of the four official languages; 2) students in non-English medium schools learn English as the second language; and 3) those in English medium schools learn their respective mother tongue as second language. This recommendation was subsequently implemented by the post-independence government from 1966 onwards, and the study of English and one's mother tongue language (MTL) became compulsory. The government had taken a conscious interventionist stance in its language planning, with the bilingual educational policy clearly designed to induce deliberate and fundamental language change in society. Considering that, in 1957, English was the mother tongue of only 1.8% of the population and 22% spoke the language to some extent, it was a highly ambitious plan to make English the country's working language and *lingua franca*. A second controversial top-down decision was the designation of Mandarin and Tamil as the official MTLs of Chinese and Indian students, respectively, although these were not the native languages of the Chinese and a large number of the Indians. Overlooking far more commonly spoken Chinese vernaculars, such as Hokkien (spoken by 30.0% of the population according to census data from 1957, in E. C. Y. Kuo 1980), Teochew (17.0%) and Cantonese (15.1%), the government decided in favour of Mandarin (0.1%) as the sole official language of the Chinese community – a move consistent with the practice of language rationalisation. In the words of K. Y. Lee (2012: 150), Mandarin was selected because it "unites the different dialect groups." In addition, Mandarin had been the standard language taught in Singapore's Chinese-medium schools since the early 20th century (L. Q. Dixon 2009). In the case of Tamil, this designated MTL was actually spoken by only 60% of all Indians in Singapore. Despite this, Tamil was chosen as the sole Indian MTL in school[1], not just because of the Tamil-speaking majority, but also because it was the Indian language "with the longest history of education in Malaysia and Singapore" (L. Q. Dixon 2009: 119).

Today, students have to study their MTLs for the entire duration of their school education and need to attain minimum MTL standards to gain admission into pre-university and university education. The main rationale for the study of the MTL was and still is to provide young Singaporeans with an identity and cultural anchor to ensure the maintenance of their core Asian values, as K. Y. Lee underlines later:

> Why did I insist on Singaporeans all needing to learn their mother tongue? For the Chinese, why did I insist that they learn Chinese? […] Because I believe language transmits values. Learning the Chinese language means imbibing the core items of Chinese history, tradition and culture. The Confucianist values of loyalty, honour, discipline, filial piety, emphasis on family, respect for authority – all vital for nation-building and for cultivated citizens with honourable personal attributes. These values will provide cultural ballast to our people as we adjust to a fast-changing world. […] Malays must learn their Malay language, Tamils their Tamil language. Our schools must teach the basic values and culture of each group's heritage using the mother tongues (2012: 70–71).

With the recent emergence of China and India as major Asian economies, the learning of Mandarin and Indian MTLs (such as Tamil or Hindi) have assumed an added economic dimension, as proficiency in these languages is expected to give Singaporeans an edge in tapping these countries' potential.

2.4 Rise in the number of bilinguals

The bilingual educational policy, implemented in 1966, had transformed Singapore's linguistic landscape and created major language shifts within the span of just one generation, for Singapore had become, by 1990, what B. B. Kachru (1983 in A. Pakir 1993) calls an English-knowing bilingual society. The census of population (CoP) of 1990 shows that 42.74% of the resident population were literate in two or more languages, not far behind the 47.60% literate in only one language. Table 1

---

1   From the 1990s onwards, non-Tamil speaking Indian students may opt to study other Indian languages, including Hindi, Bengali, Gujarati, Bengali and Urdu, in community language schools (Saravanan, 1998).

documents how the trend towards bilingualism continued beyond 1990 till 2010, when the last census was carried out.

Table 1: *Language literacy 1990–2010 for persons aged 10/15 and above (percentages of resident population) N.B. The statistics were collected from Singapore's population aged 10 and above for 1990, and from those aged 15 and above for 2000 and 2010. (SCoP 1990; CoP 2000; CoP 2010)*

Years	Not literate	Literate in one language only	Literate in two languages only	Literate in three or more languages
1990	10%	47.60%	41.87%	0.87%
2000	7.45%	40.70%	49.89%	1.96%
2010	4.14%	28.28%	61.06%	6.52%

The table shows that, by 2010, 61.06% were literate in two languages, compared to 41.87% just 20 years earlier. If we narrow the scope of the data to those who were between 15 and 44 years of age in 2010 (i.e. those who were directly affected by the policy from 1966 onwards), the percentage of bilinguals was even higher at 77.39% (CoP 2010). Table 2 provides further evidence of the policy's impact.

Table 2: *Languages literate in among bilinguals 2010 (CoP 2010)*

Languages literate in	Number	Percentage
English and Chinese only	1,305,705	68.86%
English and Malay only	390,124	20.57%
English and Tamil only	104,570	5.51%
Sub-total	1,800,399	94.94%
English and non-official language only	82,972	4.38%
Other two languages only	12,898	0.68%
Total	1,896,268	100%

As is evident from Table 2, the overwhelming majority of bilinguals (94.94%) were literate in English and an MTL. Acting on its conviction that Singaporeans need to be bilingual in English and their respective MTLs, the Singapore government has effected substantial changes in the people's language practices through its language planning and management. It has also succeeded in making English the main medium of education, with non-English medium education ceasing to exist by 1987 (W. Bokhorst-Heng 1998, L. Q. Dixon 2005). Although the extent of the language change is nothing less than remarkable, the bilingual educational policy was by no means an unadulterated success, as it had also created a language shift that is threatening to undermine the other objective of preserving Singaporeans' Asian roots and values.

2.5 Language shifts and the implications

A. Pakir (1993) had established that the proportion of the population who spoke English as their preferred home language had nearly doubled from 1980 to 1990. Table 3 shows that this trend has continued since 1990 and that English and Mandarin are fast replacing the Chinese vernaculars as the predominant home language.

Table 3: Languages most frequently spoken at home in Singapore for persons aged five and above N.B. The percentages were computed from data sourced from the census of population in 1990, 2000 and 2010

	English	Mandarin	Chinese dialects	Tamil	Malay
1990	19.18%	23.59%	39.41%	2.88%	14.30%
2000	23.03%	35.00%	23.80%	3.15%	14.08%
2010	32.29%	35.64%	14.33%	3.26%	12.19%

While 19.18% of the population had reported speaking English as the predominant home language in 1990, this percentage had grown to 32.29% by 2010. Though Mandarin remains the most frequently spoken home language in 2010, rising marginally from 35% in 2000 to 35.64%, it is apparent that English is fast drawing level, recording the largest growth between 2000 and 2010. While the Malays have preserved their mother tongue fairly well over the decades (F. Cavallaro and S. K. Serwe 2010), the percentage of those with Malay as predominant home language had dipped by over 2% from 1990 to 2010. It should be noted here that the changes documented in Table 3 are unlikely to have resulted from changes to the ratio of the major ethnic groups, as this has remained fairly constant since 1957 with approximately 75% Chinese, 13% Malays and 9% Indians despite the resident population growing from 1.4 million in 1957 to 3.9 million in 2014 (see S.-H. Saw 2012 and YoSS 2015).

Among those aged five to 44 in 2010, the language shift was even more pronounced. The percentages of those speaking English and Mandarin as home languages were almost equal at 37.21% and 37.60%, respectively (see Table 4). Indeed, it seems likely this trend will continue, with English soon overtaking Mandarin as the most frequently spoken home language. Statistics released by the Ministry of Education (MOE) appear to support this prediction: in 2009, 59% of the newly enrolled Primary 1 pupils were from English-speaking families (Oon and Kor 2009 in C. L. P. Ng 2014).

Table 4: Languages most frequently spoken at home in Singapore 2010 for persons aged five to 44 (CoP, 2010)

Language	Number	Percentage
English	775,854	37.21%
Mandarin	784,033	37.60%
Chinese dialects	125,432	6.02%
Malay	262,338	12.58%
Tamil	75,328	3.61%
Other Indian languages	31,747	1.52%
Other languages	30,336	1.45%
Total	2,085,073	100%

F. Cavallaro and S. K. Serwe (2010) report a substantial increase in the use of English among Malays in Singapore, especially among the younger generations and those from the highest socio-economic and educational levels. Citing data that reveal a rapid increase in the use of English in Malay homes from 7.9% in 2000 to 13.0% in 2005, they project that the use of Malay will decline in domains where it has always been the primary language. In a study of the language choices of Chinese, Malay and Tamil children, V. Saravanan (1999) establishes that there is a trend among the children of all three communities to use English when communicating with other children and, partly, also with their parents. V. Saravanan (1998) warns that the bilingual educational policy may have a subtractive effect, with English replacing Tamil, especially among English-speaking and socio-economically better placed Tamil families.

With the government's rigorous promotion of English as the language of administration, commerce and education, it quickly became associated with upward social mobility, economic affluence and political power (F. Cavallaro and S. K. Serwe 2010, A. Pakir 1994). Parents were quick to register the ascendancy of English and ceased to enrol their children in non-English medium schools. They were the invisible language planners (A. Pakir 1994) who were to seal the fate of non-English medium schools in Singapore, which were all closed by 1987 (W. Bokhorst-Heng 1998). The shift towards English as the main home language was not an intended outcome of the bilingual policy and was considered by the government to be a challenge to their efforts to maintain Singaporeans' Asian roots and values through the MTL medium (see K. Y. Lee 2012). H. Baetens Beardsmore (1998) cautions that the teaching of MTLs as second languages in English-medium schools may not suffice to achieve this target and that students may develop behavioural patterns that deviate from their traditional ethnic Asian cultures. To address the shift towards English, especially among Chinese families, and the difficulties students faced in MTL learning, MOE implemented a number of measures to better differentiate among students of differing abilities and to stimulate their interest in MTL learning by making curricular contents more relevant and introducing more innovative and IT-enhanced teaching methods[2]. One key policy adjustment was the introduction of a simplified MTL 'B' syllabus, which gives more emphasis to listening and speaking skills, for a minority of students with extreme difficulties coping with the MTLs.

Another important policy, targeted specifically at Chinese Singaporeans, is the Speak Mandarin Campaign, which was initiated in 1979 and has continued till the present day. The initial aim was to replace the Chinese vernaculars with Mandarin as the Chinese community's common and home language, especially among the younger generations (see S. Gopinathan 1998, K. Y. Lee 2012). The government's assumption was that the use of Chinese vernaculars at home was hindering the development of proficiency in Mandarin (K. S. Goh and The Education Study Team 1979). The sum effect of the state's policies was the huge shift from the Chinese vernaculars to Mandarin. The use of Chinese vernaculars at home decreased considerably from 39.41% in 1990 to 14.33% in 2010, while the use of Mandarin increased from 23.59% to 35.64%. By J. Platt's (1980) reckoning, a typical Chinese Singaporean in pre-independence Singapore would be capable of speaking several languages (his/her own native vernacular, one or several other vernaculars, Bazaar Malay, and possibly some Mandarin and/or English). By 2010, the individual repertoires of younger Chinese Singaporeans were mostly restricted to two languages, English and Mandarin. Multilingualism at the individual level has over the past decades largely transformed into bilingualism.

While the original target of the bilingual educational policy was to educate Singaporeans to be equally proficient in both English and their MTL, the difficulties faced by students in coping with two languages, which were sometimes not at all spoken at home, had forced the government to change tack and to adjust attainment expectations for the MTLs downwards. Today, we are informed by research (e.g. C. Baker 2011, C. Baker and S. P. Jones 1998, O. Garcia 2009) that a bilingual is unlikely to be the sum of two monolinguals and that balanced bilingualism is the exception rather than the rule. The Singapore government's downward correction in attainment expectations and the increasing differentiation in MTL instruction are thus consistent with current research perspectives.

The language developments in Singapore are complex and multi-faceted and are difficult to explain using more traditional linear models of bilingualism. The bilingual educational policy is clearly intended to be additive, aimed at helping

---

2   See the report of the Chinese Language Curriculum and Pedagogy Review Committee (2004), which recommended these adjustments to MOE.

Singaporeans acquire English. However, for the Chinese and non-Tamil speaking Indians, the policy also involves the addition of a second new language, Mandarin or Tamil, respectively. In addition, while non-Tamil speaking Indians may replace Tamil with their own mother tongues, this option is not available to Chinese Singaporeans, who have to learn Mandarin in school, resulting in the major shift from the Chinese vernaculars to Mandarin as home language. As such, the policy has had both an additive and a subtractive effect. Similarly, the shift towards English as home language can also be seen as an unintended subtractive consequence of Singapore's language planning.

Perhaps Singapore's language situation is best explained using the dynamic model of bilingualism (O. Garcia 2009), which is based on the notion that one participates in different forms of discourses in different domains and for different purposes. The languages in one's repertoire are valuable resources for the various discursive practices in one's life, and one's competencies in these languages are developed to varying degrees, depending on the amount of contact and exposure, needs and external influences. For instance, the rise of China as an economic power has elevated the status of Mandarin, and may encourage Singaporeans to invest more into the learning of Mandarin. In another plausible scenario, someone moving to Hong Kong for professional reasons may become more motivated to maintain or revive his/her knowledge of Cantonese. In a dynamic model, the domains and frequency of language use will shift with changing conditions and needs, and language competence will likewise fluctuate with increased use or neglect.

2.6 Globalisation, interculturality and foreign language learning

In 1978, MOE started offering foreign languages to Secondary 1 students who were among the top 10% performers at the Primary School Leaving Examination (PSLE). Initially, three languages, French, German and Japanese, were taught as third languages at a centralized institution, the Foreign Language Centre. Further languages were added in subsequent years – Malay (for non-Malay students in 1986), Arabic, Indonesian (both in 2008) and Spanish (2014). When the top 10% eligibility rule was introduced, it was probably formulated with view to the difficulties that beset many students in learning their first two languages. While this rule remains for the languages perceived to be of higher status and thus more popular among parents and students, namely the European languages and Japanese, it does not apply to Arabic, Indonesian and Malay, possibly because these programmes are deemed to be less attractive and require a less restrictive policy. With the introduction of Malay as a third language in 1986, the Foreign Language Centre was renamed the Ministry of Education Language Centre (MOELC).

The introduction of the third language programmes was – similar to the choice of English as first language – strongly motivated by pragmatic and economic considerations. With its increasingly export-oriented economy, Singapore was looking to increase and intensify its international contacts and to seek investments and technology from non-traditional sources, in particular, French-speaking and German-speaking countries in Europe and Japan in Asia. The first G. C. E. 'O' level German language syllabus (GLS 1987: 1) refers explicitly to Singapore's need for "increasing contact with non-English speaking countries in the world." It further states that students with foreign language competence are expected, for instance, to work for foreign investors in Singapore and Singapore's overseas missions, pursue further education in non-English speaking countries, and access technical and scientific information in the foreign languages. At the same time, a more humanistic and intercultural goal was also stated: namely, to foster intercultural competence to allow students to decentre from their own cultures, develop greater empathy towards other cultures, and acquire a more differentiated awareness of the similarities and differences between cultures (H. Funk 1987). This will in turn contribute to a better understanding of as well as closer ties and cooperation with other cultures and countries, which is of key importance against the backdrop of growing internationalisation and globalisation. A recent MOE press release confirms the continued currency of this dual objective by stating that the third language programmes are to help develop the linguistic and intercultural competence to enhance Singapore's cultural and economic relations with the target language countries and to acquire expertise in science and technology from advanced non-English countries (MOE 2012).

Besides the third language programmes, since 2005, conversational Mandarin and Malay courses have also been offered to non-Chinese and non-Malay students, respectively, as enrichment programmes in primary and secondary schools. These programmes are intended to nurture stronger interculturality, with the ultimate aim of strengthening inter- ethnic relations and social harmony. The then Education Minister, Tharman Shanmugaratnam (2005), stresses that these programmes would interest students in other ethnic communities and cultures, and increase inter-ethnic interactions both in and outside school.

At the National University of Singapore (NUS), foreign language courses – initially for Japanese – were first offered in 1981, a year after its constitution through the merger of the University of Singapore and Nanyang University. This was followed by the introduction of Mandarin, French, German, Indonesian, Malay, Tamil, Thai and Vietnamese in various area studies departments between 1991 and 1999. The Centre for Language Studies (CLS) was established within the Faculty of Arts and Social Sciences in 2001 to centralize the teaching of all foreign languages. Its main mission is to provide language teaching support to the area studies departments.

A second primary objective is to equip NUS students with knowledge of foreign languages and cultures, considered vital social and economic resources in this age of globalization and internationalization. This includes the preparation of students to participate in the university's international exchanges and interactions. As articulated in its "Framework Syllabus," the CLS has a third – explicitly intercultural – objective, namely, to help students gain insights into "the culture and conventions of the target language community" and thus obtain "a sense of how native speakers view themselves, such as how they live, how they think, what they value and what they do" (Teaching Development Committee 2006: 16). The resultant cultural awareness will not only enhance students' understanding of and interactions with foreign cultures, but also lead them to reflect on and gain a keener awareness of their own cultures and identities. The latter two overarching objectives of the CLS are thus consistent with the dual objective of MOE's third language programmes.

Today, the CLS teaches 13 languages, having added Arabic, Hindi, Korean and Spanish to its curriculum, and its total annual enrolment has grown from approximately 3,600 students in 2001 to 6,000 in 2015, which provides an indication of the growing popularity of foreign language learning among NUS students. Mirroring developments at the NUS, another major comprehensive university, the Nanyang Technological University, has also set up a Centre for Modern Languages, which currently offers courses in twelve languages. Because of MOE's eligibility restrictions for third language learning, the university courses represent the first opportunity for the majority of students to learn foreign languages in formal education. Information sourced from the websites of Singapore's tertiary institutions show that foreign languages are taught at four of five polytechnics and three of five universities, although many of these institutions currently offer only elementary courses and a limited number of instructional hours.

While no notable or large-scale research has been conducted on the foreign language learning situation and foreign language enrolment statistics of public and private institutions are not published in the public domain, there are some indicators to suggest that there is considerable interest in foreign language learning and the number of multilinguals is on the rise. One such indicator is found in the census data: the percentage of persons literate in three languages or more rose from 1.96% of the resident population in 2000 to 6.52% in 2010, representing a more than threefold increase in just ten years, although absolute numbers are still relative low at 202,606 in 2010. Other indicators include statistics from the Japan Foundation, which show a nearly twofold increase from a total of 8,414 Japanese language learners at various primary, secondary, higher and non-school educational institutions in 1998 to 15,864 by the year 2009 (*Present conditions of overseas Japanese-language education* 1998, 2009). A similar survey of the German foreign ministry puts the total number of German language learners in 2015 at 5,360, 7.24% higher than in 2010 (*Deutsch als Fremdsprache weltweit* 2015). Information from the French Embassy in Singapore indicates that there were in all 10,554 learners of French in the year 2014/2015. Korean has also gained popularity in Singapore owing to the tremendous success of Korean pop media (see W. M. Chan and S. W. Chi 2011). According to estimates of the Singapore Korean Embassy, there were close to 5,000 learners in various public and private institutions. However, for both French and Korean, no baseline data were available from the past for comparative purposes.

International exchanges and cross-cultural encounters have increased exponentially as a result of globalization and the spread of the Internet and computer-mediated communication (W. M. Chan, S. Kumar Bhatt, M. Nagami and I. Walker 2015, S. K. C. Chua 2010). Within multi-ethnic societies, the peaceful and harmonious co-existence of different cultures cannot be simply presumed and requires positive and pro-active actions, including language planning and policy interventions. Educational institutions in Singapore have thus initiated programmes to prepare students for multilingual contact and for the opportunities that emerge from this contact. The Singapore government has also been promoting programmes for the study of non-native MTLs to foster interculturality among Singapore's population of diverse ethnicity. Indeed, S. K. C. Chua (2010: 425) believes that language planning in Singapore "has evolved over the years to cater to changing local and global needs" and that the government is "moving towards trilingualism or multilingualism in Singapore as the norm."

The foreign languages that are more popular among Singaporeans are generally languages of higher status that will afford them access to the rich economic, technological and cultural resources of developed or fast-developing nations and regions such as China, France, Germany, Japan, South Korea and Latin America. The emerging trend towards the learning of a third or further languages thus seems to bear the characteristics of an elite or prestigious multilingualism, which is underscored by census data from 2010, which show that 62.04% of those literate in three or more languages possess a polytechnic, university or other professional qualification.

Conclusion

In this paper, I have traced the major developments in the linguistic landscape of Singapore from its independence to the present day and attempted to show how they have been shaped by the country's language policies and the people's responses to them. Within the space of a few decades, Singapore has transformed its people into English-knowing bilinguals, based on its conviction that English is necessary for its economic development and for inter-ethnic communication. The island nation's economic success has provided evidence of the success of this ideology and its English-knowing bilingual educational policy. Nevertheless, its efforts to advance English language competence have unintentionally led to a massive shift in the home language of its people – from the Chinese vernaculars and the official MTLs to English. This development has, in turn, threatened the second pillar of its language ideology – namely, that MTL maintenance is indispensable, if Singaporeans are to preserve their Asian identity and core values. Policy adjustments were thus undertaken by the government successively to ensure the attainability of this objective, including the marginalisation of the Chinese vernaculars, seen as 'distractions' hindering the successful acquisition of Mandarin among the Chinese community. While Singaporeans of the past were easily capable of speaking several languages, including some Chinese vernaculars, the younger generations had, by the new millennium, been transformed essentially into bilinguals with English as first language and varying degrees of proficiency in their respective MTLs.

Since the late 1970s, Singapore's language planning has been expanded to include the teaching of third languages. MOE now teaches seven different languages at a centralised language school, and the two main comprehensive universities also offer courses at various levels in 12 to 13 languages. Still, MOE's current eligibility policy is best described as restrictive and it appears unlikely that third languages will be made compulsory for students in the foreseeable future – consequences of its painful memories of the difficulties many students had in coping with two languages. Nevertheless, there appears to be growing recognition in the government and among the population of the need for additional language proficiencies. The developments in the learning of third and foreign languages are apparently motivated by two main considerations: 1) that Singaporeans need to be equipped with the linguistic resources to exploit the opportunities afforded by a globalised world; and 2) that they need to develop the competence necessary for intercultural contact, not just with other nations and cultures, but also within Singapore's own multi-ethnic society. The growing trend towards foreign language learning has the long-term potential of restoring multilingualism to its people, although for now it seems to be leading to a form of prestigious multilingualism.

To date, few studies have been conducted to investigate the foreign language learning situation in Singapore, including enrolment developments, learning outcomes, learning motivation, teaching and learning resources, and opportunities for language use and maintenance. Future research should seek to explore and shed light on these issues.

References

All-Party Committee on Chinese Education [APC]. 1956. *Report of the All-Party Committee of the Singapore Legislative Assembly on Chinese Education*. Singapore: Government Printer.

Baetens Beardsmore, H. 1986. *Bilingualism: Basic Principles* (2nd ed.). Clevedon: Multilingual Matters.

Baetens Beardsmore, H. 1998. Language Shift and Cultural Implications in Singapore. In: Gopinathan, S., A. Pakir, W. K. Ho and V. Saravanan (Eds.), *Language, society and education in Singapore* (2nd ed). Singapore: Times Academic Press. 85–98.

Baker, C. 2011. *Foundations of Bilingual Education and Bilingualism* (5th ed.). Clevedon: Multilingual Matters.

Baker, C. and Jones, S. P. 1998. *Encyclopedia of Bilingual Education and Bilingualism*. Clevedon: Multilingual Matters.

Bloomfield, L. 1933. *Language*. New York: Holt and Company.

Bokhorst-Heng, W. 1998. Language Planning and Management in Singapore. In: J. Foley (Ed.), *English in New Cultural Contexts: Reflections from Singapore*. Singapore: Singapore Institute of Management and Oxford University Press. 287–309.

Bolton, K. and Ng B. C. 2014. The Dynamics of Multilingualism in Contemporary Singapore. In: *World Englishes* 33(3). 307–318.

Carvallaro, F. and Serwe, S. K. 2010. Language Use and Language Shift among the Malays in Singapore. In: *Applied Linguistics Review* 1(1). 129–170.

Census of Population 2000. Statistical Release 2: Education, Language and Religion [CoP 2000]. 2001. Singapore: Department of Statistics, Ministry of Trade and Industry, Republic of Singapore.

Census of Population 2010. Statistical Release 1: Demographic Characteristics, Education, Language and Religion [CoP 2010]. 2011. Singapore: Department of Statistics, Ministry of Trade and Industry, Republic of Singapore.

Chan, W. M. and Chi, S. W. 2011. Popular Media as a Motivational Factor for Foreign Language Learning: The Example of the Korean Wave. In: Chan, W. M., K. N. Chin, M. Nagami and T. Suthiwan (Eds.), *Media in Foreign Language Teaching and Learning*. Boston and Berlin: De Gruyter Mouton. 151–188.

Chan, W. M., Kumar Bhatt, S., Nagami, M. and Walker, I. 2015. Culture and Foreign Language Education: An Introduction to the Book. In: Chan, W. M., S. Kumar Bhatt, M. Nagami and I. Walker (Eds.), *Culture and Foreign Language Education: Insights from Research and Implications for the Practice*. Boston and Berlin: De Gruyter Mouton. 1–34.

Chew, P. G.-L. 2013. *A Sociolinguistic History of Early Identities in Singapore: From Colonialism to Nationalism*. Basingstoke: Palgrave Macmillan.

Chinese Language Review and Pedagogy Review Committee. 2004. *Report of the Chinese Language Review and Pedagogy Review Committee*. Singapore: Ministry of Education.

Chua, S. K. C. 2010. Singapore's Language Policy and its Globalised Concept of Bi(tri)lingualism. In: *Current Issues in Language Planning* 11(4). 413–429.

Chua, S. K. C. (2011). Singapore's E(Si)inglish-knowing Bilingualism. In: *Current Issues in Language Planning* 12(2). 125–145.

Deutsch als Fremdsprache weltweit. Datenerhebung 2015. 2015. Berlin: Auswärtiges Amt.

Dixon, L. Q. 2005. Bilingual Education Policy in Singapore: An Analysis of its Sociohistorical Roots and Current Academic Outcomes. In: *International Journal of Bilingual Education and Bilingualism* 8(1). 25–47.

Dixon, L. Q. 2009. Assumptions behind Singapore's Language-In-Education Policy: Implications for Language Planning and Second Language Acquisition. In: *Language Policy* 8. 117–137.

Edwards, J. 2013. Concepts and Methodological Issues in Bilingualism and Multilingualism Research. In: Bhatia, T. K. and W. C. Ritchie (Eds.), *The Handbook of Bilingualism and Multilingualism*. Chichester: Wiley Blackwell. 26–51.

Funk, H. 1987. Deutsch als Fremdsprache in Singapur. Projektbeschreibung und Anmerkungen zu einer landeskundlichen Konzeption eines Lehrplans. In: Gerighausen, J. and P. C. Seel (Eds.), *Aspekte einer interkulturellen Didaktik*. Munich: Goethe-Institut. 170–182.

Garcia, O. 2009. *Bilingual Education in the 21st Century*. Chichester: Wiley Blackwell.

German Language Syllabus. 1987. Singapore: Ministry of Education.

Goh, K. S. and The Education Study Team. 1979. *Report on the Ministry of Education 1978*. Singapore: Government of the Republic of Singapore.

Gopinathan, S. 1998. Language Policy Changes 1979–1997: Politics and Pedagogy. In: Gopinathan, S., A. Pakir, W. K. Ho and V. Saravanan (Eds.), *Language, Society and Education in Singapore* (2nd ed.). Singapore: Times Academic Press. 19–44.

International Monetary Fund [IMF]. 2015. *World Economic Outlook: Uneven Growth – Short- and Long-Term Factors*. Washington. Available at: <http://www.imf.org/external/pubs/ft/weo/2015/01/pdf/text.pdf>.

Kuo, E. C. Y. 1980. The Social Linguistic Situation in Singapore: Unity in Diversity. In: Afendras, E. A. and E. C. Y. Kuo (Eds.), *Language and Society in Singapore*. Singapore: Singapore University Press. 39–62.

Laitin, D. D. 1992. *Language Repertoires and State Construction in Africa*. Cambridge: Cambridge University Press.

Lee, K. Y. 2012. *My Lifelong Challenge. Singapore's Bilingual Journey*. Singapore: Straits Times Press.

Li, W. 2013. Bilingualism and Multilingualism: Some Central Concepts. In: Bhatia, T. K. and W. C. Ritchie (Eds.), *The Handbook of Bilingualism and Multilingualism*. Chichester: Wiley Blackwell. 5–25.

Ministry of Education [MOE]. 2012. *MOE Language Centre to offer Spanish as a Third Language from January 2014*. Singapore. Available at <http://www.moe. gov.sg/media/press/2012/05/moe-language-centre-to-offer-s.php>.

Ng, C. L. P. 2014. Mother Tongue Education in Singapore: Concerns, Issues and Controversies. In: *Current Issues in Language Planning* 15(4). 361–375.

Pakir, A. 1993. Two Tongue Tied: Bilingualism in Singapore. In: *Journal of Multilingual and Multicultural Development* 14. 73–90.

Pakir, A. 1994. Education and Invisible Language Planning: The Case of English in Singapore. In: Kandiah, T. and J. Kwan-Terry (Eds.), *English and Language Planning: A Southeast Asian Contribution*. Singapore: Times Academic Press. 158–179.

Platt, J. 1980. Multilingualism, Polyglossia and Code Selection in Singapore. In: Afendras, E. A. and E. C. Y. Kuo (Eds.), *Language and Society in Singapore*. Singapore: Singapore University Press. 63–83.

Present condition of overseas Japanese-language education. Survey report on Japanese-language education abroad 1998. 2000. Tokyo: The Japan Foundation.

Present condition of overseas Japanese-language education. Survey report on Japanese-language education abroad 2009. 2011. Tokyo: The Japan Foundation.

Romaine, S. 1994. *Language in Society: An Introduction to Sociolinguistics*. Oxford: Oxford University Press.

Saravanan, V. 1998. Language Maintenance and Language Shift in the Tamil-English Community. In: Gopinathan, S., A. Pakir, W. K. Ho and V. Saravanan (Eds.), *Language, Society and Education in Singapore: Issues and Trends*. Singapore: Times Academic Press. 155–178.

Saravanan, V. 1999. Bilingual Chinese, Malay and Tamil Children's Language Choices in a Multi-Lingual Society. In: *Early Children Development and Care* 152(1). 43–53.

Saw, S.-H. 2012. *The Population of Singapore* (3rd ed.). Singapore: ISEAS.

Shanmugaratnam, T. 2005. *Speech at the Mother Tongue News Writing Competition on Saturday, 25 August 2005, at 2.30 p.m. at SPH News Centre*. Singapore: Ministry of Education. Available at: <http://www.moe.gov.sg/media/speeches/2005/ sp20050827.htm>.

Shi, M. H. 1991. Bilingualism in Singapore: Myth and Reality. In: *Proceedings of the thirteenth international symposium on Asian Studies*. Hong Kong: Asian Research Service. 371–382.

Singapore Census of Population 1900. Literacy, Language Spoken and Education [SCoP 1990]. 1993. Singapore: SNP Publishers.

Wee, L. 2011. Language Policy Mistakes in Singapore: Governance, Expertise and the Deliberation of Language Ideologies. In: *International Journal of Applied Linguistics* 21(2). 202–221.

Yearbook of Statistics Singapore, 2015 [YoSS 2015]. 2015. Singapore: Department of Statistics, Ministry of Trade and Industry, Republic of Singapore.

Lidija Cvikić, Jasna Novak Milić, Katarina Aladrović Slovaček
(University of Zagreb, Croatia)

The Role of Formal Language Instruction in the Maintenance of Heritage Language: The Case of Croatian Language

Introduction

Croatian is a language spoken by approximately four million users in Croatia and up to three million users in countries around the world[1]. Most of the speakers of Croatian not living on the territory of the Republic of Croatia (except minority speakers in surrounding countries such as Bosnia and Herzegovina, Serbia, some parts of Hungary and Austria) are speakers of Croatian as a Heritage Language (CHL). CHL is therefore a language of Croatian emigrants and their descendants (2nd, 3rd or sometimes even 4th generation) around the world. A Heritage Language is commonly defined as a language other than the official language of the country where a person lives, spoken by an individual, a family, or a community (www.cal. org), i.e. a language with which an individual has a personal connection (J. Fishman 2001). Although being widely used, the term has a slightly different definition and connotations in various countries, due to a different sociolinguistic situation in them (for the comparison of the meaning and usage of the term *heritage language* in USA, Canada and Australia see G. Valdés 2000, J. F. Hamers and M. H. A. Blanc 2000, J. Cummins 2005, B. Škvorc 2006, L. Cvikić, Z. Jelaska and L. Kanajet Šimić 2010).

Heritage speakers are a heterogeneous group as their connections with the heritage language can be significantly different and do not necessarily correspond with the language proficiency (K. Kondo-Brown 2003). A heritage speaker can therefore be a bilingual person with an HL as L1 or an adult learning a language of their ancestors (N. van Deusen-Scholl 2003). Most researchers, including the authors of this paper, define HL learners as "those who have acquired a certain level of oral and/or written proficiency in their ancestral language in the process of using the language at home and/or in the community, and therefore, the process and outcomes of HL acquisition are distinctly different from those of

---

1 <http://hrvatiizvanrh.hr/hr/hmiu/stanje-hrvatskih-iseljenika-i-njihovih-potomaka-u-inozemstvu/15>.

foreign language acquisition" (K. Kondo-Brown 2003: 2; see also R. Campbell and J. Rosenthal 2000; G. Valdés 1995).

In the context of Croatian, a typical heritage speaker is a second or third generation person living in a non-Croatian speaking country. He or she was raised either simultaneously bilingual (acquiring both languages from birth) or sequentially bilingual (acquiring first Croatian and then the other majority language). Croatian is typically the first acquired (in a sequence of two or more), the family or community language (not the official or majority language) and functionally the secondary language (i.e. the less dominant language), whereas the other language is the second, majority and primary language (see S. Montrul 2012, M. Polinsky and O. Kagan 2007).

Most of the Croatian heritage speakers (CHS) live in North America (USA, Canada), South America (Argentina, Chile), Australia, New Zealand, German speaking countries (Germany, Austria, Switzerland) and Scandinavia (Sweden). In the majority of the host countries Croatians and their descendants can learn Croatian. However, the type of language classes vary according to the educational policy of the host[2] country. Croatian language classes for children can be conducted as an integral part of the host country school curriculum (Austria, Australia, some parts of Germany). In this instance, the educational authorities of the host country are responsible for designing the Croatian language curriculum, organizing and financing Croatian language teaching. In the majority of European countries with considerable numbers of Croatian descendants, Croatian language classes for school-age children are supported by the Croatian Ministry of Science, Education and Sport (MSES). The teachers are formally employed by MSES and are required to apply the Curriculum for Croatian Classes Abroad[3], which is a curriculum of the Croatian language, literature and culture that has been developed by MSES. In some countries, regardless of the two mentioned models of language education in use, Croatian can be taken as a high school certificate subject (e.g. Australia, Austria). The third type of classes is organized by the Croatian community, usually with the support of the Catholic Church. These classes are held in Croatian community centres or in local public schools, often on Saturday mornings, and are commonly held by non-professional teachers (other heritage or native speakers, mostly volunteers, engaged parents, priests, etc.). The estimated total number of students included in any form of Croatian language

---

2   A country outside of Croatia where Croatian language classes are organised.
3   <http://public.mzos.hr/Default.aspx?sec=2116>.

classes is 8,500 (L. Cvikić 2012), of those, 6,300 students are included in classes offered and supported by MSES[4].

Taking into account the above mentioned factors, along with the typically small number of Croatian classes per week, teaching CHL in a classroom setting can be complex and challenging. Common issues that teachers of CHL report (L. Cvikić 2012, 2014) are similar to those reported by other HL teachers: the lack of funding, professional staff and appropriate teaching materials; little or no communication with local educational institutions, and the lack of (financial/professional) support from the homeland (J. Fishman 2001). In some countries the number of students involved in formal education is dropping due to the above mentioned issues or other reasons, most often the lack of motivation and/or a higher level of assimilation into the host culture.

1. Characteristics of heritage language learners

As mentioned earlier, heritage language speakers are a heterogeneous group, from those being bilingual to those with no command of HL. It is well-documented that in the case of taking a formal class of HL (in order to learn it or improve it), heritage language learners (HLL) differ significantly from other learners of the same language (M. Polinsky 2008, L. Isurin and T. Ivanova-Sullivan 2008). In comparison to foreign language learners, HLLs show better knowledge of the target culture as well as stronger personal identification with the language (L. Cvikić, Z. Jelaska and L. Kanajet Šimić 2010). According to M. Carreira (2001: 2) there are three defining factors of heritage language learners: a learner's personal connection with the heritage language and heritage culture, a learner's place in the heritage language community and their proficiency in the heritage language.

1.1 Heritage language learners and heritage language community

The learner's place in the heritage language community is the strongest defining factor for being HLL of an indigenous language[5]. Here, HLLs are defined as people who are members of a community with linguistic roots in languages other than English (M. Carreira 2001: 3), even though they need not have any command of the HL. According to M. Carreira (2001: 5) learning an HL in such communities

---

4 <http://public.mzos.hr/Default.aspx?sec=2116>.
5 According to J. Fishman (2001) heritage language is a superordinate term that includes immigrant languages, indigenous languages and colonial languages.

is very important since language learning goes hand in hand with the transfer of
the cultural values of the community. Heritage language learners are community
members, deeply rooted in the community. Their membership and participation
in the community is a notion that differentiates them from other groups of HLL:
learners with personal connection with the heritage language and heritage culture.
M. Carreira (2001) emphasizes that the second type of HLLs consists of people
who are not members of the community, but who have a personal relationship with
it. They learn their HL in order to establish or strengthen connections with their
family or ethnic background. N. van Deusen-Scholl (2003) recognizes the same
characteristics of HLLs making a distinction between heritage language learners
and learners with a heritage motivation.

1.2 Motivation for learning a heritage language

The influence of motivation to language learning in general has been one of the
essential research topics in language education (see R. C. Gardner 1985, Z. Dörnyei
1998, R. C. Gardner *et al.* 2004, J. S. Lee and Y.-H. Kim 2007 etc.). There is no doubt
that it is equally important in learning HLs. It is very likely, according to R. C.
Gardner's model (1985), that the learners' attitudes towards the heritage language
and culture influence their language learning. The more positive the attitudes, the
better the chances for successful and faster learning. In other words, the more the
learners can identify with the language and culture, the better the outcomes in
their HL proficiency.

Previous research for other HLs (e.g. P.-Sh. Yu 2014) has proven that the motivation for learning a heritage language in a formal setting differs among individuals.
The first type of motivation is based on learners' personal reasons: the need to be
able to speak to relatives, to understand the language of their ancestors, fulfilling
parents' wishes, etc. The other type is based on educational and professional reasons:
e.g. gaining extra school credits or better job opportunities. According to Z. Dörnyei
(1998) personal reasons most commonly create integrative motivation in learners
(they desire to belong to the community and culture), whereas others create instrumental motivation (to obtain material or practical rewards for language learning).
Both types of motivation influence language learning in a positive manner, even
though some research speaks in favour of the former, i.e. integrative motivation
(e.g. R. C. Gardner 1985).

For HLLs, integrative motivation is generally expected to be higher than
instrumental. Moreover, among them even more specific types of integrative
motivation for learning an HL can be found – identity motivation (G. Husseinali
2012, Z. Jelaska and G. Hržica 2005) and generational motivation (Z. Jelaska

and G. Hržica 2005). The former is a characteristic of HLLs, while the later is a characteristic of learners with heritage motivation.

Research on Croatian has also confirmed that in HLLs integrative motivation for learning the language (the need to be able to speak to friends and relatives) predominates instrumental motivation (learning the language for school/work) (L. Cvikić, Z. Jelaska and L. Kanajet Šimić 2010). However, identity motivation (*I learn the language because I am Croat*) was expressed as the primary aim of learning the language by the majority of research participants (L. Cvikić, Z. Jelaska and L. Kanajet Šimić 2010).

1.3 Learner's proficiency in the heritage language

In some definitions of heritage language speakers, the notion of language proficiency in an HL is a key defining factor (see G. Valdes 2000, 2005). M. Carreira (2001) claims that such a definition of HLL comes from the sociolinguistic reality of USA where Spanish is the most commonly spoken heritage language, with over 70% of the USA's Latino population speaking it at home. She argues that learners with very limited language proficiency, but with strong personal connections to the language and culture through their ancestry should also be considered as HLLs, since their learning needs significantly differ from other foreign language learners. Even if they speak an HL to a certain degree, language proficiency of HLLs is qualitatively different than the proficiency of native speakers and of foreign language learners (S. Montrul 2004). For example, studies on Russian as an HL (M. Polinsky 2008, L. Isurin and T. Ivanova-Sullivan 2008) show that HLLs have not acquired some morpho-syntactic features of the Russian language (e.g. dropping personal pronouns) or tend to use it in a different way than native speakers and L2 learners (e.g. lexicalization of one member of the aspectual pair). There is still no agreement whether this is due to the incomplete acquisition (S. Montrul 2008), language attrition (M. Polinsky 2011) or inadequate input (D. P. Y. Cabo and J. Rothman 2012).

Since an HL is acquired in a family or community, very often it is limited to particular communicative functions and HLLs lack the opportunity to acquire the whole range of linguistic modes and registers. O. Kagan and K. Dillon (2001: 5) emphasize that HLLs have the mastery of interpersonal mode, but very little or no experience with interpretative[6] and presentational[7] domain. Due to the fact that their education is mostly or entirely gained in the dominant language, HLLs often have limited literacy skills in their HL. Even when they can read and write, these

---

6 Receptive communication of oral and written messages.
7 Spoken and written communication for the audience.

skills are substantially less developed than speaking and listening comprehension. Limited or no access to education in an HL results in limited exposure to the academic language. For the Croatian language that also means limited access to the standard language, which is considerably different from the dialects spoken among families and/or communities.

All the aforementioned characteristics of HLLs' language proficiency have also been reported for Croatian as an HL. Speakers of CHL show incomplete acquisition of grammatical categories (e.g. noun declension), they tend to use dialects instead of the standard language; the level of their spelling competence is low with a noticeable difference in development between the four language skills (D. Pavličević-Franić, T. Gazdić-Alerić and K. Aladrović Slovaček 2012; D. Pavličević-Franić and K. Aladrović Slovaček 2012, 2013; Z. Jelaska and D. Vuk 2014; L. Cvikić 2014).

Taking into consideration the fact that heritage language learners are naturally exposed to language input that lacks some aspects of sociolinguistic communicative competences, as well as selected language genres and styles, formal language instruction is of great importance for fulfilling that gap.

2. The study

2.1 Aim

The aim of this paper is, based on participants' self-assessment, to investigate the role of formal language education in language learning and maintenance of the Croatian language among its heritage speakers. The authors aim to prove that, besides numerous other factors, formal education (still) has a crucial role in heritage language learning and contributes to the general language proficiency and attitudes towards language and culture.

There has been no similar research in the past for Croatian as an HL. Thus, formal education has proven to influence language proficiency in learning Croatian as a foreign language among adults (J. Novak Milić 2002, 2004, 2005, J. Novak Milić and L. Cvikić 2007). In the case of other heritage languages, formal instruction has proven to have a positive effect on the acquisition of specific grammatical structures in, for example, Spanish (S. Montrul and M. Bowles 2009) and Korean (W. O'Grady et al. 1997 in S. Montrul and M. Bowles 2009).

For the purpose of this paper three relationships were analyzed: a) between Croatian class attendance and self-assessed language proficiency; b) between Croatian class attendance and attitudes towards the use of Croatian, and c) between Croatian class attendance and the maintenance of Croatian in the participants' everyday life. According to the findings of previous research the following hypotheses were formed:

H 1: Participants who have attended Croatian language classes assess their knowledge of Croatian higher than those who had no formal education in the Croatian language.

H 2: Participants who have attended Croatian language classes have a more positive attitude to their usage of the Croatian language.

H 3: Croatian class attendance positively affects the maintenance of Croatian language – individuals who regularly attended Croatian classes use Croatian more often in everyday life.

2.2 Data collection

The research data presented in this paper was collected through the project *Croatian as a Heritage Language: Current Situation and Developmental Perspectives* conducted during the years of 2013 and 2014 and financed by the University of Zagreb[8]. The project was the first attempt to collect a larger set of data using the same methodology, and as such, a comprehensive online questionnaire was designed. The questionnaire was issued in three versions (Croatian[9], English[10] and Spanish[11]) and consisted of numerous questions addressing demographic information; self-assessment of language knowledge – Croatian and the host country's majority language; information about how and where Croatian was learnt/spoken; information on the participants' use of Croatian in everyday life; the status of the Croatian language in the participant's community; participants' attitudes towards Croatian, Croatian culture and the importance of maintaining their heritage language, etc. The questionnaire was distributed through the project website (www.nasljedni.hr) and the official Croatian Heritage Foundation's website[12]. The information about the websites and the questionnaire was also distributed through the

---

8   <http://nasljedni.hr/>.

9   <https://docs.google.com/forms/d/1en2BDlB-upU3d2yE5mtYume7Zzlh1hozfBGeO-S2rXQ/viewform>.

10 <https://docs.google.com/forms/d/1Y494uGzl3Om3Sa15caUlGBAyFizWPEYX7TJfz igklxw/viewform>.

11 <https://docs.google.com/forms/d/1ddnRwZDJuw_EXx0HzSM2643uC2laV-QK6cTx-sqP7T-Q/viewform>.

12 Croatian Heritage Foundation (CHF) is a governmental institution that supports educational, social and cultural activities of Croatian communities abroad.

authors' professional and personal contacts (e-mail, regular mail) and through the project Facebook page[13].

2.3 Participants

For the purpose of this study, only the English questionnaires were taken into consideration. Namely, the Croatian version of the questionnaire was aimed towards the people, most of whom would not be considered heritage speakers, i.e. the 1st generation of immigrants born, raised and educated in Croatia or speakers of Croatian in the countries where Croatian is either an official (Bosnia and Herzegovina) or minority language (Serbia). The Spanish questionnaire is currently being analyzed and the results are expected to be published within a year.

There were 51 responses to the questionnaire in English. Among the participants, 33 were female (65%) and 18 male (35%). Their average age was 42. The home countries of the participants included USA (24), Australia (15), Germany (3), Argentina (1), Austria (1), Canada (1), France (1), Hungary (1), Italy (1), New Zealand (1), Sweden (1), Pakistan (1).

3. Results and discussion

The participants (N=51) were divided into two groups according to their Croatian language class attendance. The results showed that just over a half of participants had attended formal Croatian classes as children (51%).

3.1 Self-assessment of the knowledge of Croatian

The participants were asked to assess their proficiency in two languages: Croatian and their other language, i.e. the majority and/or the official language of the host country. The Five-level Likert scale was used to assess the four basic language skills: listening comprehension, speaking, reading comprehension and writing (5 represents the highest and 1 the lowest proficiency level). The results of the self-assessment show that the dominant language for most participants in the survey was the language of the host country – 96.1% of all the participants have an outstanding or very good understanding of it, 94.1% claim their writing abilities in that language are very high. The average scores for each of the language skills have been shown in Table 1.

---

13 <https://www.facebook.com/nasljedni?ref=hl>.

Table 1: Self-assessment of the participants' host country language

Skill	Average score
I understand the language.	4.75
I speak the language.	4.67
I can read the language.	4.73
I can write the language.	4.67

In the self-assessment of Croatian language proficiency, the participants evaluated themselves considerably lower. Only 54.9% believe that their listening comprehension is outstanding or very good, 49% think the same for their speaking abilities and the smallest number (37.2%) can write well in Croatian. The average scores have been shown in Table 2.

Table 2: Self-assessment of Croatian language proficiency

Skill	Average score
I understand Croatian.	3.6
I speak Croatian.	3.3
I read Croatian.	3.3
I write Croatian.	3

The Mann-Whitney U test was used to compare the scores of Croatian proficiency self- assessment with Croatian class attendance. The results show a significant difference (R_{da} = 802, R_{ne} = 524) between the two groups of participants (those who attended Croatian classes and those who did not) only in regard to their writing skills ("I write Croatian", $p < .015$, $z = -2.42$).

As expected, people who had attended Croatian classes evaluated their writing skills much higher than those who had never attended formal education in the Croatian language. This partially proves the first hypothesis (H 1) according to which the formal Croatian language education has a positive effect on the self-assessment scores for specific language skills. This piece of information is very important for heritage language classes with regard to the already known fact that heritage speakers are unlikely to master all the language skills equally well. Secondary language skills, i.e. skills that are usually learnt at school, are less developed than primary skills, i.e. listening and speaking. Formal language classes, according to the self-assessment results received, have a positive effect on writing skills in the heritage language. In order to obtain more reliable results, the participants' proficiency in their heritage language should be empirically proven.

3.2 Attitudes toward the Croatian language

Croatian has three dialects (Chakavian, Kajkavian and Stokavian), two of which significantly differ from the Croatian standard language. Many Croatian speakers are therefore vertically bilingual, as they have to also learn the standard variant of the language (D. Pavličević-Franić 2005). One of the most prominent characteristics of Croatian heritage speakers is that a great number of them speak one of the dialects, and have little or no knowledge of the standard at all (L. Cvikić 2014). The awareness and knowledge of the standard language variety is commonly acquired through schooling. Heritage speakers lack this part in their education and do not get to learn the standard and the way it is used. Therefore it is interesting to explore what heritage speakers think of their knowledge of the standard language themselves.

The majority of participants in the survey claimed to know only the standard Croatian language (54.9%). Others know both the standard and one of the dialects (35.3%), while 9.8% of the participants speak only a dialect. The two groups of participants, those who attended Croatian classes and the ones who did not, do not differ in regard to what variant of the language they use. One of the possible explanations for this could be that formal Croatian education abroad lacks sociolinguistic elements, i.e. it does not dedicate (enough) time to teaching and mastering metalinguistic knowledge about the standard and other language varieties. Previous empirical research has shown that the level of proficiency in a standard language does not correlate with the time spent on learning the language in a formal setting (D. Pavličević-Franić and K. Aladrović Slovaček 2013).

Most of the participants in the survey stated that they liked speaking Croatian and are aware of the errors they make. When asked how they feel when speaking Croatian, 19.6% said uncomfortable, while 23.5% did not feel that way (they do not feel uncomfortable). No significant difference was noted between the two researched groups (the attendees of Croatian classes and the non-attendees). Only a very small number (3 participants, i.e. 5.9%) claimed not to make errors when speaking Croatian, which is interesting because of the fact that the majority of participants stated that they knew only the standard language. 7.8% of the participants said that they liked speaking Croatian but that they rarely got the chance to do so.

The results of the Mann-Whitney U test showed no statistically significant differences in the scores for the attitudes towards using Croatian ($z = -1.01$, $p > .01$) between the two groups explored (the attendees and the non-attendees of Croatian classes). This speaks against the second hypothesis according to which the attendees of Croatian classes would have a more positive attitude to their usage of the Croatian language.

3.3 Maintenance of the Croatian language

In order to investigate the effect of Croatian language class attendance on the maintenance of the Croatian language, the participants' usage of language skills in Croatian in everyday life was explored.

Table 3: Participants' use of language skills in Croatian

		Language Skills			
		Speaking	**Reading**	**Writing**	**Listening**
Language Exposure (f)	Daily	17	8	11	12
	Often	18	12	14	11
	Sometimes	11	13	10	11
	Rarely	2	12	10	10
	Never	3	6	6	7
Croatian Classes Attendance (M)	Yes	3.23	3.07	3.00	2.34
	No	3.00	2.80	2.30	2.00

The results have shown that participants are mostly exposed to the spoken language. Most of the participants listen to Croatian daily (radio, TV, music), often speak Croatian and write in it, but only sometimes read in it (including reading on the Internet). The attendees and non-attendees of Croatian classes significantly differed in the following variables: *How often do you listen to Croatian songs?* ($z = -2.61$, $p < .009$), *How often do you use Croatian on the Internet?* ($z = -2.12$, $p < .034$) and *How often do you write in Croatian?* ($z = -2.26$, $p < .023$). The Croatian class attendees listen to Croatian songs more often ($R_{da} = 31.40$, $R_{ne} = 20.81$), use Croatian on the Internet ($R_{da} = 30.40$, $R_{ne} = 21.77$) and write in Croatian ($R_{da} = 30.40$, $R_{ne} = 21.48$).

The results show significant differences in the common usage of the three different language activities by the participants who attended Croatian language classes. Two of the activities (writing in Croatian and using Croatian on the Internet) are related to secondary language skills, developed through education. This result speaks in favour of the importance of formal language education for the development of writing and reading skills in HLL.

Spearman's rank correlation coefficient has shown a positive link between the variables "attending Croatian school/Croatian classes" and the results of the self-assessment of language skills: listening, speaking and reading. A statistical significance exists between the variables "attending Croatian school/Croatian classes" and self-assessment of writing "I write Croatian" ($r = .345$, $p < .01$), as earlier mentioned. A positive correlation is also evident between the everyday use of Croatian language and the variable "attending Croatian school/Croatian classes", while it is statistically significant in "I listen to Croatian songs" (r = .389, p < .01) and "I watch Croatian TV" (r = .284, p < .01). The results have proved the third hypothesis according to which Croatian class attendees use Croatian more often in their everyday life.

Conclusion

Every immigration community aims to maintain cultural, national (ethnic) and language identity. While being strongly connected and interwoven at the community level, ethnicity, culture and language of the community can play various roles in each of the community member's life. Various relationships between cultural and language identity contribute to the heterogeneity of a group of heritage language speakers: from those who have a connection with the culture, but not a command of a language, to those who have acquired both, language and cultural values, to the same high level. A mere desire to (re)construct personal identity is one of the strongest motivations for learning a heritage language.

The aim of this paper was to investigate the role of formal language classes in the maintenance of Croatian as a heritage language. The research conducted among the speakers aimed at their self-assessment of Croatian language competence and its usage. The results showed a positive effect on both researched phenomena. The Croatian class attendees self-assessed their competence in Croatian considerably higher than the non-attendees. It is especially important that the attendees have assessed their writing in Croatian higher – the skill that is acquired in educational settings and proven to be less developed in a heritage language. Besides a more positive self-image of a Croatian language user, the research showed that the Croatian language classes attendees developed a stronger tendency to use Croatian. They are more exposed to Croatian and use it more actively.

The conducted research confirmed the importance of formal language instruction for constructing a language profile of an individual, consequently for the maintenance of the language in the community. Therefore the responsibility for the maintenance of the heritage language should not be solely on a family and individuals, but it is necessary to ensure the circumstances for learning a heritage language for all the interested community members.

References

Cabo, D. P. Y. and Rothman, J. 2012. The (Il)Logical Problem of Heritage Speaker Bilingualism and Incomplete Acquisition. In: *Applied Linguistics* 33(4). 450–455.

Campbell, R. and Rosenthal, J. 2000. Heritage languages In: *Handbook of undergraduate second language acquisition*. Mahway, NJ: Erlbaum. 165–184.

Carreira, M. 2001. Seeking Explanatory Adequacy: a Dual Approach to Understanding the Term: Heritage Language Learner. In: *Heritage Language Journal* 2(1). 1–25.

Cummins, J. 2005. A Proposal for Action: Strategies for Recognizing Heritage Language Competence as a Learning Resource within the Mainstream Classroom. In: *The Modern Language Journal* 89(4). 585–592.

Cvikić, L. 2012. Rano učenje hrvatskoga kao inoga jezika ili Što je kroatistima ostavila Mirjana Vilke? In: *XXVI. Međunarodni znanstveni skup Hrvatskoga društva za primijenjenu lingvistiku „Jezik kao informacija".* Zagreb. 11–13.5.2012.

Cvikić, L. 2014. Obilježja ovladavanja hrvatskim kao nasljednim jezikom. In: *6. Hrvatski slavistički kongres* Vinkovci i Vukovar. 10–13.9.2014.

Cvikić, L., Jelaska, Z. and. Kanajet Šimić, L. 2010. Nasljedni govornici i njihova motivacija za učenje hrvatskoga jezika. In: *Croatian Studies Review* 6. 113–127.

Dörnyei, Z. 1998. Motivation in second and foreign language learning. In: *Language Teaching* 31(3). 117–135.

Fishman, J. 2001. 300-Plus Years of Heritage Language Education in the United States. In: Kreeft Peyton, J., D. A. Ranard and S. McGinnis (Eds.), *Heritage Languages in America. Preserving a National Resource.* McHenry, IL: Center for Applied Linguistics. 81–99.

Gardner, R. C. 1985. *Social psychology and second language learning: The role of attitudes and motivation.* London: Edward Arnold Publishers.

Gardner, R. C., Masgoret, A. M., Tennantand, J. and Mihic, L. 2004. Integrative motivation: Changes during a year-long intermediate-level language course. In: *Language Learning* 54. 1–34.

Hamers, J. F. and Blanc, M. H. A. 2000. *Bilinguality and Bilingualism.* Cambridge: Cambridge University Press.

Husseinalli, G. 2012. Arabic Heritage Language Learners: motivation, expectations, competence and engagement in learning Arabic. In: *Journal of the National Council of Less Commonly Taught Langauges* 11. 98–110.

Isurin, L. and Ivanova-Sullivan, T. 2008. Lost in Between: the Case of Russian Heritage Speakers. In: *Heritage Language Journal* 6(1). 72–104.

Jelaska, Z. and Hržica, G. 2005. In search for a missing part: Identificational and generational motivation in learning the L2. In: Medved Krajnovic, M. and

J. Mihaljevic Djigunovic (Eds.), 15 *EUROSLA*: book of abstracts. Zagreb-Dubrovnik: Filozofski fakultet. 101–102.

Jelaska, Z. and Vuk, D. 2014. Nasljedni govornici injiho v hrvatski jezik – utjecaj jezične povijesti napisanu proizvodnj. In: *XXVII. Međunarodni znanstveni skup HDPL-a "Višejezičnost kao predmet mutlidisciplinarnih istraživanja".* Zagreb. 25–27.4.2014.

Lee, J. S. and Kim, Y.-H. 2007. Heritage language learners' attitudes, motivations and instructional needs: The case of postsecondary Korean language learners. In: Kondo-Brown, K. and J. D. Brown (Eds.), *Teaching Chinese, Japanese, and Korean heritage language students: Curriculum needs, materials and assessment.* New York: Lawrence Erlbaum Associates.

Kagan, O. and Dillon, K. 2001. A New Perspective on Teaching Russian: Focus on the Heritage Learner. In: *Slavic and East European Journal* 45(3). 507–518.

Kondo-Brown, K. 2003. Heritage Language Instruction for Post-secondary Students from Immigrant Backgrounds. In: *Heritage Language Journal* 1(1). 1–25.

Montrul, S. 2004. Subject and object expression in Spanish heritage speakers. A case of morpho-syntactic convergence. In: *Billingualism: Language and Cognition* 7. 125–142.

Montrul, S. 2008. Second language acquisition welcomes the heritage language learner: Opportunities of a new field. In: *Second Language Research* 24. 487–506.

Montrul, S. 2012. Is the heritage language like a second language? In: Roberta, L., Ch. Lindqvist, C. Bardel and N. Abrahamsson (Eds.), *12 EUROSLA Yearbook.* Amsterdam: John Benjamins Publishing Company. 1–29.

Montrul, S. and Bowles, M. 2009. Is grammar instruction beneficial for heritage language learners? Dative case marking in Spanish. In: *The Heritage Language Journal* 7(1). 47–73.

Novak Milić, J. and L. Cvikić. 2007. Gramatika u nastavi hrvatskoga kao ne-materinskoga jezika. In: Cvikić, L. (Ed.), *Drugi jezik hrvatski.* Zagreb: Profil International. 145–149.

Novak Milić, J. 2002. Učenje glagolskih oblika u hrvatskome kao stranome jeziku. In: *Suvremena lingvistika* 53–54(1–2). 85–101.

Novak Milić, J. 2004. Alibi za gramatiku (Utjecaj gramatičkoga poučavanja na razvoj glagolske morfologije u hrvatskome kao stranome ili drugome jeziku). In: Stolac, D., N. Ivanetić and B. Pritchard (Eds.), *Suvremena kretanja u nastavi stranih jezika: Zbornik radova Hrvatskog društva za primijenjenu lingvistiku.* Zagreb and Rijeka: Hrvatsko drustvo za primijenjenu lingvistiku. 341–350.

Novak Milić, J. 2005. Djelotvornost gramatičkoga poučavanja. In: Jelaska, Z. (Ed.), *Hrvatski kao drugi i strani jezik.* Zagreb: Hrvatska sveučilišna naklada. 351–357.

Polinsky, M. 2008. Gender under Incomplete Acquisition: Heritage Speakers Knowledge of Noun Categorization. In: *The Heritage Language Journal* 6(1). 40–72.

Polinsky, M. 2011. Reanalysis in adult heritage language: A case for attrition. In: *Studies in Second Language Acquisition* 33. 305–328.

Polinsky, M. and Kagan, O. 2007. Heritage Languages: In the 'Wild' and in the Classroom. In: *Language and Linguistics Compass* 1(5). 368–395.

Pavličević-Franić, D. 2005. *Komunikacijom do gramatike.* Zagreb: Alfa.

Pavličević-Franić, D. and Aladrović Slovaček, K. 2012. Mastering morphological competence in the acquisition of Croatian as L2. In: Akbarov, A. and V. Cook. (Eds.), *Approaches and Methods in Second and Foreign Language Teaching* Sarajevo: International Burch University. 187–198.

Pavličević-Franić, D. and Aladrović Slovaček, K. 2013. Learning and teaching of Croatian as a heritage language (L2) in children of Croatian emigrants abroad. In: *International Symposium on Language and Communication: Exploring Novelties – Book of Proceedings.* Izmir: Izmir University. 137–150.

Pavličević-Franić, D., Aladrović Slovaček, K. and Gazdić-Alerić, T. 2012. Jezične kompetencije učenika u hrvatskoj nastavi u inozemstvu. In: *Napredak* 153(2). 163–185.

O'Grady, W., Song, M., Cho, S. and Lee, M. 1997. The learning and teaching of Korean in community schools. In: Kim, Y.-H. (Ed.), *Korean language in America 2.* American Association of Teachers of Korean. 111–127.

Škvorc, B. 2006. Hrvatski uokviren engleskim: jezika ustralskih Hrvata kao prvi i drugi jezik. In: *Lahor* 1. 15–26.

Van Deusen-Scholl, N. 2003. Toward a Definition of Heritage Language: Sociopolitical and Pedagogical Consideration. In: *Journal of Language, Identity and Education* 2(3). 211–230.

Valdés, G. 2000. The Teaching of Heritage Languages: An Introduction for Slavic Teaching Professional. In: Kagan, O. and B. Rifkin (Eds.), *The Learning and Teaching of Slavic Languages and Cultures.* Bloomington: Slavica. 375–405.

Valdés, G. 2005. The teaching of minority languages as academic subjects: Pedagogical and Theoretical Challenges. In: *The Modern Language Journal* 79(3). 299–328.

Yu, P.-Sh. 2014. Heritage Language Learning Motivation, Self-Perceived Identity and Maintenance among Chinese-American College Students. In: *Journal of Language and Cultural Education* 2(1). 26–47.

Kyria Finardi
(Federal University of Espirito Santo, Brazil)
Virág Csillagh
(University of Geneva, Switzerland)

Globalization and Linguistic Diversity in Switzerland: Insights from the Roles of National Languages and English as a Foreign Language

Introduction

Globalization contributed to the emergence of the information society (P. Lévy 1999) and knowledge economy (N. V. Varghese 2013), which in turn, led to the internationalization of higher education (J. C. Shin and U. Teichler 2014). The role of languages in this scenario must be analyzed with care since globalization generates wealth as well as misery (J. Blommaert 2010) once it privileges some languages at the expense of others and this privilege in turn, generates power and capital (P. Bourdieu and J. Thompson 1991).

The status of a given language is a form of cultural and symbolic capital, described by P. Bourdieu as the knowledge, skills, qualifications and prestige associated with a language. Linguistic capital is described by J. Blommaert (2010) as being linked to globalization and to the notion of linguistic imperialism or linguicide (R. Phillipson 1992) which usually assumes that a powerful/global language (such as English) may threaten minor/local ones. Yet, and still according to J. Blommaert (2010), this assumption is shortsighted since it ties a speaker to a local language, reinforcing the presumed fixed connection between people and their environment when we know that an important characteristic feature of the globalized world we live in is mobility. In the contemporary society people move both in real and in symbolic, social space and this mobility bears important implications for the language. Thus, the problem of globalization in relation to the language can be summarized as being a choice between saving speakers from their economic predicament or saving a language from its death (J. Blommaert 2010).

J. Blommaert (2010) seems to be aligned with P. Bourdieu's view of linguistic capital when he proposes that linguistic inequality is not related to different values of languages in general but to specific resources such as registers, varieties, accents, genres and skills, or linguistic capital in P. Bourdieu's view. These linguistic resources (linguistic capital for P. Bourdieu) follow the predicament of their users, that is, if they are socially mobile, their resources will follow this trajectory; if they are socially marginal, their resources will also be qualified as such. Though an analysis of these resources or of the notion of linguistic capital in relation to the languages used in Switzerland is beyond the scope of this paper, we would like to retain this idea in the ensuing study.

1. Language skills and economic value

Though the notion of symbolic power and linguistic capital are very interesting per se, not all the wealth carried by languages is symbolic and not all the connections between linguistic and financial factors are indirect. Language economics, this relatively young branch of mainstream economics, examines the interrelationships between economic and linguistic phenomena (F. Grin 2003) while benefiting from the tools and advantages of decades of developments in the field of economics. Language economists (F. Grin 1999; 2003) have developed a system of values that categorizes the assets accessed through proficiency in a given language according to two central dimensions. On the one hand, gains can be obtained either at the individual or the social level. On the other hand, benefits can be of market or non-market type in nature. Due to a number of difficulties related to the investigation of non-market values (V. Csillagh 2015), research in language economics tends to focus on the assessment of market values both in terms of individual and social benefits (F. Grin 2003).

As an example of non-market values in higher education that can be enhanced by multilingualism, it is enough to think of potential friendships with international students at the student level or a culturally more diverse atmosphere at the level of the institution. Neither of these can be directly translated to financial gains and yet they are important assets in individual life and institutional portfolios. The list of market values is traditionally headed by individual salary differentials linked to proficiency and increases in national GDP as a result of multilingualism. Both are crucial to a country's wealth and are therefore important elements of language policy decision-making. However, before we consider these aspects, we would like to briefly address some of the questions the above classification raises in terms of language learning motivation.

2. Economic value and motivation

A detailed review of the wide range of influences that processes of multilingualism, globalization and internationalization have on foreign language learning at the level of the individual is beyond the scope of this paper. Yet, we would like to draw attention to some of the most important findings of contemporary research on this issue. Motivation has traditionally been categorized as internal and external and language learning motivation theories undoubtedly contain important references to the learning environment (for a review see V. Csillagh 2015).

Research has shown that international openness (T. Yashima 2009) and positive attitudes towards learning English (V. Csillagh 2010; J. Kormos and K. Csizér 2008) as well as a sense of social obligations (V. Csillagh 2010; 2016) and interest in English and American culture (V. Csillagh 2010; J. Kormos and K. Csizér 2008), among a host of other factors, positively impact learners' motivation, whereas ethnocentric attitudes (V. Csillagh 2010; S. Ryan 2009) tend to diminish it. Learners thus reap considerable non-market benefits through their enjoyment of language learning and cultural interest, but also by fulfilling their social goals. On the other hand, their international aspirations and perceptions of the role they are to fill in society also have a strong financial overtone.

It is important to point out that the influence of these factors was always indirect, as they acted through learners' self-concept. Indeed, dynamic theories of motivation (Z. Dörnyei 2009) emphasize the relevance of identity creation as an aspect of foreign language learning. E. Ushioda (2015) draws attention to the fact that learners live in complex interrelations with and are inseparable from their multiple contexts. In learners' quickly expanding world, the motivational impact of global and local, cultural and ethnic, social and economic contexts has become a primary feature of foreign language learning.

While these findings have clear implications for educators and learners, V. Csillagh (2016) suggests that they are also central to the efficiency and profitability of an educational system. As a consequence, they have an essential role to play in the success of language education policies. M. Kelly (2013: 15) argues that "[h]igher education is at the forefront of mobility" and diversity, and it is crucial for institutions to adapt their policies to the swiftly changing cultural and social environment.

3. Globalization and language policy

Language policy is described by J. Blommaert (2010) as the production and enforcement of norms for language use, and its success is measured by the degree to which these norms are accepted and spread. Traditionally, the state is the major player in the field of language policy regulating issues such as which language(s) and forms of literacy are official and national. In the case of Switzerland, the linguistic scenario is that of a country with three official languages (German, French and Italian), four national languages (the official ones plus Romansh) and where English and Spanish are taught as foreign/additional languages together with other national languages in school. As such, Switzerland can be described as the personification of linguistic diversity and multilingualism in Europe and according to F. Grin (2003), any form of linguistic diversity entails some sort of conflict which calls for some kind of intervention in the form of language policy. F. Grin (2003) also reminds us that language policies have direct economic implications which is why a language economics viewpoint is more frequently required to evaluate possible courses of action in language policy and diversity.

K. Finardi and M. C. Porcino (2014) suggest that globalization and the advent of the internet changed the way we teach, learn, view and use languages in general and English in particular. So as to check if this applies to Switzerland the present study analyzes the role of national and additional languages (L2) in university education for life both from the perspective of the local setting of multilingual Geneva and in today's globalized world. With that aim the study explores language practices at the University of Geneva in relation to motivation, career prospects and Swiss language policies.

3.1 Swiss linguistic panorama and language policies

According to G. Lüdi (1998), the idea that Switzerland is a multilingual country is both commonplace and based on the principle of territoriality, which means that the country is seen as a mosaic of four monolingual geographical areas. However, in Switzerland as in other Western European countries, the increasing mobility of the population as a result of globalization has led to a gradual destabilization of the national linguistic and cultural landscape. Switzerland has received many immigrants since the 1960s whose language backgrounds change the traditional image of a country made up of culturally and linguistically homogeneous regions. The homogeneity of these areas may no longer exist since all Swiss cities are more or less multilingual nowadays, Geneva probably being the most multilingual of all, which explains our choice for this study.

As regards the linguistic compositions of the Swiss population, census results show that 63.7% are German L1 speakers, while 20.4% have French, 6.5% Italian and 0.5% Romansh as their mother tongue (G. Lüdi and I. Werlen 2005). The majority or 90.8% of German-speaking residents speak the German dialect instead of

Standard German at home (G. Lüdi and I. Werlen 2005: 36), and though the Swiss German dialects were traditionally used for the home and everyday life while Standard German was usually used in the professional sphere, V. Csillagh (2015) explains that German dialects started to gain ground and became an emblem of Swiss ideological and economic independence gradually replacing Standard German in a number of contexts, so much so that French speakers have started to question the learning of Standard German as a national language.

Also according to V. Csillagh (2015) and as opposed to the linguistic duality of the German cantons, French-speaking areas are highly multilingual. On average 18.4% of the population are of non-French mother tongue and 8% of residents speak another official language (G. Lüdi and I. Werlen 2005). Nationwide, foreigners constitute one fifth of the population and while most of them have French or Italian as a mother tongue, 37.7% speak a language other than the four official languages at home (ibid.). Such multilingual settings provide a unique background to language learning but also pose challenges to communication.

In 2000, the non-official languages with the largest group of native speakers were Serbo-Croatian with 103,000 speakers, followed by Albanian with 95,000, Portuguese with 89,500, Spanish with 77,500, English with 73,000, Macedonian 61,300, and a total of 173,000 speakers of other languages, amounting to roughly 10% of the population with a native language not among the four official languages. These percentages have since then grown and pose serious implications for the balance among national languages and perhaps even more so for the balance between national and foreign languages.

In 2009 the number of foreigners in Switzerland soared to 22%, 85% of whom were of European origins with the largest group of foreigners coming from Italy (15.4%), followed by Germany (15.1%), Portugal (13.1%) and France (5.7%). The proportion of non-European nationals doubled since 1980 to reach 14.9% today, according to the information displayed in the Federal Statistical Office of Neuchâtel in 2015. The percentage of non-national language speakers varies greatly from one canton to another, and is headed by the canton of Geneva (18.7%), followed by the canton of Vaud (12.5%), Basel City (12.1%) Zurich (9.9%), Ticino (5.4%), Obwalden (5.3%), Jura (4.8%), Nidwalden (4.6%) and Uri (4.5%) and is particularly important in large cities. A look at the density of Spanish and Portuguese at the district level shows that they concentrate in the French-speaking region, whereas Turkish and Slavic languages are concentrated in the German speaking region.

In Switzerland, compulsory education is regulated by each canton but there is a general agreement that the two majority national languages (German and French), will be taught as first foreign/additional languages as a way to guarantee national cohesion. Yet, the role of English as a foreign language seems to be threatening this agreement as shown by the project to include English as a first foreign language in the canton of Zurich.

Opinions seem to be divided in relation to the role of English in Switzerland. Some claim that if English was used as an instrumental language between language groups in Switzerland it would threaten national cohesion and the mutual cultural understanding. What is more, the increasing use of English phrases in the media and advertising could downplay the use of French or German. On the other hand, there are those who feel that the teaching of English as a foreign language could help, instead of hinder, national cohesion (M. Heller 2003), if it were used as an instrumental language or lingua franca, defined by D. Crystal (1995: 454) as a medium of communication for people who speak different first languages. Indeed, C. Hoffmann (2000) claims that English has been used as a lingua franca in multilingual countries such as Belgium, where a certain amount of tension exists between the country's main two languages, or between countries with similar languages such as Denmark, Sweden and Norway, or Belgium and the Netherlands, for speakers who want to avoid encountering negative linguistic attitudes. Other parts of Europe, such as, for instance Catalonia or the Basque Country in Spain, seem to be moving in the same direction.

The reason for this feeling in Switzerland may be related to the fact that the German speaking Swiss who learn French can usually communicate well in that language with the French speaking Swiss whereas the French speaking Swiss who learn Standard German cannot really communicate with the German speaking Swiss in German since German speaking Swiss speak Swiss German and not standard German in non-official environments. Some German speaking Swiss feel that it is easier to speak English to French speaking Swiss who learned Standard German rather than trying to communicate with them in Standard German. Of course that causes a number of reasons for resentment, especially on the French side who not only has to invest more years to learn standard German that is not really spoken by the German speaking Swiss but also who feel that the German speaking Swiss who proposed the teaching of English as a first foreign language (before the teaching of French) breached the contract and good will implied in the policy to teach German or French first as foreign/additional languages.

A survey conducted in September 2000 and reported by Heather Murray, Ursula Wegmüller and Fayaz Ali Khan in 2001 found that the introduction of early teaching of English in the canton of Zurich was broadly accepted by the German speaking Swiss. Regarding the choice of foreign/additional languages to teach the study revealed that attitudes towards English are complex and related to ideas of national languages. As for the teaching of foreign/additional languages in Swiss schools, the study showed that the German speaking Swiss respondents judge their skills in

French and English better than that of Romansh in German and English and that in both regions respondents feel they speak English more fluently than the national language counterpart. The German speaking Swiss spend more on the teaching of English than the French speaking Swiss or the Italian speaking Swiss on the teaching of German or French. Finally, the study reports interesting data for the role of English in the world of work in Switzerland with a growing demand for English among employees identified. The same was identified for the role of English in the academic field, which is undeniably growing, as evidenced by the proliferation of publications, and courses offered in that language in Swiss universities.

Yet, there are some who resent the increasing use of English as a threat to national cohesion, world multilingualism and to the role of French as a scientific language (L. Gajo 2013). As can be seen in this portrait, the roles of national languages and that of English as a foreign/additional language in Switzerland (and anywhere else we would add) are complex and multifaceted. So as to offer a glimpse of how this complexity is materialized in a given context we now focus on the Swiss example of multi and plurilingualism.

Plurilingualism refers to a situation where a person has competence in more than one language whereas multilingualism is a situation where multiple languages coexist though are stored separately. The Common European Framework of Reference for Languages, CEFR (Council of Europe 2001) promotes plurilingualism as a shift in perspective towards the use of additional languages by removing the pressure to achieve perfection since this concept emphasizes the fact that a person's competence in a given language interacts and contributes to the growth of communication skills as a whole. According to the Council of Europe this perspective entails that the aim of language education is not seen as simply to achieve 'mastery' of one or two, or even three languages, each taken in isolation, with the 'ideal native speaker' as the ultimate model. Instead, the aim is to develop a linguistic repertoire, in which all linguistic abilities have a place. In line with the Council of Europe's view of plurilingualism, we now turn to the Swiss example.

3.2 The value of Swiss plurilingualism

Another side to the argument, however, is that of the economic reality, which is often contrasted with the pleas driven by patriotic sentiment. However and surprisingly, research has shown that the global language (English) is not always the pragmatic choice (F. Grin 2014). F. Grin (1999), investigating salary differentials linked to language proficiency in Switzerland, found that in French-speaking cantons skills in English can result in a salary increase of as much as 10.23%. What was more surprising was the 13.82% raise that was associated with proficiency in

German. Admittedly, these figures are for men and not all sectors display the same demand for language skills (G. Lüdi and I. Werlen 2005). However, a recent large scale study of Swiss firm's hiring needs (F. Grin, C. Sfreddo and F. Vaillancourt 2009) identified similar trends as regards the number of companies reporting a shortage of language skills.

With language education comprising 10% of total federal education spending, the stakes amount to around CHF 1500 per student per year (F. Grin and C. Sfreddo 1997). Therefore, the argument for economically sensitive language education policies is definitely valid and relevant to the case. On the other hand, these research findings also demonstrate that plurilingualism is highly valuable from an economic perspective, its market value being higher than that of an English-only policy. V. Csillagh (2016) identifies Swiss plurilingualism as the lifeblood of the country's economy. This was further confirmed by G. Lüdi *et al.* (2009), who showed the importance of German and Italian, in addition to English, in Swiss corporate communication. Last but not least, we would like to cite F. Grin, C. Sfreddo and F. Vaillancourt's (2009) shocking statistics, which show that if, from one day to the next, all Swiss residents lost their skills in other languages, the loss would result in a drop of as much as 10% of the country's GDP.

3.3 The role of English

Though Switzerland is often viewed as the personification of multilingualism and successful L2 teaching, questions of language use and learning are linked to identity and values and also to questions of global and local multilingualism. As suggested by V. Csillagh (2016), no examination of modern foreign language learning can be complete without taking into consideration the global role of English whose unprecedented status implies serious consequences on social and economic processes permeated by globalization. Indeed, at least one book was dedicated to understand its use in Europe (J. Cenoz and U. Jessner 2000) and another to understand its use in relation to globalization (M. Saxena and T. Omoniyi 2010).

Many different names and adjectives have been linked to English, among which we have: international language (T. Cain 2008; E. J. Erling 2005; T. McArthur 2004; S. L. McKay 2002); international language of social inclusion (K. Finardi 2014); lingua franca (M. El Kadri and T. Gimenez 2013; J. Jenkins 2006; B. Seidlhofer 2001) world or global language (D. Graddol 2006; K. Rajagopalan 2010); academic language (A. Mauranen and E. Ranta 2008); language of imperialism (B. Kumaravadivelu 2006); minor English (J. Zaidan 2013) and the most spoken and studied language worldwide (C. Kramsch 2014). Though these studies are relevant for pointing out some of the implications of adopting a certain view of English, they say little about how these views are materialized in different contexts.

As suggested by K. Finardi (2014), much has been said about the spread of English and its implications (T. Cain 2008; D. Graddol 2006; J. Jenkins 2006; S. L. McKay 2003) in a world where non-native speakers of English are said to outnumber native speakers by double (B. B. Kachru 1996), triple (A. Pakir 1999 in T. Cain, 2008), or quadruple (B. B. Kachru 1996) depending on the source of statistics. If the spread of English continues as projected (D. Graddol 2006), language policy makers, implementers and critical users must consider the implications of using, teaching and learning this language in a variety of local and global contexts.

Though a detailed review of the role of English in the globalized scenario is beyond the scope of this paper, we can say that in general terms the view of the status of English can be divided in two main lines, the first represented by those who see it as a language that can connect and empower people (D. Crystal 2003; D. Graddol 2006; K. Finardi 2014) and the other as a language that separates people and threatens other languages or communities (R. Phillipson 2009; L. Gajo 2013). Yet, and despite the view of English adopted, the analysis of language use in multilingual contexts cannot make do without considering the role of English in the globalized world and local scenario. So as to offer a contribution in this direction, the present study analyzes the multilingual context of a Swiss university in relation to global trends and local uses of national and foreign languages. With that aim and in what follows, a glimpse of this national scenario will be zoomed in a particular local scenario where the data of this study was collected, namely, the University of Geneva (UNIGE).

4. UNIGE

UNIGE is one of Europe's leading universities, one of the three best French speaking universities in the world and one of the 100 best universities in the world according to at least four different ranking institutions: Leiden Ranking (56th), Shanghai Ranking (66th), Times Higher Education (107th) and World University Rankings (85th). With around 18,000 students of more than 150 nationalities, UNIGE is Switzerland's second largest university right after the University of Zurich with 26,000 students.

Regarding the internationalization of UNIGE in 2014 there were 40% of international students, 52% of international teaching staff, 65% of international doctoral students and 153 nationalities represented with 797 incoming students, 431 outgoing students and 733 exchange agreements. As we can see from these figures UNIGE has a strong tradition of receiving international students with diverse linguistic backgrounds.

The Faculty of Letters at UNIGE offers courses about or in seventeen languages, namely: English, Armenian, French, Greek, Italian, Latin, Portuguese, Romansh, German, Arabic, Chinese, Japanese, Russian, Spanish, Korean, Mesopotamian and Hebrew. Fifteen of these languages are offered for graduate programs: Arabic, Armenian, Chinese, English, French as a foreign language, German, Hebrew, Italian, Japanese, Latin, Medieval French and Latin, Mesopotamian, Greek, Russian, Spanish and eighteen of these are offered at Master's level: Ancient Science and Latin, Ancient Science and Mesopotamian, Arabic, Armenian, East Asian languages and philology, Chinese, English, French as a foreign language, German and Swiss Culture, German, Italian, Japanese, Latin, Medieval studies, Mesopotamian, Greek, Russian and Spanish with Portuguese offered both at BA and MA levels. There are a total of four Teaching Diplomas and four languages offered as foreign or additional languages: French, Korean, Italian and Romansh.

As regards the use of languages at UNIGE in general, we can say that the most spoken languages per course in a decreasing order are French in all courses (especially in the Medicine area), English (especially in Economics and Social Sciences), German (especially in Law) and Italian (especially in Science). The highest number of L2 speakers in a decreasing order are English, German, French and Italian and the highest number of L1 speakers in a decreasing order are French, followed by German and Italian with the same proportion and finally by English.

Regarding the language policy at UNIGE, a document found in the site of the institution[1] states language policy measures in regards to six aspects: 1) Admission, 2) Language teaching, 3) Language of instruction, 4) Language of research, 5) Language of administration and 6) Language of external communication. In what concerns admissions, the document states that non-French speakers must take a French proficiency test prepared by the university for bachelor's level whereas for the master's level students the faculties are free to impose the test.

In what concerns the teaching of languages, the following policies apply: 1) Non-francophone students have access to French classes, 2) External financial sources are sought to guarantee the offer of French courses to non-francophone students through international agreements with UNIGE, 3) Credits can be given for language studies and each faculty/course can decide how much credit to assign, 4) In all cases the credit must be given to students who have a language certificate, language certificate with course title, completed a mobility program in a university whose language of instruction is different from French, 5) the university supports alternative models of language acquisition such as the tandem, 6) when the language of

---

1   Available at: <http://www.unige.ch/rectorat/static/politique_langues.pdf>.

instruction is English or German (in Masters and Doctorate courses), the students can benefit from a linguistic support from the university, 7) when courses are taught in English or German students can have linguistic support from the university to write papers and make oral presentations, 8) the university can propose a service of linguistic assistance to non-francophone professors or students in the preparation for the French proficiency tests. Such a service can also be offered if the language of instruction is considered weak by the professor or faculty.

Regarding the language of instruction, bilingual courses (those which are at least 25% taught in another language) are encouraged. Exceptionally and when justified, a bachelor level course can be taught in another language. The bilingual courses are certified with a diploma with a special mention to the language certificate.

With regards to the language of research, UNIGE offers linguistic support to write scientific papers in French, English and German. In what concerns the administrative language, the policy is that the language of the university (used for all communications with students, faculty and personnel) is French but English can be used with the non-francophone public. Important information regarding ethics or health is translated at least into English.

Finally, regarding the language of external communication, the document states that the official relations of UNIGE are made in the national languages and other languages can be used with international universities and the choice is made on a case basis. The language of promotion and recruitment is French but the university supports the translation of papers and presentations in other languages. Documents aimed at mobility and employability may be translated into English.

5. Research methods

The aim of the study was to look at the linguistic diversity at UNIGE. With that aim, a mixed methods design (Z. Dörnyei 2007) was used, the primary source of which originated from a questionnaire survey of 375 university students from four faculties at UNIGE. The online questionnaire was entirely in French and consisted of a total of 102 items, most of which belonged to eleven multi-item scales focusing on students' attitudes towards English. In these items, respondents were asked to signal their agreement or disagreement with a set of statements or indicate the regularity with which they practised certain activities in English. For the purposes of the present study, we examined a portion of the answers in the light of federal, local and institutional policies as well as from the perspective of lifelong learning.

In total, 375 students answered the call, seven of whom pursued studies at several faculties, therefore they were excluded from the comparisons. As shown in Table 1, the remaining 368 participants came from the faculties of Law and Medicine, Science and Social and Economic Sciences (SES).

Table 1: Participants

Gender	Law	Medicine	Science	SES	Total
Male	27	19	51	50	147
Female	64	42	95	20	221
Total	91	61	146	70	368

Participants represented all levels of university education and age groups. Their age ranged from 16 to 65, with an average of 23. The majority (256) of them had completed their secondary education in Switzerland, 187 in the canton of Geneva. An important number, 119 came from other countries, mostly (69) from France. The responses were recorded in LimeSurvey® (2012, V. 2.0) and data clearing took place in Microsoft Excel (2010). SPSS® (2013, V. 22.0) was used to analyze the data and compute statistics. Some of the results of the descriptive statistics are discussed below.

6. Results of the study

6.1 Language use

Regarding the participants' L1, most of them were French speakers, with around the same number of German, Italian and English speakers and a large number of speakers of other languages. On average students demonstrated a high level of multilingualism with as much as three L1s and two L2s. Figure 1 shows the number of responses in each category.

Figure 1: Mother tongues

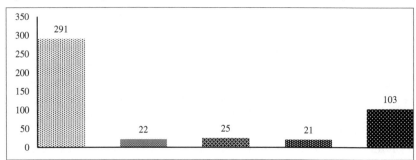

As displayed in Figure 2, language practices differed greatly, with the only exception of French, which was used *very often* at the university by students of all the four faculties. German was used most (between *rarely* and *sometimes*) at the faculty of Law and Italian at the faculty of Medicine, though its occurrence was still below *rare*. Science students used English most frequently (towards *often*), with medical students running a close second. All in all, English was used more often than *sometimes* by students of three faculties, with Law students using it considerably less often during their studies but still *sometimes*

Figure 2: Language use at the four faculties. Note: 1 corresponds to never or almost never and 5 to very often or always

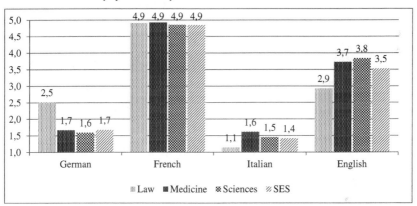

In addition and as Figure 3 shows, there were important differences in students' L2 skills. For a clearer interpretation of the results, students with no proficiency were included in the analysis, whereas native speakers were excluded. Medical students excelled in French, while their peers at the faculty of Science finished last when it came to the main language of the university. Nevertheless, even the lowest levels in French reached C1 in the Common European Framework of Reference.

The case of German is radically different, although again Science students were the ones who achieved the lowest scores. The overall level was A2. It is important to note that as V. Csillagh (2016) explains there were a lot of heritage learners in the sample, who indicated German as a mother tongue and an L2. With the inclusion of these participants, the results are considerably higher and show a clear B2 (ibid.).

As with the regularity of its use, average levels in English show the same pattern. Law students and participants from the SES reported the highest level of English, but even low-scoring Science students' skills were close to B2. As for the third official language of the country, the average proficiency levels in Italian were low when considering participants with skills in the language only, and with the inclusion of all non-native students, they virtually disappeared.

Figure 3: Foreign language skills at the four faculties. Note: 1 denotes A2 and 6 C2

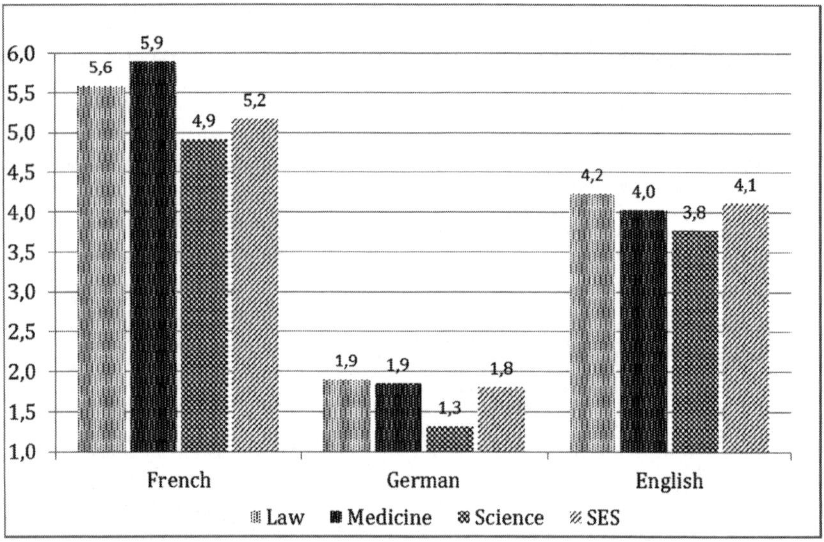

Participants' attitudes to English also showed interesting patterns as shown in Figure 4. Students' motivation being generally quite high, they also had favourable attitudes to the idea of a global language. In addition, the item linking English to career prospects obtained the highest mean value in the whole questionnaire (V. Csillagh 2016).

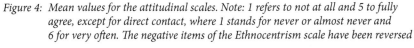

Figure 4: Mean values for the attitudinal scales. Note: 1 refers to not at all and 5 to fully agree, except for direct contact, where 1 stands for never or almost never and 6 for very often. The negative items of the Ethnocentrism scale have been reversed

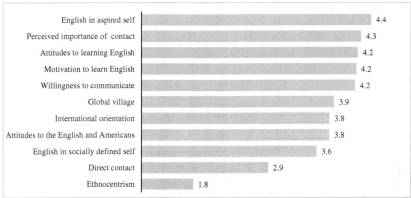

On the whole, the analysis of the attitudinal scales revealed that English is an important part of participants' self-concept, as the items linking it to their aspired self-obtained the strongest agreement among all the scales. Additionally, the questions investigating the place of English in students' socially defined self also elicited responses that were singularly high when compared to other contexts (V. Csillagh 2015). It is not surprising to see high levels of agreement when it comes to questions of positive attitudes and motivation to learn the global language. However, given the particularly multilingual local context and the importance of official languages in federal language policy on the one hand and the almost exclusive use of French at the University of Geneva on the other, participants' remarkably positive attitudes to the global village and the extent of their international openness might come as a surprise.

What is even more interesting is that, in light of the language data discussed above, we know that many of them are not taught the language nor taught in English at the university. This might mean that their valuable skills and their positive attitudes are therefore untapped, their potential wasted. Moreover, English is only one of the many languages UNIGE students master. Thus, their skills, when put to use, might increase their chances manifold not only at the labor market but also in their life in a globalized world.

6.2 Discussion

6.2.1 The market value of university students' language skills

Participants' attitudes towards English reflect global values associated with the language, but also show the relevance of the language in the local context, as a means to achieve professional goals and coveted social status. Their motivation to learn English is linked first and foremost to their sense of responsibility in their social milieu (V. Csillagh 2016), of which economic considerations form an important part. As a standalone factor, however, market benefits do not fully explain students' motivational patterns.

6.2.2 Economic value and university students' attitudes

The results show English skills in surplus compared to the local market demand. On the other hand, there is a considerable shortage of Italian and a slight shortage of German skills. These patterns of surplus and shortage reflect some of the issues at the heart of the current debate on Swiss language education policy. The surplus of English skills, coupled with the shortage of German skills (a national language) in our sample can be a manifestation of the tension between national languages versus English (a global language).

6.2.3 Language skills and university education for life

Plurilingual language policies are needed to change the balance of university language use and, potentially, learning. The analysis of language policies at UNIGE suggests that these guidelines still fall short of fulfilling this expectation. Widely available language education would help develop language skills in areas of shortage, while more extensive use of a greater variety of languages would help hone existing ones. We argue for enhancing awareness in policy making of both market and non-market benefits as well as global and local values.

Conclusion

This paper was motivated by the desire to reflect on multilingualism in the current global setting. With that aim, a study on the linguistic diversity of Switzerland and the linguistic practices of its second largest university in its most multilingual city was proposed against the backdrop of the current scenario of globalization. The construction of multilingualism in Switzerland in general and in Geneva in particular as well as the roles of national languages in contrast to the role of English as a foreign/additional language were analyzed in that context and in relation to motivation, career prospects and UNIGE's language policies. The results of this study showed that social and economic considerations on a local but also on a global scale play an important role in the attitudes and language practices of UNIGE students. Based on these results, the study argues for a review of language policies to reflect both global and local considerations as well as to prepare the citizens for the challenges of multilingualism in the current scenario of globalization.

In that sense, we agree with M. Kelly (2013) that language policies should be carefully tailored by universities since they are an essential element of academic life and also provide a valuable support for the study of other disciplines. Moreover, language policies support the mission of the institution by helping students become more employable and with more valuable life skills, not to mention that languages can help the university achieve its international (and universal) ambition.

References

Blommaert, J. 2010. *The Sociolinguistics of Globalization. Cambridge Approaches to Language Contact.* Cambridge: Cambridge University Press.

Bourdieu, P. and Thompson, J. 1991. *Language and Symbolic Power.* Cambridge, MA: Harvard University Press.

Cain, T. 2008. Do You Speak Global? The Spread of English and the Implications for English Language Teaching. In: *Canadian Journal for New Scholars in Education* 1(1).

Cenoz, J. and U. Jessner (Eds.) 2000. English in Europe: The Acquisition of a Third Language. In: Multilingual Matters: Bilingual Education and Bilingualism 19, Series Editors N. Hornberger and C. Baker.

Council of Europe. 2001. *Common European framework of reference for languages: Learning, teaching, assessment.* Cambridge: Cambridge University Press.

Csillagh, V. 2010. *World citizenship as a factor affecting the motivated learning behavior of adult Hungarian learners.* Unpublished master's thesis. Eotvos Lorand University, Budapest, Hungary.

Csillagh, V. 2015. Global trends and local realities: Lessons about economic benefits, selves and identity from a Swiss context. In: *Studies in Second Language Learning and Teaching* 5(3). 431–453. doi: 10.14746/ssllt.2015.5.3.5.

Csillagh, V. 2016. Love or money? Reinterpreting traditional motivational dimensions in modern social and economic contexts. In: Gkonou, C., D. Tatzl and S. Mercer (Eds.), *New directions in language learning psychology.* Dördrecht: Springer Science and Business Media.

Crystal, D. 1995. *Encyclopedia of the English language*. Cambridge: Cambridge University Press.

Crystal, D. 2003. *English as a global language* (2nd ed.). Cambridge: Cambridge University Press.

Dörnyei, Z. 2007. *Research methods in applied linguistics: Quantitative, qualitative, and mixed methodologies*. Oxford: Oxford University Press.

Dörnyei, Z. 2009. The L2 motivational self-system. In: Dörnyei Z. and E. Ushioda (Eds.), *Motivation, language identity and the L2 self*. Bristol: Multilingual Matters. 9–42.

El Kadri, M. and Gimenez, T. 2013. Formando professors de inglês para o context do inglês como lingua franca. In: *Acta Scientarium. Language and Culture* 35(2). 125–133.

Erling, E. J. 2005. The many names of English: A discussion of the variety of labels given to the language in its worldwide role. In: *English Today 81, 21*(1). 40–44.

Finardi, K. and Porcino, M. C. 2014. Tecnologia e Metodologia no Ensino de Inglês: Impactos da Globalização e da Internacionalização. In: *Ilha do Desterro* 66. 239–284.

Finardi, K. 2014. The slaughter of Kachru's five sacred cows in Brazil and the use of English as an international language. In: *Studies of English Language Teaching 2*. 401–411.

Gajo, L. 2013. Français, plurilinguisme et science: une problématique émergente. In: *Synergies Europe* 8. 7–10.

Gajo, L. 2013. Le plurilinguisme dans et pour la science: enjeux d'une politique linguistique à l'université. In: *Synergies Europe* 8. 97–110.

Graddol, D. 2006. *English Next: Why global English may mean the end of 'English as a foreign language'*. London, UK: British Council.

Grin, F. 1994. Conséquences économiques de l'intégration linguistique des immigrants. *IVᵉ Conférence internationale sur le droit et les langues: Droit et langue(e) d'enseignement*. Fribourg, 14–17.9.1994.

Grin, F. 1998. Language Policy in Multilingual Switzerland: Overview and Recent Developments. Paper presented at the *Cicle de conferencies sobre política linguística. Direcció general de política linguistica*. Barcelona, 4.12.1998.

Grin, F. 1999. *Compétences et récompenses: la valeur des langues en Suisse*. Fribourg: Editions Universitaires.

Grin, F. 2003. Language planning and economics. In: *Current Issues in Language Planning 4*(1). 1–66. doi: 10.1080/14664200308668048.

Grin, F. 2014. Dépasser les idées reçues. *Le Débat* 178(1) 127–135. doi: 10.3917/deba.178.0127.

Grin, F. and Sfreddo, C. 1997. *Dépenses publiques pour l'enseignement des langues secondes en Suisse.* Aarau: CSRE-SKBF.

Grin, F., Sfreddo, C. and Vaillancourt, F. 2009. *Langues étrangères dans l'activité professionnelle: Rapport final de recherche.* Geneva: Université de Genève.

Heller, M. 2003. Globalization, the new economy, and the commodification of language and identity. In: *Journal of Sociolinguistics* 7(4). 473–492. doi: 10.1111/j.1467-9841.2003.00238.x.

Hoffmann, C. 2000. The spread of English and the Growth of Multilingualism with English in Europe. In: Cenoz, J. and U. Jessner (Eds.), *English in Europe: The Acquisition of a Third Language.* Multilingual Matters: Bilingual Education and Bilingualism 19, Series Editors N. Hornberger and C. Baker. 1–21.

IBM Corp 2013. IBM SPSS Statistics for Windows, Version 22.0 [Computer software]. Armonk, NY: IBM Corp.

Jenkins, J. 2006. Current perspectives on teaching world Englishes and English as a lingua franca. In: *TESOL Quarterly* 40(1). 157–181.

Jordao, C. M. 2014. ILA – ILF – ILE – ILG: quem dá conta? In : *Revista Brasileira de Linguística Aplicada* 14(1). 13–40.

Kelly, M. 2013. Issues for Language Policy in Higher Education. *Darnioji Daugiakalbystė 2.* 12–22. Sustainable Multingualism 2/2013. 12–22.

Kachru, B. B. 1996. World Englishes: Agony and ecstasy. In: *Journal of Aesthetic Education* 30(2). 135–155.

Kormos, J. and Csizér, K. 2008. Age-related differences in the motivation of learning English as a foreign language: Attitudes, selves, and motivated learning behavior. *Language Learning* 58(2). 327–355. doi: 10.1111/j.1467-9922.2008.00443.x.

Kramsch, C. 2014. Teaching Foreign Languages in an Era of Globalization: Introduction. In: *The Modern Language Journal 98.*

Kumaravadivelu, B. 2006. *Understanding language teaching: from method to post-method.* Mahwah, New Jersey: Lawerence Erbaum Associates, Inc. Publishers.

LimeSurvey Project Team 2012. Lime Survey: An Open Source survey tool, Version 2.0 [Computer software]. Hamburg: LimeSurvey Project.

Lüdi, G. 1998. De la Suisse quadrilingue à la Suisse plurilingue: Bases démographiques, modèles de développement et problèmes de gestion. In: *DiversCité Langues. En ligne.* Vol. III. Available at: <http://www.uquebec.ca/diverscite>.

Lüdi, G., Werlen, I. and Franceschini, R. 1997. *Le Paysage linguistique de la Suisse. Recensement fédéral de la population 1990.*

Lüdi, G. and Werlen, I. 2005. *Recensement fédéral de la population 2000: le paysage linguistique en Suisse.* Neuchatel: OFS, Avril.

Lüdi, G., Barth, L. A., Höchle, K. and Yanaprasart, P. 2009. La gestion du plurilinguisme au travail entre la 'philosophie' de l'entreprise et les pratiques spontanées. In: *Sociolinguistica* 23. 32–52.

Lévy, P. 1999. *Cibercultura*. São Paulo: Editora 34.

Mauranen, A. and Ranta, E. 2008. English as an Academic Lingua Franca – the ELFA project. *Nordic journal of English Studies* 7(3). 199–202.

McArthur, T. 2004. Is it *world* or *international* or *global* English, and does it matter? In: *English Today* 79, 20(3). 3–15.

McKay, S. L. 2002. *Teaching English as an international language: rethinking goals and approaches*. Oxford: Oxford University Press.

Microsoft Corporation 2010. Microsoft Excel 2010 [Computer software]. Redmond, WA: Microsoft Corporation.

Murray, H., Wegmüller, U. and Khan, F. A. 2001. *L'anglais en Suisse: Rapport de recherche*. Bern: Office fédéral de l'éducation et de la science.

Muji, A. 2003. Le débat suisse sur l'enseignement des langues étrangères. Vers une réflexion sur l'auto-constitution du collectif helvétique. In: *Bulletin VALS-ASLA (Association suisse de linguistique appliquée)* 77. 67–81.

Phillipson, R. 1992. *Linguistic Imperialism*. Oxford: Oxford University Press.

Phillipson, R. 2009. *Linguistic imperialism continued*. New York, NY: Routledge.

Rajagopalan, K. 2010. The rigmarole of intelligibility in world English(es) – or, on making sense of it all or, if you like, making the very idea of intelligibility intelligible. In: *Revista Letras and Letras. Uberlândia-MG* 26(2). 477–492.

Ryan, S. 2009. Self and identity in L2 motivation in Japan: The ideal L2 self and Japanese learners of English. In: Dörnyei Z. and E. Ushioda (Eds.), *Motivation, language identity and the L2 self*. Bristol: Multilingual Matters. 120–143.

Saxena, M. and Omoniyi, T. (Eds.) 2010. *Contending with globalization in world Englishes*. Multilingual Matters 9.

Seidlhofer, B. 2001. Closing the conceptual gap: The case for a description of English as a lingua franca. In: *International Journal of Applied Linguistics* 11(2). 133–158.

Shin, J. C. and Teichler, U. (Eds.) 2014. *The Future of the Post-Massified University at the Crossroads. Restructuring Systems and Functions*. Cham: Springer International Publishing.

Ushioda, E. 2015. Context and complex dynamic systems theory. In: Dörnyei, Z., P. MacIntyre and A. Henry (Eds.), *Motivational dynamics in language learning*. Bristol: Multilingual Matters. 47–54.

Ushioda, E. and Dörnyei, Z. 2012. Motivation. In: Gass, S. and A. Mackey (Eds.), *The Routledge handbook of second language acquisition*. New York, NY: Routledge. 396–409.

Varghese, N. V. 2013. Globalization and higher education: Changing trends in cross border education. In: *Analytical Reports in International Education* 5(1). 7–20.

Yashima, T. 2009. International posture and the ideal L2 self in the Japanese EFL context. In: Dörnyei Z. and E. Ushioda (Eds.), *Motivation, language identity and the L2 self*. Bristol: Multilingual Matters. 144–163.

Yonezawa, A. 2013. The Internationalization of the University as a Response to Globalization: an East Asian Perspective. In: Shin, J. C. and U. Teichler (Eds.), *The Future of the Post-Massified University at the Crossroads. Restructuring Systems and Functions*. Cham: Springer International Publishing. 59–71.

Zaidan, J. 2013. *Por um Inglês Menor: a desterritorialização da grandelíngua*. Unpublished PhD dissertation. Universidade Estadual de Campinas. Brazil.

Jeanette King, Una Cunningham
(University of Canterbury, Christchurch, New Zealand)

Intergenerational Transmission of Minority Languages in New Zealand: Methodological Issues

Introduction

This paper reports the research aims and methods of the Intergenerational Transmission of Minority Languages (ITML) Project at the University of Canterbury, which is studying the extent to which speakers of minority languages in New Zealand are passing their language on to their children. We are planning a number of interrelated projects, but here we report on our 'bilingual teens' project, which focuses on the experiences of parents and their teenage children in situations where intergenerational transmission has been successful. These questions are being addressed respectively by examining census data on language ability and by conducting interviews with families who speak a minority language. The phrase 'minority language' is used here to refer to languages other than the three official languages of New Zealand: English, Māori and New Zealand Sign Language.

One of the initial motivations for the current project was a report from the Office of Ethnic Affairs where it was suggested that migrant families should consider speaking English to their children to improve their level of English (2013: 16). This report leans heavily on work by H. Esser which claims that "school performance is not enhanced by proficiency in the language of the country of origin in addition to that of the host country" (2006: 72). Our concern is that advice such as this may encourage migrant families to abandon intergenerational language transmission without considering the long-term personal and societal benefits of competence in the heritage language (U. Cunningham 2011). It is also worth noting that in comparison with other jurisdictions there is a dearth of public understanding and knowledge about multilingualism in New Zealand and a lack of information for professionals working with parents and children.

The data sources for the 'bilingual teen' ITML project are twofold: recent census data on the number of child speakers and interviews with parents and their minority language- speaking teenagers. Information from both sources (outlined below) will allow the ITML project to address the deficits in current knowledge with pamphlets and presentations to parents and relevant professional bodies. The project also aims to set up a website which includes information, resources, advice and encouragement drawn directly from the interviews to encourage parents to raise their children as speakers of their minority languages (e.g. U. Cunningham 2015; TeRūnanga o NgāiTahu 2007).

1. New Zealand's linguistic and cultural background

New Zealand, situated in the South Pacific, was the last major land mass in the world to be discovered and settled by humans. Polynesian ancestors of the Māori arrived about 1,000 years ago and European explorers from the late 18th century (J. M. Wilmshurst *et al.* 2008). Settlement, mainly by British citizens, started in the 1840s after 25 years of missionary interaction, and the Māori populace began to shift from speaking Māori to speaking English from the early 20th century onwards (R. Benton 1991). However, this shift has been somewhat countered as a result of concerted efforts at language revitalisation aimed at raising new generations of children as speakers of Māori. Of particular note, and internationally lauded and replicated, are the early childhood language nests, kōhanga reo, and other Māori immersion educational initiatives (R. Benton and N. Benton 2001).

Along with continuous British immigration, other nationalities have also settled in New Zealand, with numbers particularly increasing after changes to immigration policies in 1975 and 1987 (J. Phillips 2013). As of 2013 the total population of New Zealand was 4.2 million comprising 74.6% European, 15.6% Māori, 12.2% Asian, 7.8% Pacific (Statistics New Zealand 2015a)[1]. There have been increasing numbers of migrants, particularly from Asia, coming to settle in New Zealand in the last 15 years. For example, the number of people who could speak Hindi nearly tripled between 2001 and 2013, while speakers of Northern Chinese (including Mandarin) almost doubled in the same time period (Statistics New Zealand 2014: 24).

As a consequence of the increased levels of immigration New Zealand is now regarded as a superdiverse country (Royal Society of New Zealand 2013: 1; P. Spoonley and R. Bedford 2012). Superdiversity refers to increased levels of complexity in a population, particularly in reference to country of origin, ethnicity and language (S. Vertovec 2007). However, New Zealand's superdiversity is largely manifested in Auckland, the largest urban region in the country. Auckland

---

1   These percentages do not sum to 100 percent because people can and do identify with multiple ethnicities.

is home to 33% of New Zealand's population (Statistics New Zealand 2015b: 1) and is the most ethnically diverse part of the country, having the highest proportion of overseas born people (39%), over half of all the country's multilingual speakers, 66% of Pacific peoples, and 65% of those who stated that they couldn't speak English (Statistics New Zealand 2014). The high levels of people of Pacific origin gives Auckland the distinction of being the largest Polynesian city in the world.

Despite this apparent diversity it is claimed that New Zealand is one of the most monolingual countries on earth, in that 82% of the population at the 2001 census were monolingual in English (D. Starks, R. Harlow and A. Bell 2005: 18–19). Indeed, perhaps partly to do with insularity, many immigrants who speak languages other than English have reported much pressure to speak English and, in general, shift towards English has been within 2–3 generations (for a comprehensive overview, see M. Roberts 2005). This insularity and pressure towards language shift, particularly amongst minority languages, is manifested in a recent study that reveals a hierarchy amongst languages other than English in New Zealand with "the arguments in favour of minority language promotion [being] most widely accepted for the Māori language, followed by New Zealand Sign Language, then Pacific languages, and finally community languages" (J. de Bres 2015: 1).

Generations of migrants from many of the Pacific Islands have led to the situation where "there are more Pacific people from Niue, the Cook Islands, and Tokelau living in New Zealand than in their respective home countries" (Statistics New Zealand and Ministry of Pacific Island Affairs 2010: 11). However, apart from Samoan and Tongan, the situation with regard to most Pacific languages in New Zealand is of concern, with very low proportions of these populations able to speak their language (J. McCaffery and J. McFall-McCaffery 2010). This situation has led some commentators to note that New Zealand has a responsibility to protect Pacific languages, particularly those languages which to which New Zealand has a special responsibility, namely, Cook Islands Māori, Niuean and Tokelauan (Human Rights Commission 2008: 3).

Within this context it is perhaps not surprising to know that New Zealand lacks a national language plan, despite a well-received framework being published in 1992 (J. Waite 1992). The need for a national languages policy has been noted by a number of institutions, including the Human Rights Commission (2008) and the Royal Society of New Zealand (2013). Recognition of Auckland's super-diversity has led to a recent draft Auckland Languages Strategy being produced by an Auckland Council working party (Tāmaki Makaurau Auckland Languages Strategy Working Group 2015). Concern about the decline in Pasifika languages led to the publication of a Pacific Languages Framework in 2012 (Ministry of Pacific Island Affairs).

2. Census data

From 1996 onwards there has been a question on language ability included in the five yearly New Zealand census. The question reads: in which language(s) could you have a conversation about a lot of everyday things? Within the tight framework of questions in the census, this question has been designed as the best probe to elicit data about language ability.

Clearly there are limitations with the responses gathered from such a question. Firstly, as the question relies on self-reporting it is not objective and relies on people's own assessment of their ability to speak a language, as well as how they interpret what it means 'to have a conversation about a lot of everyday things'. These differences in interpretation can lead to under and over reporting (see, for example, W. Bauer 2008: 39–40 for an analysis with respect to the Māori language). Also, ability to speak a language does not mean that the respondent actually speaks it regularly. So the information provided gives us no indication as to the number of languages actually being spoken regularly in New Zealand, nor whether the language was learned as a first or second language. In addition, although respondents are able to list as many languages as they wish, it is likely that many multilinguals do not give the full list of languages they can speak. Nevertheless, within these caveats, the census information can provide a useful overview about aspects of reported language ability. In this paper we present an analysis of data from the 2013 census[2]. The work presented in this paper is based on and includes customised Statistics New Zealand's data which are licensed by Statistics New Zealand for re-use under the Creative Commons Attribution 3.0 New Zealand licence.

The 2013 census reveals that there are speakers of over 190 languages in New Zealand and that there are at least 168 languages spoken by children. In order to provide a more manageable dataset this paper contains information on 23 minority languages in New Zealand commonly spoken by children. The languages for the dataset were selected as the 20 languages other than English, Māori and NZ Sign Language which are reported to have more than 1,000 child speakers in New Zealand in the 2013 Census. Cook Islands Māori, Niuean and Tokelauan were also included as they are languages for which New Zealand arguably has a

---

2   The census which would have normally been held in March 2011 was cancelled due to the Christchurch earthquakes and was held instead in March 2013.

special protective relationship, thus bringing the total number of languages analysed here to 23.

Half of the languages in the dataset are from countries in the Asian continent: Gujarati, Hindi, Japanese, Khmer, Korean, Northern Chinese, Panjabi, Persian, Russian, Tagalog, Urdu and Yue. There are five Polynesian languages: Cook Islands Māori, Niuean, Samoan, Tokelauan and Tongan, and five European, or European derived languages: Afrikaans, Dutch, French, German and Spanish. Arabic is the only language from the Middle East and North Africa.

The parameters of the commissioned dataset from Statistics New Zealand are shown in Table 1.

Table 1: Parameters of commissioned dataset drawn from 2013 Census, Statistics New Zealand

Tongue	The subject language spoken within the family.
Geography	2013 boundaries: Auckland, rest of NZ, New Zealand as a whole
Child language	Does child speak the subject language? Yes, no.
Birthplace	Birthplace of child: NZ or overseas.
Age group	Age group of child: 0–1, 2–6, 7–12, 13–18.
Family language	The parent(s) concerned speak the subject language: yes, no.
Other language	Another adult in the household speaks the subject language: yes, no.
Children	Aged 0 to 18 inclusive, and in a child role in a family nucleus.

If any family member speaks the language, the family was included as part of the reference population. The commissioned dataset therefore includes families where no adult speaks the subject language but where it is reportedly spoken by at least one child in the household. This meant that languages taught in secondary school, such as French, German, Japanese and Spanish showed 1,000 to 2,000 more speakers in the 12–18 year old age group compared to those in younger age groups. Since we are interested in the success of intergenerational transmission these speakers have been excluded in the data presented here.

Also note that children and families can be counted more than once if they are reported as speaking more than one language and will appear in the dataset for each language. 'Northern Chinese' includes those answering either 'Chinese' or 'Mandarin' or 'Northern Chinese'. Consequently, the data may also include answers that might properly belong to some other Sinitic language, so caution must be used when comparing this group. 'Yue' includes Cantonese. Responses for ethnic group or descent are not considered in this dataset. While the child's birthplace is one of the parameters in the dataset we do not have any information about the birthplace of the parents.

The dataset parameters enable us to present information about the role of birthplace, place of residence and number of adult speakers in the family in intergenerational transmission of these languages.

2.1 The role of community in intergenerational transmission

There is a great range amongst the populations of child speakers for the 23 languages in the dataset. As shown in Figure 1, there is only one language with over 20,000 child speakers (Samoan 23,052), and only another two languages with around 10,000 child speakers (Hindi 10,338 and Tongan 9,834). The language with the median number of child speakers in the dataset is Spanish (2,655) and the overall mean amongst the languages is 4,295 child speakers, reflecting the fact that there are several larger languages, but a majority of languages with smaller numbers of child speakers.

Considering the range of languages in our sample it would be expected there would be a range of success in intergenerational transmission. The scatterplot in Figure 1 plots each language according to the numbers of child speakers (horizontal axis) and the rates of intergenerational transmission for that language (vertical axis). It is worth noting that the phrase 'rates of intergenerational transmission' is the number of children who report as speaking the languages a percentage of the total population of children who are raised in a household where at least one adult speaks that language. In other words, the wider population for this calculation is total number of children who have the possibility of being raised as speakers and the percentage thus gives an indication of the rate of intergenerational transmission.

Figure 1: Scatterplot of 23 minority languages in New Zealand by numbers of child speakers (horizontal axis) and rates of intergenerational transmission (vertical axis)

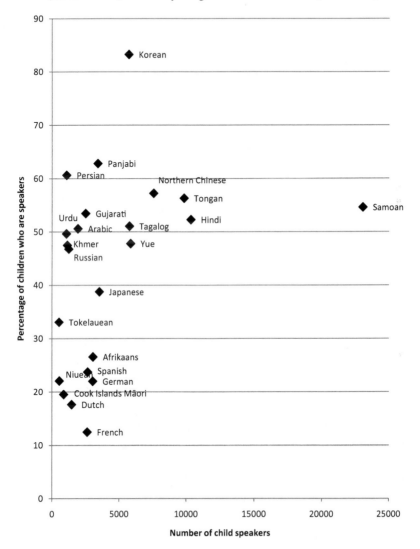

We can see in Figure 1 that Samoan is in quite an exceptional position having over double the number of child speakers than the next highest language (Hindi). The four languages with the most speakers (Samoan, Hindi, Tongan and Northern Chinese) also have good rates of intergenerational transmission with over 50% of their children being raised as speakers. For languages with fewer than 7,000 speakers, the rates of intergenerational transmission vary widely, but, in general if your language has fewer than 7,000 child speakers then the rate of intergenerational transmission is likely to be less than 40%. The Korean community is the exception here. With 5,724 child speakers it has the highest rate (83%) of intergenerational transmission of any of the 23 minority languages analysed here. A caveat is that there is no information about the birthplaces of the parents, thus we cannot be sure whether the parents are first, second or third generation migrants to New Zealand, as this may affect their likelihood of transmitting their language to their children.

We also notice that Panjabi, spoken largely in Pakistan as well as parts of India, has a higher rate of transmission than Urdu and Hindi. While Urdu and Hindi are official languages of India and Pakistan respectively these languages are frequently used in diglossic situations in those countries by populations whose home language is usually another language, such as Panjabi. Accordingly, in the diaspora, multilingual parents who speak these languages will typically speak Punjabi at home rather than Urdu or Hindi (Shaista Rashid 25 June 2015, personal communication).

As discussed more fully below, the high rates of intergenerational transmission of some languages is likely attributable to high levels of within-group marriage. Most of the languages shown in Figure 1 which have transmission rates of 50% or greater are spoken by groups who also have high levels of within group marriage, namely, the Korean, Tongan, Samoan, Indian and Chinese ethnic groups (P. Callister, R. Didham and D. Potter 2005). In contrast one of the lowest levels of within-group marriage is with French people, who also have the lowest rate of intergenerational transmission in our dataset. Other languages with low rates of intergenerational transmission are also spoken by ethnic groups with low levels of within-group marriage, namely, German, Niuean, Cook Island Māori and Dutch (P. Callister, R. Didham and D. Potter 2005).

As noted, Auckland is a superdiverse city, and it is a place where increasing numbers of children (currently 29%) speak more than one language. Over New Zealand as a whole, 53% of multilingual children reside in Auckland[3]. We therefore considered whether rates of intergenerational transmission may be higher in Auckland where there are likely to be larger language communities.

---

3   Figures calculated from commissioned Census data.

However, as shown in Figure 2, this is not the case for most languages. For just under half of the languages, children living in Auckland speak their community languages at about the same rate as children living elsewhere in New Zealand. For about a third of the languages children living in Auckland have a much higher chance of being a speaker of their minority language compared with children living in other areas of the country. These languages are: Arabic, Hindi, Japanese, Korean, Northern Chinese, Russian, Samoan and Yue. The most marked differences between the rates of intergenerational transmission in Auckland and the rest of New Zealand are with Northern Chinese (61% in Auckland, 46% elsewhere) and Russian (55% in Auckland, 38% elsewhere). Analyses of the level of statistical significance in these results will be presented in future publications.

Figure 2: Rates of intergenerational transmission in Auckland (black) and the rest of New Zealand (grey) of 23 minority languages

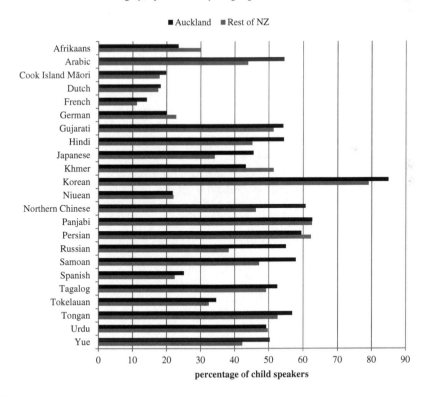

On the other hand there are two languages which are much more likely to be spoken by children living outside Auckland: Afrikaans and Khmer. It is unclear why this is the case for Afrikaans, since G. Barkhuizen and U. Knoch (2005) report that most Afrikaans speakers live in Auckland. Nevertheless, "although scattered across New Zealand, the Afrikaans community has very strong ties, boosted through the community activities of the Afrikaans Club, an organisation which issues regular newsletters and organises frequent cultural activities. There are also regular Afrikaans church services in various towns and cities" (G. Barkhuizen and U. Knoch 2005: 218).

With regards to Khmer speakers it seems that "despite being small, communities have established various associations in their main cities of residence. There are groups in Auckland, Hamilton, the Manawatū, Wellington and Christchurch. Because they unite people and provide places to celebrate religion and culture, these associations have played a large part in preserving traditional identity" (M. H. Liev and R. Chhun 2014: 2).

2.2 The role of birthplace in intergenerational transmission

As shown in Figure 3, and as expected, children born overseas are much likely to be speakers of the minority home language than children born in New Zealand. Note that 'born overseas' here means being born in any other country other than New Zealand, and does not automatically mean being born in the country where the heritage language is spoken by a majority. The differences are substantial in 13 languages: Afrikaans, Cook Islands Māori, Dutch, German, Khmer, Niuean, Russian, Samoan, Spanish, Tagalog, Tongan, Urdu and Yue. These results appear to confirm that the situation in New Zealand is not conducive for intergenerational transmission or maintenance of minority languages.

Figure 3: Rates of intergenerational transmission of 23 minority languages by child's birthplace

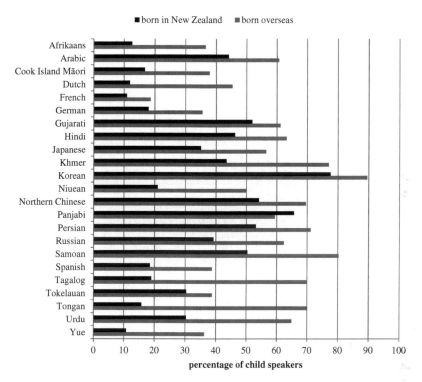

Analysis of the age ranges within the New Zealand born dataset also shows that for over a half of the languages the rates of intergenerational transmission generally decrease from the younger age groups through to the older ones. That is, as shown in Figure 4, there are proportionately more speakers in the 2–6 year old age range and this decreases over apparent time in the 7–12 and 13–18 year old age groups. Children under the age of two have not been included in this table since most in this age group are too young to converse.

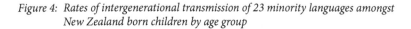

Figure 4: Rates of intergenerational transmission of 23 minority languages amongst New Zealand born children by age group

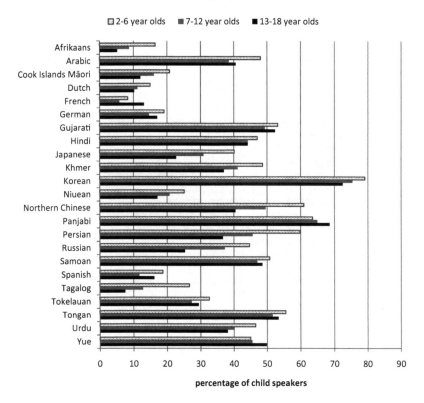

percentage of child speakers

There are only three languages which report higher proportions of speakers in the teenage age group when compared to 2–6 year olds: French, Panjabi and Yue. For the French group this might suggest this data includes families where both the parents and the teenage children learnt the language at school, thus not being an example of intergenerational transmission. It is unclear why Panjabi and Yue have larger numbers of New Zealand born teenage speakers. There are six other languages which appear to maintain similar rates of intergenerational transmission throughout the three age groups: German, Gujarati, Hindi, Korean, Samoan and Tongan.

2.3 The role of mothers and other adults in intergenerational transmission

It is often stated that mothers have an important role in transmitting language(s) to their children (E. Caneva and S. Pozzi 2014). However, A. de Houwer (2007: 417–418) contends that parents' gender does not have an effect on transmission as her data shows no difference between mothers and fathers in this respect. Figure 5 shows the likelihood of a child being a speaker of a minority language in New Zealand when either the father or mother also speaks the minority language. It appears to confirm A. de Houwer's results claim since for most languages the likelihood of intergenerational transmission is about the same regardless of the parent's gender. Tagalog is the only language where having a father who speaks the language gives a far greater likelihood of the child also being a speaker.

Figure 5: Rates of intergenerational transmission of 23 minority languages when father speaks the minority language (black) and when mother also speaks the minority language (grey)

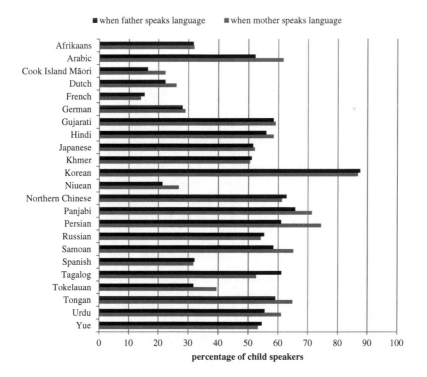

However, it is important to note that a large proportion of children who speak a language live in households where both parents are speakers. So the gender differences in Figure 5 are somewhat masked since child speakers whose parents both speak the language will be counted in both the male and female parent data. Figure 6 shows that when households where both parents speak the language are removed the gender differences become more marked. The groupings for the mother (but not father) settings include couples where the mother, but not the father speaks the language, as well as households where there is more than one mother, or a solo mother. The parameters for the 'father only' data are the same.

Figure 6: Rates of intergenerational transmission of 23 minority languages when the child's father (but no mother) speaks the minority language (black) and when the child's mother (but no father) speaks the minority language (grey)

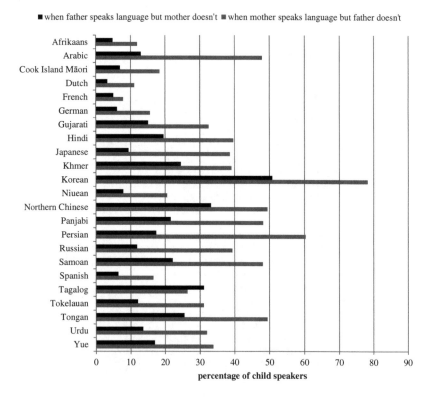

In all cases, except Tagalog, children being raised in a situation where only one parent speaks the language are much more likely to speak that language if it is their mother who speaks the language rather than their father. However, it is worth pointing out that the numbers of child speakers involved here are much more numerous in mother (not father) settings than the reverse, by a factor of two to ten times. For example, there are 192 children who speak Panjabi who live with a Panjabi speaking father, but no Panjabi speaking mother, whereas there are 429 Panjabi speaking children who live with a Panjabi speaking mother but no Panjabi speaking father (a twofold difference). The greatest difference is with the Japanese speaking children where only 117 live with a Japanese speaking father but no Japanese speaking mother, whereas 2237 Japanese speaking children live with a Japanese speaking mother but no Japanese speaking father (a twelvefold difference).

However, while, in most cases, mothers have a stronger role in intergenerational transmission in situations where there is no father who speaks the language (rather than the reverse), these rates of transmission are still much less for children in situations where both parents are speakers of the minority language. Indeed, this is the most optimal circumstance which increases the likelihood of transmission. Figure 7 shows that the effect of having both parents as speaker of the minority language in the household greatly increases the rate of intergenerational transmission. In fact, for most languages this well over doubles the likelihood of the child also being a speaker. The differences are particularly high for Afrikaans, Dutch, French, German and Spanish – the only European languages in the dataset, where having both parents in the household as speakers the language increases the rate of intergenerational transmission by at least five times when compared to having just one adult speaker in the home.

Figure 7: Rates of intergenerational transmission of 23 minority languages by the number of adult speakers of the target language in the household

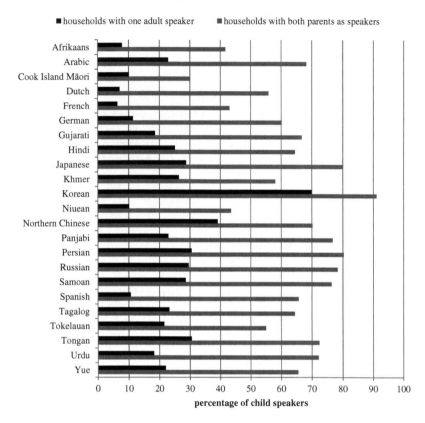

While figure 7 shows the likelihood of intergeneration transmission when both parents speak the language, the results are largely similar if there are two or more adults (whatever their relationship) in the household who speak the minority language.

3. Interview data

To complement the analysis of the census data the 'bilingual teen' ITML sub-project is carrying out a selection of interviews with minority language speaking families in Christchurch. The aim of the interviews is to gather data about the experiences of families who have successfully raised children as speakers of minority languages. Accordingly, both parents and/or caregivers and their teenage children are being interviewed. Here we outline information about how the interviews will be conducted and some of the methodological constraints.

3.1 Recruitment of interviewers

Through connections in teacher education courses and in the local community the project has recruited interviewers for six languages: Chinese[4], Dutch, French, German, Korean and Spanish. Each interviewer is a native speaker of the respective language and was born and raised in a country where that language was the majority language. They are also competent speakers of English. The Korean interviewer is undertaking the project for her Masters' thesis while the other interviewers are paid research assistants. At present the project group meets weekly to discuss equipment, progress in recruiting participants, and so on. The interviewers are responsible for translating the information sheets and consent forms into the target languages, recruiting participants, conducting interviews, transcribing, and, where necessary, translating the interviews.

3.2 Recruitment of participants

For each minority language, the project is looking for five families in the Christchurch region who have successfully raised a New Zealand born 16–18 year old as a speaker of the minority language. Thus there are a number of parameters to take into consideration in identifying potential families to interview.

Participant recruitment is by means of the 'snowball' method (C. Mutch 2013). The interviewers start with any contacts they may have personally. In fact, many of the interviewers have connections within some of the other minority language communities so this information is also shared amongst the group. Contact members of the communities are asked whether they know of any families who fit the criteria. In order to avoid any perception of coercion the contact is asked to get in touch with the potential participants, give them a brief overview of the project and ask if they wish to be contacted with a view to participating. If the response is positive the community contact gives the interviewer the contact information for the potential participants. Families who agree to participate can also be asked if they know other families who fit into the criteria and if they would mind contacting them to see if they would mind being approached by the interviewer.

---

4   As the interviewer can speak both Mandarin and Yue it is possible that we may have participants from both major language groups.

If parents agree to participate their permission is also sought to interview their 16–18 year old child or children. The young people are also asked to give assent to be interviewed. Parents will be interviewed regardless of whether the young person participates or not.

Except for the case of Korean, recruitment of participants for the other languages has been difficult. This is largely because Christchurch, and not Auckland, is the project home. The other major constraint is that we are looking for New Zealand (rather than overseas) born teenagers who speak the minority language. Due to the difficulty in recruiting families it is likely that some of the required parameters will be stretched. For example, we may have to interview some families where the young adult is in fact over the target age of 16–18, and is in their twenties. We may also need to conduct some interviews by Skype with families in other parts of the country if we are unable to recruit enough participants in Christchurch.

Consent forms give participants the option of allowing parts of the audio recording to be: (a) used in an online resource to support parents raising their children as speakers of their community languages and/or (b) shown to students enrolled in a university class or a professional audience at a conference, and/or (c) used as part of other research work by the research team.

3.3 Questions

The interviews with the parents and young adult are semi-structured and largely involve the same material. Both will cover the participants' language background and experiences of being a speaker of a minority language in New Zealand. Parents will be asked details of the decision to raise the child as speaker of a community language in New Zealand, including factors and reasons in the decision. Both parents and the child will be asked for information about experiences with this decision over the child's life, as well as how well they think the child achieves in English as a school subject and whether they think that being raised as a speaker of their community language has affected the child's schooling. These questions will be asked in order to provide a perspective on suggestions that speaking a minority language may negatively affect the teenager's acquisition of English.

Both parents and child will be asked for advice for new parents. It is the response to the last question which we expect will be of particular use in the pamphlet and web material the project will produce.

3.4 Recording of interviews

One of the conditions of the project's Human Ethics permissions from the University of Canterbury is to conduct interviews in public places. This is to obviate any pressure to behave hospitably or provide hospitality if an interview were to take place in an interviewee's home. However, finding an appropriate public place can be difficult. We need to choose venues that are appropriate to the participant and also easily accessible. Cafés can be noisy and although the recording devices being used are equipped with a lapel microphone for the participant, too much background noise may make the recordings less than optimal for use on the website (if the participant has agreed to this use). In order to provide a safe environment, interviews with the teenagers are to be conducted in the presence of another adult or friend of the teenager. The other person needs to be in visual proximity but not necessarily within earshot. At this stage several interviews with the 16–18 year old participants have taken place after school at local high schools.

Parents and children are being interviewed separately since the perspectives of the parents and children will differ and the project is interested in these differences. For the adult interview it is not necessary for all parents or caregivers to participate, but we would especially wish to interview at least one adult who is a speaker of the minority language.

It is expected that the interviews with adults will largely be in the minority language and that interviews with the teenager will be in English. The interviewers have been asked to start the interview in the minority language but to follow the lead of the interviewee in respect of language choice.

3.5 Data analysis

The interviewers will transcribe the interviews, and then translate them, where required, into English. The interview data will be analysed using a thematic analysis with a top down application of U. Bronfenbrenner's model (1999). We also plan further statistical analysis of the census data presented here.

4. Methodological issues

The Intergenerational Transmission of Minority Languages project has addressed a number of methodological issues in its first year. In the first instance, the analysis of census data is constrained by the limitations of the question posed in the census questionnaire. Nevertheless, much useful information can be gleaned from the data available. The project has also been fortunate to secure funding which enabled commission of a dataset from the 2013 New Zealand Census. In commissioning such a dataset, careful thought had to be given to the parameters requested, and to how and whether the requested data would allow calculations about the rates of intergenerational transmission. For example, as the numbers of child speakers of most of these languages is low, it is not fruitful to request parameters that are too fine-grained because some cells in the dataset can be randomly rounded to protect confidentiality. In addition, great care is needed when manipulating the data provided to ensure the correct data points are being extracted.

By focussing the dataset on families where minority languages were spoken and applying a number of other parameters as outlined in Table 1, we were able to calculate rates of intergenerational transmission in 23 minority languages. It is hoped that wider promulgation of the census statistics and the rates of successful intergenerational transmission, which vary widely between the languages in this dataset (from 12% for French to 83% for Korean), may help raise critical awareness amongst the minority language populations in New Zealand. In language planning, critical awareness "about the value of language and the implications of language choices for sustaining a language" (Ministry of Pacific Island Affairs 2012: 7) is regarded as being important to improve the health of a language (R. L. Cooper 1980: 113–125).

With regard to the interview data, the project is constrained by the fact that the team is situated in Christchurch, rather in the superdiverse city of Auckland. This means that identifying potential participants can be constrained due to the small populations. This is especially true of the European languages for which we have interviewers available.

Conclusion

The ITML project is a good example of how both quantitative and qualitative data can complement each other in providing a comprehensive summary of the situation of minority languages in New Zealand. The Census data gives an overview of differences between the rates of intergenerational transmission amongst the languages under study here, as well as an indication as to some of the important parameters which affect these rates. We have found that the situation which will give the optimum likelihood of intergenerational transmission is for the child to be born overseas before migrating to New Zealand, and to have two speakers of the minority language (preferably parents) in the child's household. The fact that, for most languages, the numbers of speakers in the teenage age group is lower than it is in younger age groups suggest that parents find it difficult to maintain transmission as the child grows up. If supportive information were available this might help parents negotiate some of the transitions and maintain language transmission. However, these results need to be interpreted cautiously as there may be other reasons why teenage respondents do not indicate linguistic ability in a language they may have been reported as speaking when they were younger. Of course the children in the different age groups are not the same individuals – the census gives a snapshot – but these figures may anyway show that many young people do not continue to develop language skills in their home language beyond childhood.

While the Census data gives a macro viewpoint, the interview data will provide nuanced information at the micro level of the family (U. Bronfenbrenner 1999). We expect the interviews with the parents to highlight a wide range of personal, cultural and linguistic factors which have affected their choices, beliefs and practices as they have raised their child. The wealth of information will provide a good basis for tailoring helpful information for both specific language groups as well as the wider minority language community. Making best practice material and tips and audio clips of first person accounts by parents and adult children available on a website will provide practical support to families who are raising, or intending to raise, young children as speakers of their language. We feel that it is also important to raise the awareness levels about intergenerational transmission of minority languages in the wider New Zealand society, particularly amongst professionals such as midwives, doctors and early childhood teachers, through a series of pamphlets and talks to professional bodies. Thus the ITML project aims to encourage a supportive climate to aid intergenerational transmission amongst minority languages in New Zealand.

Acknowledgements

The ITML project wishes to thank the New Zealand Institute of Language, Brain and Behaviour for funding of $6,000 to pay for the commissioned census data from Statistics New Zealand and for research assistants for the interviews. We would like to thank our Masters students, research assistants and language advisers Jin Kim, Novia Bin, Marie-Ève Therrien, Julia Hinrichs, Anneke Campo, Lia de Vocht, Rong Wang, Carolina Tornero Martos, Diane Fletcher and Shaista Rashid, along with Andrew McLaren from Statistics New Zealand.

References

Barkhuizen, G. and Knoch, U. 2005. Missing Afrikaans: 'Linguistic Longing' among Afrikaans-speaking immigrants in New Zealand. In: *Journal of Multilingual and Multicultural Development* 26(3). 216–232.

Bauer, W. 2008. Is the health of Te Reo Māori improving? In: *Te Reo* 51. 33–73.

Benton, R. 1991. *The Māori language: dying or reviving?* Honolulu: East West Center. (Reprinted by New Zealand Council for Educational Research in 1997).

Benton, R. and Benton, N. 2001. RLS in Aotearoa/New Zealand 1989–1999. In: Fishman, J. (Ed.), *Can threatened languages be saved? Reversing language shift, revisited: A 21ˢᵗ century perspective.* Clevedon: Multilingual Matters. 422–449.

Bronfenbrenner, U. 1999. Environments in developmental perspective: theoretical and operational models. In: Friedman, S. L. and T. D. Wachs (Eds.), *Measuring environment across the life span: emerging methods and concepts.* Washington, D.C.: American Psychological Association Press. 3–28.

Callister, P., Didham, R. and Potter, D. 2005. *Ethnic intermarriage in New Zealand.* Wellington: Statistics New Zealand.

Caneva E. and Pozzi, S. 2014. The transmission of language and religion in immigrant families: a comparison between mothers and children. In: *International Review of Sociology* 24(3). 436–449.

Cooper, R. L. 1980. Sociolinguistic surveys: the state of the art. In: *Applied Linguistics* 1(2). 113–128.

Cunningham, U. 2011. *Growing up with two languages.* London: Routledge.

Cunningham, U. 2015. *Growing up with two languages* [website]. Available at: <http://cw.routledge.com/textbooks/9780415598521/>.

De Bres, J. 2015. The hierarchy of minority languages in New Zealand. In: *Journal of Multilingual and Multicultural Development.* doi:10.1080/01434632.2015.1009465.

De Houwer, A. 2007. Parental language input patterns and children's bilingual use. In: *Applied Psycholinguistics* 28. 411–424.

Esser, H. 2006. Migration, language and integration. In: *AKI Research Review* 4. 1–117.

Human Rights Commission. 2008. *Languages in Aotearoa New Zealand: Tewaka reo, Statement on Language Policy.* Available at: <http://www.hrc.co.nz/files/3414/2388/3771/25-Aug-2008_11-45 14_Language_Policy_Aug_08.pdf>.

Liev, M. H. and Chhun, R. 2014. Cambodians – fitting in: work, community and culture. In: *TeAra – the encyclopedia of New Zealand* updated 17.9.2014. Available at: <http://www.TeAra.govt.nz/en/cambodians/page-2>.

McCaffery, J. and McFall-McCaffery, J. 2010. O tatou ō aga'iifea?: 'Oku tau ō kife?; Where are we heading?: Pasifika languages in Aotearoa/New Zealand. In: *Alter-Native: An International Journal of Indigenous Scholarship* 6(2). 86–121.

Ministry of Pacific Island Affairs. 2012. *The Pacific Languages Framework.* Wellington: Ministry of Pacific Island Affairs.

Mutch, C. 2013. *Doing educational research: A practitioner's guide to getting started* (2ⁿᵈ ed.). Wellington: New Zealand Council for Educational Research Press.

Office of Ethnic Affairs. 2013. *Language and integration in New Zealand.* Available at: <http://ethniccommunities.govt.nz/sites/default/files/files/LanguageandIntegrationinNZ.pdf>.

Phillips, J. 2013. History of immigration. In: *TeAra – the Encyclopedia of New Zealand*, updated 21.8.2013. Available at: <http://www.TeAra.govt.nz/en/history-of-immigration>.

Roberts, M. 2005. Immigrants' attitudes to language maintenance in New Zealand. In: Bell, A, R. Harlow and D. Starks (Eds.), *Languages of New Zealand*. Wellington: Victoria University Press. 248–270.

Royal Society of New Zealand. 2013. *Languages in Aotearoa New Zealand*. Wellington: Royal Society of New Zealand.

Spoonley, P. and Bedford, R. 2012. *Welcome to our world? Immigration and the reshaping of New Zealand*. Wellington: Dunmore Publishing.

Starks, D., Harlow, R. and Bell A. 2005. Who speaks what language in New Zealand? In: Bell, A, R. Harlow and D. Starks (Eds.), *Languages of New Zealand*. Wellington: Victoria University Press. 13–29.

Statistics New Zealand. 2014. *2013 Census QuickStats about culture and identity*. Wellington: Statistics New Zealand.

Statistics New Zealand. 2015a. *National ethnic population projections: 2013(base)–2038*. Wellington: Statistics New Zealand.

Statistics New Zealand. 2015b. *Quickstats about Auckland region: 2013 census*. Wellington: Statistics New Zealand.

Statistics New Zealand and Ministry of Pacific Island Affairs. 2010. *Demographics of New Zealand's Pacific population*. Wellington: Statistics New Zealand and Ministry of Pacific Island Affairs.

Tāmaki Makaurau Auckland Languages Strategy Working Group. 2015. *Ngā reo o Tāmaki Makaurau Auckland Languages Strategy*. Available at: <http://www.cometauckland.org.nz/webfiles/CometNZ/files/Nga_Reo_o_Tamaki_Makaurau_Draft_Action_Plan_-_revised_draft_updated_March_2015_2.pdf>.

Te Rūnanga o Ngāi Tahu. 2007. *Generation Reo* [website]. Available at: http://www.generationreo.com/.

Vertovec, S. 2007. Super-diversity and its implications. In: *Ethnic and Racial Studies* 30(6). 1024–1054. doi: 10.1080/01419870701599465.

Waite, J. 1992. *Aoteareo; speaking for ourselves*. (Two parts). Wellington: Ministry of Education.

Wilmshurst, J. M., Anderson, A. J., Higham, T. F. G. and Worthy, T. H. 2008. Dating the late prehistoric dispersal of Polynesians to New Zealand using the commensal Pacific rat. In: *Proceedings of the National Academy of Sciences USA* 105(22). 7676–7680.

Ana Cristina Neves
(University of Saint Joseph, Macau, China)

(Re)Reading Otherness: Translanguaging Processes in the Linguistic Landscape of Macau

Introduction

Multilingual settings are especially interesting for the study of linguistic landscape, particularly when different writing systems and completely different cultures come together. This is the case of Macau, one of the richest cities in the world, where traditional Chinese, Cantonese, Portuguese and English coexist.

Located in the southern tip of *Zhongshan* island, about 60 km across Hong Kong and circa 140 km from Guangzhou, Macau has seen an economic development since the handover in late 1999. This progress was due mainly to the liberalization of the gambling industry in 2001. In fact, Macau has surpassed Las Vegas and is now home to over 35 casinos, the main attraction to the Chinese tourist. This tourism segment was also reinforced by China's decrease of travel restrictions, also easing the employment market mainly to mainland immigrants. In the peak season, the tourist inflow can reach 2,000 tourists daily, stemming mainly from the Mainland, followed by Hong Kong, Taiwan, South Korea and Japan (MGTO 2014).

Macau is nowadays known as the Las Vegas of the Far East, once considered "as the Eastern Vatican" due to its high number of churches under Portuguese rule (C. M. B. Cheng 2002: 65). Indeed, the Portuguese set presence in this peninsula in the 1550s and remained in there under not always so clear circumstances until 1999, after the *Joint Declaration of the Government of the People's Republic of China and the Government of the Republic of Portugal on the question of Macao* had been signed in 1987. This document grants a high level of autonomy to Macau until at least 2049, except with respect to the military defense and foreign affairs that are of the responsibility of the State Council of the People's Republic of China.

The co-existence of Portuguese and Chinese for over four centuries and the fast economic development of Macau allowed the present sociolinguistic pattern of different linguistic communities that are outnumbered by the Chinese varieties, followed by Portuguese, English and Tagalog.

At the national level, these linguistic varieties find a place in the Constitution of China, which grants the use of the local "languages in common use in the locality" (Constitution of People's Republic of China, Section 6, Art. 121). At the local level, these linguistic communities are protected against discrimination based on language by Art. 25 of the Basic Law of Macau, a mini-constitution that grants the partial co-official status of the Portuguese language, which can be used by "the executive authorities, legislature and judiciary of the Macao Special Administrative Region" (Basic Law of Macau, Ch. I, Art. 9).

It was, nevertheless, the handover in 1999 that enhanced the growing interest in the Portuguese language. This language became more and more a landmark of the Macau identity in contrast with both Mainland China and Hong Kong. However, it was not the only language whose importance grew. English, one of the official languages of Hong Kong, gained ground in the Macau territory on account of both its geographical and cultural proximity to Hong Kong and the general international status of the English language (A. Moody 2008).

The sociolinguistic data analysis of A. Moody (2008) clearly points out the growing use of English in Macau, Cantonese impact on the English language, which could also be extended to Portuguese, and the importance of Portuguese not only as a cultural identity but also for career advancement among civil servants.

Besides Moody's sociolinguistic study, one more study was found so far on this topic, although from a different research field. In their tourism research study, L. Yan and M. Y. Lee (2014) identified implications for policy makers, based on the perceptions of tourists on Macau street names.

1. Literature review

In the field of linguistic landscape, particular attention has to be given to the categorization of the data, as this might influence the results, as L. Edelman showed (2009). Although there is a tendency to present data in a quantitative manner, especially when the aim is to identify the extent to which English is the *lingua franca* of the millennium, there is room for a qualitative-driven approach, as several papers in the field have proven.

In a multilingual setting, translation assumes a particular undeniable significance (B. Spolsky 2009: 37). Conveying information presupposes translation, and even transliteration, where different scripts are put in use. Translation is, however, a strategy that usually implies costs.

P. Backhaus (2006) already reported a major difference between top-down and bottom-up signs regarding the usage of mutual translation, which is much more common among the official or top-down signage. However, the German marketing agency Endmark (2006 *in* L. Edelman 2009) demonstrated that English slogans are often not clear to consumers, who were not able to provide an accurate translation in a study carried out by this agency. This means that factual information moves to the background in favour of emotionally more appealing linguistic devices.

Within translation as a strategy of conveying information in the public space, the translation of proper names shows that these can actually belong to any language, making their translation superfluous. Among researchers of linguistic landscape it is common to assign the proper name to the language of origin, which affects the research results and conclusions (L. Edelman 2008: 152). L. Edelman (2009), referring to studies carried out by M. K. El-Yasin (1994) and R. S. Mahadin (1996), concludes that foreign names are associated with a better product quality, often implying a more costly price. This same author goes further stating that proper names have the major function of conveying feelings, which explains the usage of functional words in some of the shop names (2009: 144). Indeed, the fact that proper names have a special status is well documented and demonstrated by the periodic international conference, namely the United Nations Conference on the Standardization of Geographical Names, which reinforces the use of Romanization.

Taking into account studies carried out in Asia, it has been proven that the coexistence of more than one language generates a symbiotic process at different levels, in which sometimes the target language becomes so familiar that it penetrates into the source language. P. Backhaus (2009) gives an extensive discussion of the implications of strategies such as translation and transliteration in the linguistic landscape of Tokyo and Québec. The effects of this practice can go further and affect the source language, as it happens with Thai whose syntax is being influenced by English in the linguistic landscape of Bangkok (T. Huebner 2006). On the other hand, where there is no official translation of proper names, locals create themselves an informal translation, as reported by M. L. Curtin (2009: 227) on Taiwan. In the case of multilingual advertising in India, T. K. Bhatia (1987: 35 in T. Huebner 2009: 87) came to the conclusion that product naming is usually in English, whereas the language of the headlines could be either English, Sanskrit or Persian, varying according to the product, and the remaining body text is usually in Hindi. This means that code-mixing is rather the rule than the exception. And as there is variety in the degree of translation, which can be total or partial, this reflects well how the public space becomes "a product of social translation" (E. Soja 1989: 79–80 in A. Pennycook 2009: 310).

R. Jakobson (1959) distinguishes between three types of translation, that, as we will see, can be easily applied to describe the linguistic landscape: 1) intralingual or rewording, 2) interlingual or translation proper, and 3) intersemiotic or transmutation. The first one presupposes rephrasing within the target language; the second one refers to what we commonly understand by translating from a source to a target language; and the third one implies the usage of nonverbal signs. However, the question of the proper names, especially brand names, remains open: Should they be treated as intersemiotic translations?

Considering the translation type, there is another category of analysis that is also relevant, namely the number of languages displayed on a sign. While T. Huebner (2006: 34) claims that signs can be either monolingual or multilingual, M. Reh (2004 in B. Spolsky 2009: 28) – considering his study on a Ugandan city – groups information according to the arrangement of multilingual information: 1) duplicating or signs where all the information is given in both languages; 2) signs where there is partial or overlapping translation; and 3) complementary or signs where different information is given in each language. Taking into account this taxonomy, official signs in Tokyo (P. Backhaus 2007) give the same information in both languages which means that public signage is intended to monolingual readers of the two languages. This is a good example for the importance of linguistic landscape and what it can tell us about the state of public and private literacy of the stakeholders.

This categorization brings us to the question of the presence of code-mixing, which was well documented in T. Huebner's paper on Bangkok (2006), according to which English is affecting the Thai syntax. Other than code-mixing there are strategies worth mentioning, such as code-switching and interlanguaging, which are not so commonly referred to in linguistic landscape. Although both terms, code-mixing and code-switching, are often used in an interchangeable manner and have found various, at times contradictory, approaches (E. Botztepe 2003), we do make a distinction in the sense of S. Poplack (1980) and A. Y. Aikenwald and R. M. W. Dixon (2006: 333). By code-mixing we understand a hybrid form of two codes, which can entail lexical transfer, accommodation, syntactic change, borrowings and alike. In turn, code-switching should be understood as the movement of a speaker from one language or code to another or the "seemingly random alternation of two languages […] where juxtaposition of L1 and L2 elements does not violate a surface syntactic rule of either language" (S. Poplack 1980: 581). Unlike S. Poplack (1980), we consider the distinction between code-switching and borrowing not a critical one.

All these concepts move around a continuum between source and target language (from the point of view of translation), with different degrees of hybrid forms imposed by code- mixing (from the sociolinguistic point of view), and different types of translation which can be based on a focus-on-the-target-language or not. When we consider that one of the languages is not the native language of the community, the term of interlanguage might be useful in the description of the data produced by speakers that have not reached a proficiency level in the target language. Interlanguaging goes back to L. Selinker (1972) to define the learner's interpretation and understanding of the target language, i.e. while learning or acquiring a second language the learner creates his own independent grammar of the target language, which is neither the grammar of his mother tongue nor the grammar of the target language, rather an intermediary hybrid stage between both languages. According to R. Ellis (1997), this stage can be one of transition. As there are different learners, this presupposes different interlanguages, or better, different hybrid codes that are between the primary or source and the secondary or target languages, if these are regarded as the opposite extremes of a continuum. Either seen as a *system* or a *transition*, interlanguaging finds its best theoretical background in psycholinguistics, unlike the term of international language that presupposes a sociolinguistic approach (A. Davies 1989: 448). According to the same author (ibid. 461), an interlanguage cannot, however, be an international language – at least, in applied linguistics – as it is not a full language, but rather a natural language with a high degree of permeability.

The question of interlanguaging, especially when applied to linguistic land-scape, as it is the case, becomes more obvious but also more complex regarding the existence of slogans produced in the target or recipient language and that are not necessarily subject to the process of translation. T. Dubovíviciene and P. Skorupa (2014) demonstrate how the definition of advertising slogan is not a clear-cut one, as it depends from the author and suggests a definition based on the shared perception that a slogan is "a short catchy phrase related to a specific brand" that helps the customer to recall the brand's key points. According to their study based on a corpus of 100 native English slogans, they identify as main features of the slogan language several figures of speech (simile, metonymy, metaphor, pun, personification, apostrophe, paradox), sound techniques (rhyme, alliteration, assonance, consonance, rhythm, onomatopoeia) among other rhetori-cal devices (repetition, anaphora, epistrophe, comparison, parallelism, antithesis and hyperbole), whereas the first group, the one of figurative language, is the most representative one, led by the occurrence of puns or word plays, followed by the occurrence of repetitions, alliterations, rhymes, apostrophes, metaphors and comparisons. Capitalization and unconventional spelling are other common devices. It is important to refer that most studies on slogans did not focus on lin-guistic landscape neither on multilingual contexts, nor did they consider slogans produced by non-native speakers.

The above-mentioned phenomena have been registered in several research studies worldwide and we perceive them as translanguaging processes, depend-ing on the degree of fluency and proficiency, in the sense of O. García (O. García 2007 in A. Creese and A. Blackledge 2010: 106), that defines translanguaging based on the lack of a "diglossic functional separation". Taking into consideration these processes under the umbrella term of translanguaging and the fact that the analysis of specific linguistic categories, such as proper names and their co-texts or slogans, has been reported to deserve a special attention (E. Shohamy and D. Gorter 2009), this piece of writing is an attempt to contribute to these issues.

2. Corpus and methodology

The corpus is based on 494 pictures, which resulted in 699 tokens. These were categorised according to its flow: bottom-up or private signs, and top-down or official signs. Top-down imprints stemmed from governmental institutions reaching a total of 152 tokens. In turn, the private businesses reached the total of 275 establishments making up a total of 546 tokens.

Following previous studies, one of the categories of the data analysis was grouping the tokens according to the number of languages displayed, which resulted in the following table:

Table 1: Number of languages displayed per flow

	Multilingual	Bilingual	Monolingual	Total
Top-down	61	77	14	152
Bottom-up	28	216	300	544
Total	89	293	314	696

The difference in the total of bottom-up monolingual signs between Tables 1 and 2 is accounted for the fact that there were signs displaying other languages such as: one Czech, two French, one Dutch, one Japanese, three symbols (Nike, H2O, Circle K) and two Italian words whose companies stem from Hong Kong (Giordano, Staccato). One missing value had to be reported as such due the fact that one sign displayed absolutely no imprinting. Similarly to other studies, proper names were assigned according to the language of origin.

Table 2: Single language signs per flow

Monolingual signs	Only Cantonese	Only Portuguese	Only English	Total
Top-down	12	1	1	14
Bottom-up	244	2	44	290
Total	256	3	45	304

The number of tokens found displaying only Portuguese were two: one embroidery shop and one restaurant. The 44 tokens displaying only English stemmed from industry sectors such as mostly fashion, but also health care, telecommunications and catering.

Taking into consideration that top-down signs are to their majority multilingual or bilingual, as Table 1 shows, and often display a mutual interlingual translation, we will focus this analysis on the bottom-up signage, particularly on the bilingual signs. In order to do so, we will perform a descriptive, linguistic analysis whereas translanguaging phenomena (code-mixing, code-switching, interlanguaging, syllabification) will be used to illustrate the data. Special attention will be given to proper names and co-texts or longer stretches of words stemming from non-official local signs, namely the examples on Table 3.

3. Data analysis

3.1 Code-mixing

The number of signs displaying code-mixing, where proper names are kept in their Romanized form, is numerous (Picture 1).

Another form of code-mixing is the general tendency to display the Arabic numbers (Picture 2), instead of the Chinese, probably because the numerical Chinese characters are also assigned other meanings, depending on their context; but also because speakers of other languages than Chinese would easily understand them, as they are used worldwide. There are besides the Arabic numerals, two indigenous numeral systems in use in China: the Suzhou numerals – that are being replaced by the Arabic ones; and, the Modern Chinese numerals, which can be simple (used in a general way) or complex (used in finance).

Code-mixing as in Picture 3, where one can see the adverbial Latin abbreviation AM/PM being displayed in a Portuguese sign, is not uncommon.

We consider these three examples more than code-mixing: script-mixing, as it involves the usage of different scripts.

Picture 1	Picture 2	Picture 3
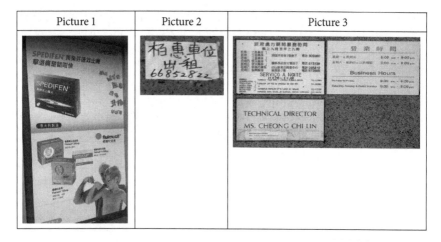		

3.2 Intralingual translation

Only in the case of English, one could find intralingual translation or rewording. If we compare these two imprints, we see that there is a difference in size, sequence and intralingual information of the displayed languages. Shops displaying English as the main and only language are relatively common, especially when they stem from Hong Kong or have as a referent a locally well-known brand, such as *City Chain* or *Milan Station* or even Adidas. However, this is not the case here. What is also worth mentioning is that those English names are usually built upon monosyllabic or at the most disyllabic English words.

Picture 4	Picture 5
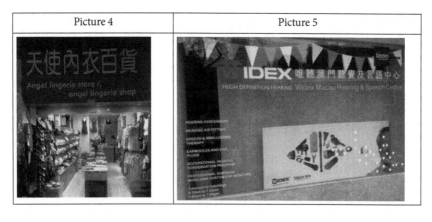	

3.3 Intersemiotic translation

If the way we categorize proper names has been considered relevant for data analysis, it is also worth considering the intersemiotic, non-redundant value they are assigned to by not being followed by a translation or any type of body text. This applies particularly to 1) the names of internationally well-known brands, whose names have become global or cross- lingual, to such an extent that 2) even displaying the brand name turns out to be superfluous. Examples of the first situation are Haagen-Dazs, Swarovski, Joy & Peace, Levis, just to name a few, as we can see on Picture 6. A good example of the second case is the Nike swoosh, which is more than enough to identify the shop (Picture 7). Cases like these are also associated with the most commercial and business oriented areas of Macau.

Picture 6	Picture 7

3.4 Interlingual translation and non-indexicality

On Picture 8, one can see one of the multilingual signs displayed in bottom-up signage, where both traditional and simplified Mandarin set their presence. It is noteworthy that the proper names, brands and captions are not subject to this process of multilingual, interlingual translation, especially if not stemming from Chinese.

Picture 9 demonstrates a rare case of non-indexicality which consists here of the inexistence of any verbal or non-verbal index nor of a reference that identifies the shop, in an agglomeration that has been growing at a fast pace, whereas, however, the word of mouth still plays a role.

114 Ana Cristina Neves

Picture 8	Picture 9

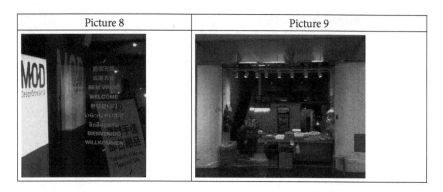

3.5 Slogans

English is not necessarily displayed in names of the shops. However, it appears in what could be considered a slogan. These slogans or co-texts occur in the business-oriented surroundings and among private business signs. Curiously, international brands like the Dutch ice cream *Häagen-Dazs*, do not display any of their well-known slogans, which once again assigns to the brand name – a proper name – an intersemiotic connotation. If international brands do display a slogan, then there is a higher probability that this occurs on a billboard, but not next to the shop sign or caption.

Table 3. Slogans used by shops

No.	Slogans	Location
1	Go online, no limit (3G)	billboard
2	Thinking green. Going clean. Living cool. (China Bank)	billboard
3	Allure of eyes (ColourMix)	billboard
4	We unlock the power of the sea and distill it into our scientifically proven formulas. (H2O)	billboard
5	Just do it. (Nike)	billboard
6	Making life beautiful (Sasa)	billboard
7	Adidas is all in. (Adidas)	billboard
8	Pass the torch. Play it forward. (Giordano)	billboard
9	Bras n' things. (San Vo)	shop sign
10	Welcome, how are you today? (B Plus Cafe)	shop sign
11	In service to overseas workers worldwide. (Pacific Ace)	shop sign
12	Character King – Macau Souvenirs Shop	shop sign
13	Something about tea. (local tea house)	shop sign
14	No. 1 selling souvenirs in Macau (Pastry shop Koi Kei)	shop sign
15	Health, by the Kuokei begins (Kuokei juice shop)	shop sign

Taking into consideration the 15 co-texts collected among the bottom-up signage, there is obviously a distinction between locally and globally or internationally rooted slogans. The placement of the slogan is also indicative of a difference between these two types of slogans, as showed in Table 3.

We will focus our analysis on the local co-texts (no. 9–15). By doing so, we notice a disregard of action words, imperative forms, any type of figure of speech or sound technique, when compared to slogans 1–8. In turn, there is a preference for nouns with the main function of conveying information or supremacy. Other than that, there is a general tendency for 5-word slogans.

In fact, the local slogans or phrases (from 9 to 15) can be broken down in 3 different groups according to specific functions that are not mutually exclusive:

a) (9)   Bras n' things.
    (11)   In service to overseas workers worldwide.
    (13)   Something about tea.
    (14)   No. 1 selling souvenirs in Macau
b) (12)   Character King – Macau Souvenirs Shop.
    (14)   No. 1 selling souvenirs in Macau
    (15)   Health, by the Kuokei begins
c) (9)   Welcome, how are you today? B plus Café (Picture 11)
    (15)   Health, by the Kuokei begins (Picture 10)

In group a), the main function is to give extra information on the type of product, whereas in group b) the attention goes to words that emphasize supremacy such as "king" and "no. 1", without the need of using adjectives or any other type of modifier or intensifier, and the beginning of something positive (15). One should, however, notice that the Chinese language is not inflected and a noun in Chinese can also assume the role of an adjective or another word class. Group c) includes other functions such as the association of health to the name of the shop and hereby to the product (fresh fruit juices) and the use of a question that obviously intends to engage the customer in an active role, where the use of a pronoun is unavoidable. By doing so, (9) also tries to establish a personal relationship and gives a conversational tone to the slogan, in which the potential customer, or rather, the reader is addressed with a direct question. The last two groups are definitely the ones that appeal the most to the emotions of the consumer, whereas the first one is mainly informative. Other than that, there is a general tendency for 5-word slogans.

If we focus on the local slogans (no. 9–15), we see a disregard of action words, imperative forms, any type of figure of speech or sound technique, that were proven to be the commonest features, as discussed in the previous section on literature review. In turn, there is a preference for nouns with the main function of conveying information or supremacy of the product and/or service. Only further research can give an answer to the question whether these can be considered general features of different interlanguages in this specific context.

Picture 10	Picture 11

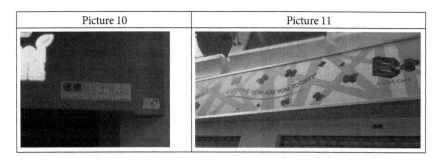

3.6 Romanization

Local proper names or better, their Romanization is actually what allows us to identify Cantonese as the Chinese variety *par excellence*, setting presence in Macau. For the sake of a better understanding of what happens with the translation of Chinese proper names, let us look closely at the examples of *chong fok* on Picture 12 and *tin yat* on Picture 13. In the first case, *chong + fok* (Cantonese) or *zhong + fu* (Mandarin) can be literally translated by MIDDLE/CENTER + BLESSING/ GOOD LUCK, respectively; in the second case, *tin + yat* (Cantonese) or *tian + yi* (Mandarin) find their literal equivalents in SKY/DAY + ONE, respectively. Both word phrases have seemingly no meaning in the source language, if translated literally word by word as we did, although their choice is usually the result of a personal meaning to the shop owner, and both undergo a simple process of Romanization in the target language, that has little meaning in the target language. Not only do these proper names have a personal meaning, they also meet one of the functions registered among the slogans, namely group b), by emphasizing a supremacy or by appealing to the emotions of the consumer. In any case, the fact that these nouns are simply Romanized and not translated results in a loss of meaning in the target language and even in a gap between both cultures.

Pictures 12 and 13 are, in contrast to Pictures 4 and 5, examples of proper translation, the one that accompanies the Portuguese language.

Picture 12	Picture 13
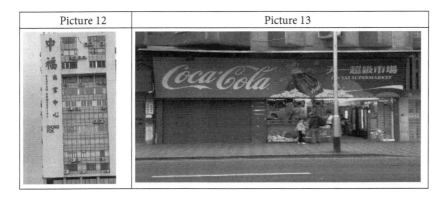	

3.7 Syllabification

In the case of Portuguese, the syllabification process is eye-catching for a native speaker. In Picture 14, the caption seems to be split in a way that makes an even division of the letters: 11 letters to the right side and other 11 to the left, resulting in an uncommon syllabification of the word *comercial* in Portuguese, that according to the Portuguese grammar rules should be *co-mer-ci-al*. A similar phenomenon is displayed in Picture 15, where *de* in *licençade* does not seem to be a separate word.

Picture 14	Picture 15

Conclusion

The demonstrated presence of translanguaging phenomena, either through translation or code-mixing, Romanization, etc., reveals the complexity of linguistic landscape. A descriptive linguistic analysis of the data points out, above all, a process of appropriation that is materialized through these strategies and possibly interlanguaging. Local bottom-up co-texts and slogans and proper names in a general way assume a unique role in this context by being particularly permeable to specific translanguaging processes.

A qualitative and sheer linguistic analysis of the types of translation in the bilingual signs shows that transliteration or Romanization of the proper names is very common when Portuguese is the target language. Co-texts, slogans and an intersemiotic value of the proper name, or rather, the brand name, are rather associated with English.

The signage displayed in the public space conveys more information than one at first might be able to realize. It is also a meeting point for an interdisciplinary analysis, allowing a data exploration from different perspectives such as sociolinguistic, psycholinguistic, semiotic, translatological, among other.

References

Aickenwald, A. Y. and Dixon, R. M. W. 2006. *Grammars in Contact: A Cross-linguistic Typology*. Oxford: Oxford University Press.

Backhaus, P. 2006. Multilingualism in Tokyo: A Look into the Linguistic Landscape. In: D. Gorter (Ed.), *Linguistic Landscape: A New Approach to Multilingualism*. Clevedon: Multilingual Matters. 52–67.

Botztepe, E. 2003. Issues in Code-Switching: Competing Theories and Models. In: *Working Papers in TESOL and Applied Linguistics* 3(2). 1–27.

Cheng, C. M. B. 2002. Cultural Significance: The Identity of Macao. The Conservation of Urban Heritage. In: *Macao Vision: Conference proceedings*. Macao. 10.–12.9.2002. Macao: Cultural Affairs Bureau. 23–69.

Cook, G. 2001. *The Discourse of Advertising*. London and New York: Routledge.

Creese, A. and Blackledge, A. 2010. Translanguaging in the Bilingual Classroom: A Pedagogy for Learning and Teaching?. In: *The Modern Language Journal* 94 (1). 104–115.

Curtin, M. L. 2009. Languages on display: Indexical signs, identities and the linguistic landscape of Taipei. In: Shohamy, E. and D. Gorter. (Eds.), *Linguistic Landscape: Expanding the Scenery*. New York: Routledge. 221–237.

Davies, A. 1989. Is International English an Interlanguage?. In: *TESOL Quarterly* 23(3).

Duboviciene, T. and Skorupa, P. 2014. The Analysis of some Stylistic Features of English Advertising Slogans. In: *Man and the Word* 16(3). 61–75.

Edelman, L. 2009. What's in a Name? Classification of Proper Names by Language. In: Shohamy, E. and D. Gorter. (Eds.), *Linguistic Landscape: Expanding the Scenery*. New York: Routledge. 141–154.

Ellis, R. 1997. *Second Language Acquisition*. Oxford: Oxford University Press.

Gorter, D. (Ed.). 2006. *Linguistic Landscape: A New Approach to Multilingualism*. Clevedon: Multilingual Matters.

Huebner, T. 2006. Bangkok's linguistic landscapes: Environmental print, code-mixing, and language change. In: Gorter D. (Ed.), *Linguistic Landscape: A New Approach to Multilingualism*. Clevedon: Multilingual Matters. 31–51.

Jakobson, R. 1959. On Linguistic Aspects of Translation. In: Brower, R. A. (Ed.), *On Translation*. Cambridge, Massachusetts: Harvard University Press. 232–239.

Macau Government. 1987. *Joint Declaration of the Government of the People's Republic of China and the Government of the Republic of Portugal on the question of Macao*: Available at: <http://bo.io.gov.mo/bo/i/88/23/dc/en/default.asp>.

Macau Government. 1999. *Basic Law of the Macau Special Administrative Region*: Available at: <http://bo.io.gov.mo/bo/i/1999/leibasica/index_uk.asp>.

MGTO, Macau Government Tourism Office. 2014. *Tourism Indicators*: Available at: <http://industry.macautourism.gov.mo/en/Statistics_and_Studies/list_statistics.php?id=39,29&page_id=10>.

Moody, A. 2008. Macau English: status, functions and forms. In: *English Today* 95, 24(3). 3–15.

National People's Congress. 1982. *The Constitution of the People's of China*. Available at: <http://www.npc.gov.cn/englishnpc/Constitution/node_2825.htm>.

Pennycook, A. 2009. Linguistic Landscapes and the Transgressive Semiotics of Graffiti. In: Shohamy, E. and D. Gorter. (Eds.), *Linguistic Landscape: Expanding the Scenery*. New York: Routledge. 302–312.

Poplack, S. 1980. Sometimes I'll Start a Sentence in Spanish y Termino Español: Toward a Typology of Code-switching. In: *Linguistics* 18(7/8). 581–618.

Selinker, L. 1972. Interlanguage. In: *International Review of Applied Linguistics* 10. 209–231.

Scollon, R. and Scollon, S. W. 2003. *Discourses in Place: Language in the Material World*. London: Routledge.

Shohamy, E. and Gorter, D. (Eds.). 2009. *Linguistic Landscape: Expanding the Scenery*. New York: Routledge.

Spolsky, B. 2009. Sociolinguistic Theory of Public Signage. In: Shohamy, E. and D. Gorter. (Eds.), *Linguistic Landscape: Expanding the Scenery*. New York: Routledge. 25–39.

Yan, L. and Lee, M. Y. 2014. Tourist Perceptions of the Multi-Linguistic Landscape in Macau. In: *Journal of China Tourism Research*. 432–447.

Michał B. Paradowski, Aleksandra Bator, Monika Michałowska
(University of Warsaw, Poland)

Multilingual Upbringing by Parents of Different Nationalities: Which Strategies Work Best?

Introduction

The majority of the peoples on earth are multilingual, not mono- or even bilingual (S. Bagga-Gupta 2013: 36). In many corners of the world people have long been growing up speaking more than merely two tongues. In the scientific literature today, too, bilingualism is seen as a specific – not only quantitatively, but also qualitatively different – case of multilingualism, rather than vice versa (P. Herdina and U. Jessner 2002; U. Jessner 2006: 35). This has led some researchers (e.g. H. Widła 2015) to talk of the twilight of *bi*lingualism in favour of *multi*lingualism. Multilingual and multicultural couples are no longer surprising or shocking. The topic of this chapter, a very current and complex issue, is the efficiency of language acquisition in the process of multilingual upbringing by parents of different nationalities.

The article aims at presenting, assessing and discussing the effectiveness of the methods that the parents may choose if their aim is to raise their children multilingually. The theoretical introduction focuses on the early development of bilingualism with the emphasis on the role of the parents and the possible models of education that they may introduce in their households. The subsequent empirical section presents the results of a survey conducted among 37 multilingual families in which the parents are of two different nationalities.

1. Multilingualism and bilingualism

1.1 Becoming bi-/multilingual

Some may claim that the most natural surrounding for a child is a unilingual environment. As B. Z. Pearson (2008: 4) highlights, it is a widespread stereotype, especially in countries with a mainstream culture characterised by monolingualism, such as the United States. Examples of people using one language exclusively are relatively rare and "now hard to find even in the mountains of Papua New Guinea" (V. Cook 2002: 23). In some regions of the world, such as Singapore, families are accustomed to using two or three languages in their households interchangeably and from the very beginning, and it is the usage of one language that turns out to be exceptional there (A. F. Gupta 1994: 161).

It is vital to mention that in order to raise a bilingual or multilingual child, a parent does not have to be bilingual her-/himself. The growing culture of globalisation permits the application of many means which render the task feasible, even if the parent does not know the language of concern (B. Z. Pearson 2008: 5).

Many people wrongly believe that multilingualism can be accomplished only if the acquisition of languages begins in childhood. It may indeed be easier when the process starts early, but a later age of onset is not an excluding factor; what matters is the actual experience in using the language (G. Luk, E. de Sa and E. Bialystok 2011; M. Consonni et al. 2013; L. Sheng et al. 2013; F. de Carli et al. 2014; T. A. Gibson, E. D. Peña and L. M. Bedore 2014; S. Unsworth et al. 2014). Life circumstances such as migration, education or intermarriage force many to adjust to the new situation, and an adult may attain a level of linguistic proficiency comparable to that of a child who has been acquiring her/his languages all life long, with the possible exception of native-like pronunciation (as the attainment here may depend on the individual differences regarding the articulatory rehearsal component of working memory and phonetic coding ability)[1]. Likewise, bilingual exposure from birth does not necessarily lead to a 'balanced' bilingual, as A. de Houwer (2003, 2007) showed that around one in four bilingually raised infants will be productive in only one language.

1.2 Debunking the myths surrounding multilingualism

Many myths and much prejudice has grown up around the notions of bi- and multilingualism. It is essential to dispel some of the most commonly heard misconceptions.

One frequently encountered opinion, especially prevalent in territories marked (whether historically or contemporarily) by high linguistic homogeneity[2],

---

1 But consider the lesser relevance of NS-oriented norms in contexts of English used as a lingua franca (M. B. Paradowski 2013).

2 Such as current-day Poland, as if forgetting that before the aftermath of World War II the country had eternally been a cauldron of nationalities, religions and languages, with a centuries-old tradition of openness and tolerance towards other ethnic groups (H. Komorowska 2014), and that under the partitions of the Polish-Lithuanian Commonwealth between Russia, Prussia and Austria – with the former kingdom consequently erased from the maps of Europe for 123 years – it was common to function in both the strongly defended native language and the imposed language of the occupant (while

is that bi- or multilinguals are exceptions to the default monolingual norm (M. B. Paradowski 2011: 331*f.*). This pervasive monolingual bias (M. Silverstein 1996, 1998; V. Cook 2002; P. Auer and W. Li 2006; F. Grosjean 2008) can be traced back to: i) the formation of nation states in the 18th and 19th c. with the accompanying imposition of nationalistic one country – one language policies aiming at linguistic unification of the citizens and creation of a national identity centred around the majority/official language and culture (D. Singleton and L. Aronin 2007; R. Mesthrie 2010), ii) the growth of colonialism, iii) the associated prestige ascribed to the privileged languages, and iv) the Saussurean-Chomskyan linguistic tradition taking as its reference point the idealised monolingual native speaker (A. Otwinowska 2015). Yet, the opposite is true: multilingualism is a natural potential available to every normal human being; monolingual speakers are but the consequence of environmental factors that have failed to provide the opportunity to acquire another language (M. B. Paradowski 2011: 332).

Another misconception, going back to L. Bloomfield's (1933: 56) definition that held sway over the field for many decades, has been that in order to deserve the label 'bi-/multilingual', one needs to have an equal, 'perfect', 'native-like' command of both/all her/his languages. Such a stance would at once imply that code-switching or a 'foreign' accent are undesirable signs of linguistic sloppiness or 'contamination' (S. Jarvis and A. Pavlenko 2007). The still widespread fallacy of the monolingual reference point means that despite using two or more languages on a regular basis, many bilinguals themselves evaluate their own linguistic competences as inadequate and do not perceive themselves as bilingual (*cf.* V. Cook 1999; S. Canagarajah 2004; J. Jenkins 2006; F. Grosjean 2008: 224; A. de Houwer 2015). Nowadays most linguists have departed from this static fractional/coordinate view of bi-/multilinguals as 'many monolinguals in one person' with separate competencies (U. Jessner 2006: 130) and identities (M. Gawinkowska, M. B. Paradowski and M. Bilewicz 2013) in each language, and from considering the aim of second language acquisition to be "learning how to behave monolingually in the new language" (L. Ortega 2010; *cf.* W. Li and M. G. Moyer 2008; A. de Houwer 2009), in favour of a dynamic compound perspective on multicompetent users (V. Cook 1991, 2008; E. Macaro 2009; G. Luk and E. Bialystok 2013), tilting towards less rigorous expectations. Unbalanced bilingualism is expected and normal (*cf.* A. de Houwer 2009; F. Grosjean 2010; J. Paradis, F. Genesee and M. Crago 2011), especially given differential, probabilistic

---

learning Greek and Latin at school and modern languages at university; E. Schramm 2008, not to mention elite multilingualism, A. Otwinowska 2015).

success even in native bilinguals, as opposed to guaranteed, categorical success in all – healthy – monolinguals (L. Ortega 2014). D. Crystal points out that "people who have perfect fluency in two languages do exist, but they are an exception, not a rule" (1987: 362), F. Grosjean stresses the importance of frequency, defining bilinguals as "those who use two or more languages (or dialects) in their everyday lives" (2010: 22), and even language policies recognise that individuals are "social agent[s] who [have] *gradually varying* competences in several languages and experience with several cultures" (E. Sauer and V. Saudan 2008: 5; emph. added).

Some parents fear that exposing their child to more than one tongue may cause language impairment or deficits, or that for children already diagnosed with impairments two languages mean too much unnecessary pressure and effort (E. Haman *et al.* 2015). The reality is that language impairments, if they do occur, are completely independent of bi- or multilingualism (L. M. Bedore and E. D. Peña 2008; J. Paradis 2010); in fact, children diagnosed with SLI who regularly use two or more languages have been shown to make significantly fewer errors in certain areas of both their languages compared to age-matched monolingual SLI peers (J. Paradis, M. Crago and F. Genesee 2006; S. Chilla 2008a, b; S. Armon-Lotem, G, Gordishevsky and J. Walters 2010; K. F. Peets and E. Bialystok 2010; F. Grosjean and P. Li 2012; T. Roeper 2012; K. Jensen de López and A. E. Baker 2015; S. Armon-Lotem, J. de Jong and N. Meir 2015). It is true that bi-/multilinguals outperform monolingual peers in some cognitive aspects: they i) achieve lower scores in receptive vocabulary tests in each of their respective tongues (D. K. Oller and R. E. Eilers 2002) – but this vocabulary deficit only concerns home- and not school-related lexis and the difference level is at approximately 10% (E. Bialystok *et al.* 2010), ii) are slower in vocabulary recall (lexical access time as measured in picture naming tasks; by around 40ms in their L_1 and 80–90ms in their L_2; I. Ivanova and A. Costa 2008, as well as more frequent experience of the 'tip of the tongue' phenomenon; T. H. Gollan and N. Silverberg 2001, T. H. Gollan and L.-A. R. Acenas 2004) – these are natural given the relatively lower input in each of the languages and the necessity to suppress the influence of the other language(s) in cases of lexical conflict[3], and iii) are later to develop some syntactic structures (E. Nicoladis 2006). However, with time they manage to catch up (at least to a level where these deficits can no longer be spotted in daily functioning), and overall the total lexical resources and linguistic repertoires of persons speaking more than

---

3   As well as in the case of the so-called emotion-related language choice (*cf.* M. Gawinkowska, M. B. Paradowski and M. Bilewicz 2013).

one language are much larger than in monolinguals (B. Z. Pearson, S. C. Fernández and D. K. Oller 1993; A. de Houwer 2009).

2. Models of education adopted by parents

If they want to succeed in their children's multilingual language acquisition, the parents not only need to create a favourable environment providing the necessary exposure, but also to actively participate in the process. B. Z. Pearson cites two attitudes that are indispensable in bilingual upbringing (2008: 123). Firstly, the parents have to show a "positive attitude towards bilingualism", meaning that they really want their children to be bilingual, are dedicated to the process, persistent, and determined to succeed, not allowing others to lead them astray by unfavourable opinions or criticism. The second necessary attitude is an "impact belief" – assumption that their own language practices influence those of their children; the parents had best therefore put an effort in developing and maintaining their own linguistic skills.

Some may think that it is the mother's language which turns out to be the most important for the offspring Nevertheless, a survey conducted by A. de Houwer (2007) failed to prove this point. Both parents have equal chances of transmitting their language to the child if the language is actively used at home.

There are two ways in which bilingual children can learn their two languages: either the child is exposed to both languages from the very beginning and acquires them at the same time (*simultaneous bilingualism*), or one language is learnt after the other (*successive bilingualism*). The starting point for differentiating one type of bilingualism from the other is usually the age of three (L. Arnberg 1987: 66).

Parents who wish to raise their children bilingually can choose from among several strategies. Each of them suits different needs and has its advantages and disadvantages.

2.1 One parent – one language (OPOL)

One of the earliest methods of bilingual upbringing to be reported (F. Grosjean 1982: 173) has been the *one parent – one language* approach, also known as *one person – one language*. In this strategy while communicating with the child each parent uses her/his native language. The method is based on a strict separation of the two languages that should lead to achieving the ability to use both in a fluent, balanced and native way (J. M. González 2008: 635). Because the child can "associate each language with a specific person" (L. Arnberg 1987: 87), it is easier for her/him to "keep the languages separated and to avoid mixing them." The model has been widely supported as an effective method that can lead to the acquisition of the minority language and active bilingualism (J. M. González 2008: 636). Adopting this strategy may also be advantageous to parents who, by addressing their child in their native languages, want to establish a mutual emotional relationship (*ibid.*).

The fact that many families have managed to raise bilingual children with the use of this method does not mean that it is not without problems. One potential danger is that the majority language, spoken either by the mother or the father, may start to dominate as soon as the child goes to school or strikes up acquaintance with other speakers of the language (F. Grosjean 1982: 175). As a consequence, the child may become reluctant to use the minority language (L. Arnberg 1987: 89).

The method also raises the question of which language the parents should speak to each other. According to L. Arnberg (*op. cit.*: 87), the minority language is advisable, as it gives the child an additional opportunity to be exposed to the less-used tongue. Yet, many everyday situations may force the bilingual parent to use her/his spouse's language in the child's presence. When the child has her/his playmates over, the parent may decide to speak the language that is comprehensible to everyone so as not to "single her/his child out" (L. Arnberg 1987: 88). Similarly, while spending time together or with friends, if the only persons who use the minority language are mother and daughter, the others should not feel excluded from the conversation (J. M. González 2008: 636). Because of these concerns many researchers have been wondering whether absolute consistency is mandatory, and the general consensus seems to be that the application of the "pure" OPOL method turns out to be difficult and therefore rare (L. Arnberg 1987: 88). B. Ramjoue (1980), for instance, allowed exceptions to the rule as long as the child knows why the parent switches to the other language. B. Abdelilah-Bauer (2008: 95) goes even further in postulating that absolute consistency should be avoided, claiming that trying to remain consistent at all costs may have a detrimental effect on the spontaneous interaction between the parent and the child. Nevertheless, in the initial stage of the child's bilingual development consistency does play an important role, as it helps her/him learn how to separate both language systems (L. Arnberg 1987: 88).

2.2 Minority language at home (mL@H)

The *minority language at home* method aims at introducing two languages. The child is supposed to acquire the minority language at home and the majority language outside – for example at the playground or school (C. Baker 2011: 100). The main objective is to provide maximal input of the former at home and to counteract the dominating influence of the majority language from the external environment (L. Arnberg 1987: 90): both parents are supposed to use the minority language, even if it is not the mother tongue of both. The strategy is usually implemented by parents who both have a high degree of proficiency in the language. The method leads to sequential bilingualism, since the acquisition of the second language begins when the child goes to nursery or school.

mL@H may be a good solution for families that emigrated, if they wish to keep their native language alive. It enables the acquisition of the minority language regardless of its prevalence in the local community. Furthermore, unlike the *one parent – one language* method, it does not cause disorientation concerning the choice of code, since everyone uses the same one, although it may become confusing for the children if the parents decide to use the minority language at home, but not outside.

However, the method also has disadvantages. First of all, many of the benefits associated with simultaneous bilingualism remain out of easy reach of children who have been educated with the use of mL@H. What is more, due to the delay in the acquisition of the majority language, the method demands a greater dose of parental indulgence, since the children may have problems with communicating in their L_2 until the age of around five (*ibid.*). Nevertheless, after a sufficient period of exposure, they typically manage to catch up with their peers.

2.3 Initial one-language strategy

Some parents assume that being exposed to two languages from the very beginning may be too confusing for the child. For that reason, they initially decide to use one language, and only then introduce the second (usually between the age of three and five; F. Grosjean 1982: 174). However, the successive way of presenting both languages may also be problematic in some respects. One difficulty is that one of the parents will have to speak a new language to the child than that which has hitherto been used. As language serves to establish an emotional bond between parents and children, the latter are usually resistant to a parent communicating with them in a new language (L. Arnberg 1987: 91).

2.4 Time and Place (T&P)

The *Time and Place* method is based on two other main criteria according to which parents may choose the language of communication (R. Rosenback 2015). The family can alter the language depending on the time of day, month or year, or according to the activity or place. For example, one language is spoken during the day, another one in the evening, or one during the week and the other over the weekend (F. Grosjean 1982: 174). One language may be spoken outside the house, another one inside, or one upstairs, the other downstairs or only in a particular room (L. Arnberg 1987: 93). In some families, it is common practice to use the minority language only during certain activities (*ibid.*).

Although this model also requires persistence plus organisational skills on the part of the parents, it allows substantial creativity in establishing the household and encourages a diversity of options. The advantage is that it can be easily adapted to the ideas or needs of the family. What is more, every person—including the child—can be engaged in the organisation of their multilingual household. As it is less restrictive, the method may be an option for parents who wish to introduce a language they are not quite proficient in, or want to pass to their offspring numerous languages they know (R. Rosenback 2015). Finally, it is easily adaptable to the needs of a monoparental family. Nevertheless, compared with the previous methods, this one seems far less natural and based on an arbitrary factor (F. Grosjean 1982: 174), and has therefore not enlisted many supporters among scholars.

2.5 Mixed strategy

The mixed strategy is based on interchangeable use of the languages by the parents; however, most often it is primarily the parent speaking the minority language who has to switch between the languages (L. Arnberg 1987: 86). Which language is used at a particular moment depends on such factors as the topic of the conversation, situation, interlocutors, and so on (*ibid.*). This strategy of "free alternation of languages" is adopted in some bilingual families because the parents consider this solution the most natural (F. Grosjean 1982: 174) or do not want to impose any particular rules with regard to the use of the languages in the home (L. Arnberg 1987: 86). Still, the mixed strategy has one weakness: the lack of a plan for the use of the languages may contribute to the dominance of the majority language at the expense of the minority one (F. Grosjean 1982: 174). As a solution B. Ramjoue (1980) postulated that the minority language be used between the parents, or that the majority language-speaking parent use the language to the child at least part of the time.

3. The survey

The preceding sections aimed at presenting the general theoretical view on bilingualism and multilingualism as well as the issue of multilingual upbringing. This section will describe the results of an online survey conducted among 37 families who decided to raise their children bilingually or multilingually and in which the parents are of different nationalities.

3.1 Methodology

3.1.1 Purpose

The survey was conducted for three main reasons. First of all, it was to gather information on the methods applied by parents and the behaviour of the children. Additionally, the results included parents' opinions on the efficiency of the chosen strategies and their children's linguistic development. The survey also aimed at establishing whether the parents would change anything if they had a chance to go back in time.

3.1.2 Families

The survey was completed by mothers from 37 bilingual or multilingual families. The main condition was for the parents to have different nationalities. In only one case was the native language of both parents the same. In 23 families (62.2%) the native language of either the mother or the father was also the dominant language spoken in the community. Only two mothers indicated that they are monolingual. Among the remaining 35 families, 11 (29.7%) were bilingual and 24 (64.7%) multilingual.

It is vital to highlight that in 16 families (43.2%) the mothers who were filling in the questionnaire have higher linguistic education, which may have contributed to the thoroughness of the observations and answers given in the survey.

The 37 families sent the results from twenty countries on four continents. The majority – 18 families (48.65%) – currently live in Europe: in the United Kingdom (4), Germany (2), Belgium (2), Greece (2), the Czech Republic (1), Norway (1), Finland (1), France (1), Spain (1), Croatia (1), Poland (1), and the Netherlands (1). 14 families (37.8%) presently reside in North America: in the United States (9), Canada (4) or Mexico (1). 4 live in Asia: in the United Arab Emirates (1), Lebanon (1), Turkey (1), and Japan (1). One family resides in Australia.

3.2 Results

3.2.1 Reasons for multilingual upbringing

In the case of multinational marriages it is obvious that one of the most important reasons for raising children multilingually is mutual communication. Since in the majority of cases the parents also have different mother tongues, the child is often required to know both of them on a communicative level in order to be able to communicate. *[The] child [should] be capable of talking and exchanging information [not only] with his or her parents, but also with other members of the community*, whose dominant language is often different from the ones already spoken at home. However, in the survey only nine families (24.3%) indicated this motive in the question about the reasons for the decision to raise their children multilingually.

The reason that turned out to be the most popular one is *the need to communicate with the rest of the family from both sides*. Even if the parents of the child are themselves multilingual, it is rare that their relatives, or even friends, are able to use multiple languages too. In the questionnaire, seventeen families (45.9%) gave this reason as the one which convinced them to choose multilingual upbringing.

Language is more than just a means of communication, it is also *part of [one's] heritage*. It is almost never separated from the culture. When a child grows in a country distant from the native one of her/his parents, they try *to convey the culture of the country* via the use of language and encourage the child to remember her/his roots. It is also a natural thing to communicate with the child in one's own mother tongue, as it creates a more genuine connection; some mothers also described communication in a non-native tongue as "uncomfortable." The reason involving one's roots and culture was indicated by twelve mothers (32.4%).

Being multilingual has many advantages and can be beneficial not only for children, but also adults (E. Bialystok, F. I. Craik and M. Freedman 2007; M. B. Paradowski 2011; A. Alladi *et al.* 2014). Being able to use more than one language is in itself a very useful skill, but it also *enhances the operation of the brain and favourably influences cognitive development* (*cf.* also M. B. Paradowski and M. Michałowska, in press). Multilingualism can also make people *more open-minded and capable of understanding different cultures and acknowledge their diversity*. Additionally, knowledge of many languages can play *a crucial role in the future career*, as it provides more possibilities and paths, including education abroad, which may sometimes be better or less expensive than in the home country. Those benefits were listed as the reason for applying multilingual upbringing by thirteen mothers (35.1%).

Figure 1: Popularity of the reasons for multilingual upbringing

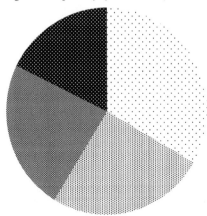

· ˙ The need to communicate with the rest of the family from both sides

▧ Enhanced operation of the brain, bigger tolerance, richer career opportunities

▨ Language to convey the culture of the country and as a part of the heritage

▨ The need to communicate with the parents and other members of the local community

3.2.2 Parents

The closest environment of the children was culturally very rich from the beginning of their lives. The mothers who filled in the survey present in total 21 nationalities: Polish (4), Mexican (4), American (3), Canadian (2), British (2), Spanish (2), German (2), Italian (2), Bulgarian (2), Icelandic (1), French (1), Greek (1), Croatian (1), Estonian (1), Danish (1), Dutch (1), Swedish (1), Serbian (1), Brazilian (1), Indonesian (1), Chinese (1), and Peruvian (1). In one case, the mother has double nationality, Turkish and Finnish. Their partners present in total 19 different nationalities: American (6), Canadian (5), British (4), German (3), French (2), Greek (2), Dutch (2), Turkish (2), Finnish (1), Irish (1), Spanish (1), Slovak (1), Mexican (1), Australian (1), Peruvian (1), Lebanese (1), and Japanese (1). In two cases, the fathers have double nationalities – one is Moroccan and Greek, the other Venezuelan and Spanish.

With all those nationalities comes a great linguistic variety. The mothers speak in total 19 different native tongues: English (7), Spanish (6), Polish (4), German (2), French (2), Italian (2), Portuguese (1), Icelandic (1), Indonesian (1), Swedish (1), Turkish (1), Greek (1), Cantonese (1), Dutch (1), Serbian (1), Bulgarian (1), Estonian (1), Bulgarian (1), and Danish (1). In one case the mother has two native tongues, Spanish and Catalan. Their partners use in total 12 different mother tongues: English (16), French (2), Spanish (4), Greek (2), Turkish (2), Arabic (2), Finnish (1), Slovak (1), Swabian (1), Japanese (1), German (1), and Dutch (1). In three cases the fathers have two native languages – English and German, English and French, and Dutch and English. Among the 37 families in only two do the parents share the same mother tongue; in one of these cases the father has two native tongues.

Only two mothers admitted that they are monolingual, but, interestingly enough, one of them claimed to be using two different languages while communicating with the child[4]. Among the remaining 35 mothers, the most popular pattern is the knowledge of two or four languages (11 mothers – or 29.7% – in each case). A slightly smaller number use three languages (8 mothers, 21.6%). Two mothers admitted that they know five languages and three claimed they know six.

3.2.3 Linguistic environment

The number of languages that a child is exposed to depends on many factors. The first crucial one is the language in use between the parents. In many cases one of the parents' mother tongues already serves as a means of communication in the family. However, parents quite often communicate in a third language, different from their native ones, that is known to both of them. Another key factor here is location. Depending on where the family currently reside, the child can be exposed to a higher or lower number of languages. If in the area where the family live one of the languages used at home is at the same time the dominant language of the community, the number is reduced. Nevertheless, if the concerned country or region is bi-, tri- or quadrilingual, the number of languages the child is exposed to rises considerably. In the case of this survey, the most frequent case was exposure to three languages (17 families; 45.9%). A slightly smaller number of children are exposed to two languages (12 families; 32.4%), whereas five families (13.5%) expose their children to four languages. Exposure to five, six or seven languages is rare, concerning one family in each case (Fig. 2). There is a moderate positive correlation (.6259) between the number of languages spoken by the mother and the number of languages the child has contact with.

---

4 This may be due to the fact that many people use very strict definitions of bilingualism or multilingualism, and associate these labels with early language acquisition. Such people very often consider themselves monolinguals, even if they can justifiably be classified as late sequential bilinguals.

Figure 2: The number of languages the children are exposed to in each family

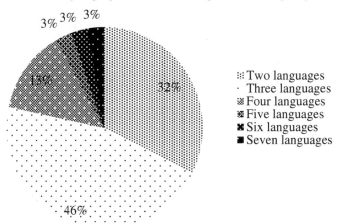

3% 3% 3%
3%

:: Two languages
· Three languages
※ Four languages
※ Five languages
※ Six languages
■ Seven languages

32%

46%

Most of the mothers choose to use either one or two languages while communicating with the children. Seventeen (45.9%) use only one language as the means of communication, which in most cases (88.2 per cent) is their mother tongue. Fourteen (37.8%) use two different languages. In two cases the second language occurs only when a third person is involved in the conversation and there is a possibility that s/he will not understand what has been said. Only six mothers (16.2%) use three languages to communicate with their children. However, sometimes the second or third language occurs only rarely, to provide small exposure. One mother claimed that the only case in which she uses a language other than her L_1 is when she provides a translation of what she has just said in Bulgarian into English or Japanese.

The total number of languages that the children have contact with is thirty, whereas all the parents concerned have in total only twenty four different native tongues. Hence, it is visible that exposure to parents' non-native tongues is quite popular (23 families; 62.1%) and, interestingly enough, not always connected with the place of residence of the family (in only 8 cases among these (34.8%) is it connected with the place of residence of the family). The languages the families expose their children to present as follows: English (37), Spanish (15), French (11), German (7), Dutch (6), Polish (4), Greek (4), Arabic (3), Turkish (3), Italian (2), Bulgarian (2), Portuguese (1), Czech (1), Slovak (1), Catalan (1), Icelandic (1), Russian (1), Indonesian (1), Swabian (1), Hochdeutsch (1), Norwegian (1), Swedish (1), Finnish (1), Croatian (1), ASL (1), Cantonese (1), Serbian (1), Japanese (1), Estonian (1), and Danish (1). It is vital to highlight that in all 37 families the children have contact with English, which also underlines the importance and role of this language in today's world (M. B. Paradowski 2008)[5].

A good opportunity for the child to be exposed to different languages and, at the same time, to have contact with other peers who also communicate in those languages is sending her/him to a bilingual kindergarten or school. However, among the families who took part in the survey only eight (21.6%) decided to choose this kind of educational institution. This may be due to financial reasons: despite their growing popularity, the tuition fees at such establishments tend to be quite high.

3.2.4 Profile of the children

The survey took into consideration 48 children in total. In 29 cases (78.4%), there is only one child in the family. In five (13.5%), there were two children, and in three cases three children.

All the families claimed that their children have had contact with at least two different languages from the first days of life, but the acquisition of the third or latter languages was delayed in six families (16.2%). The mothers gave diversified reasons for this. In three cases they claimed that it came naturally with the beginning of nursery, kindergarten or school – a perfect example of sequential multilingualism. One mother also underlined that she does not talk in Greek to her child because it is not her native language and she was afraid of transferring her accent, so waiting until the beginning of school seemed a good solution. In two cases the acquisition of a new language resulted from moving countries. Two families deliberately delayed the acquisition of the third language as they had thought it could turn out to be too confusing for the children, but one of them (even though the child is just 18 months old) already regrets the decision and has started to introduce the third language. One mother also highlighted that she wishes to expose her child to two more languages, but this is greatly hindered by unfavourable conditions (as she does not have a driving licence and is unable to take the child around and enable contact with native speakers).

3.2.5 Methods applied in the process of upbringing

The *one parent – one language* method is applied by only 23 families (62.2%), 11 of whom (47.8%) do not apply the "pure" version, since the mothers claim to use more than one language while communicating with their children. Instead

---

5   This result may have also been influenced by the fact that English was the language of
    the survey.

of this, reading to a child is the most often used activity by parents. The analysis showed that only one family does not use readings. All the mothers read in their native language(s), but additionally 27 (73%) read in non-native tongues as well[6]. In the remaining nine cases, in which the mothers read only in their native tongues, all the children listen to stories read in another language or languages as well. There is a moderate positive correlation (.5423) between the presence of reading performed by the mother and the child's ability to communicate effectively with the mother's family in the mother's native language.

Among the other methods, the survey mentioned error correction, encouragement and rewards. Correcting errors is applied by 33 families (89.2%). Encouraging the child to speak more than one language is only a little less popular (31 families; 83.8%). Rewarding children for speaking more than one language does not have many supporters; only four families (10.8%) declare using it.

One of the mothers has another method that she considers efficient in the process of multilingual upbringing. As the family live in Washington, DC, in order to provide extra exposure to German the mother decided to hire an *au pair* who speaks German exclusively. She has also introduced German play times. The mother claims the method to be effective, as the father also uses German and additionally English while communicating with the child.

3.2.6 Children's linguistic skills and behaviours

The most important outcome of language acquisition is the ability to communicate. In the case of the families that took part in the survey it was also the main reason for which they decided to apply bilingual or multilingual upbringing – to render possible communication between them, their children and families. The analysis has shown that, in general, they have succeeded. Among the 37 families, only three mothers report having problems with understanding their children's speech, and only two evaluate communication with their families in their native languages as unsuccessful[7]. The situation is very similar when it comes to the father's family: in this case 33 mothers (89.2%) claim that communication with this side of the family in the fathers' native language is successful, and only one mother admitted otherwise.[8]

---

6   Interestingly enough, 16 of those 27 (59.3 per cent) declare that they are applying the OPOL method.
7   In one case the child does not have contact with this side of the family.
8   In three cases children do not have contact with the father's family.

The methods applied by the families turned out to be effective not only with regard to communicative skills, but also general linguistic skills. 21 mothers (56.8%)
claim to be content with their children's writing skills. Among them 14 (37.8%)
describe themselves as very satisfied and 7 (18.9%) satisfied. There is a moderate
positive correlation (.4472) between the level of satisfaction and parents' patience.
In the remaining 16 cases (43.2%) the children have not yet developed a written
form of the language. Regarding speaking, only one mother is not happy with her
child's speaking skills. 26 (70.3%) claim to be very satisfied, 8 (21.6%) satisfied, and
3 to be neutral about it. As far as pronunciation is concerned, also only one mother
admitted that she is not content with her child's performance, but still remains
neutral about it, and the remaining mothers are either very satisfied (21 mothers;
56.8%), satisfied (12 mothers; 32.4%), or neutral (3 mothers). Children's vocabulary was widely appreciated as well. In this case again only one mother claimed
she is not happy. Among the remaining mothers 24 (64.9%) are very satisfied,
9 (24.3%) satisfied, and the remaining 4 (10.8%) neutral. Grammar is also satisfac-
tory; 16 (47.1%) described themselves as very satisfied, 11 (32.4%) as satisfied and
7 (20.6%) as neutral towards the issue. Three mothers refrained from answering
the question and one claimed she is not contented with her child's performance.

The questionnaire also tackled three issues concerning children's linguistic
behaviour: code-switching, lexical transfer, and grammatical transfer. One mother
refrained from answering. 19 elaborated on the topic and gave examples from
their children's idiolects. Code-switching was observed in exactly 50 per cent of
the cases (18 families), lexical transfer in 20 families (55.5%) and grammatical
transfer in 19 families (52.8%).

Code-switching appeared in all possible forms – as a shift for a word, phrase
or sentence. The mothers underlined that this takes place when the child is unable to find the word in the language currently spoken or when a notion is better expressed in another language – reasons coherent with those enumerated by
scholars. Lexical transfer is the most common behaviour of all three. There is a
moderate negative correlation (–4.000) between the presence of lexical transfer
and the acquisition of languages from birth. Grammatical transfer, only a little
less ubiquitous than lexical transfer, was very keenly described by the mothers.
There is a moderate positive correlation between observed lexical transfer and
observed grammatical transfer (.4976).

The mothers also highlighted some other behaviours. For example, one child
tends to use two words, one after the other, in both languages. One mother pointed
out that, based on her observations, her daughter code-switches and applies lexical transfer only while talking with her or her husband, never with other people,
probably because she knows that both her parents speak those languages and will

understand her without difficulty. Finally, one mother stated that the whole family code-switch and apply lexical transfer, not only her daughter. She also underlined that sometimes this is used as an inner joke.

3.3 Parents' opinions

The parents seem to be very contented with the applied methods and their outcomes. The process turned out to be effective despite some inconsistencies highlighted above. 27 mothers (70.3%) claim to be very satisfied with the effects of upbringing, 9 (24.3%) are satisfied, and 2 remain neutral. The mothers describe their children as very bright and keen learners who are curious and inquisitive. In general, the children are able to communicate fluently and efficiently in two, three or four languages, have rich vocabulary and learn new words, rules and languages quite fast and with ease. The mothers also claim that the children have no foreign accent in their speech. One mother believes that her daughter's skills in every single one of her three languages do not differ from those of her monolingual peers; another underlined that her daughter's Norwegian is not worse than her classmates'. Some children are considered even more advanced than their peers – in one case a boy's communicative skills were evaluated as better that the other children's in the playgroup. The children, even very little ones, also understand that different people may speak different languages and have to be addressed accordingly. With passing time, children also tend to mix languages less. The mothers feel proud of their children and confident about their further linguistic development or success in adult life. None of the mothers judged the early exposure to more than two languages to be problematic or confusing. On the contrary, one mother claims that it was the delayed introduction of the third language that turned out to be challenging. Parents who refrained from introducing further languages at the beginning claim they would not delay the introduction of a new language again.

Sometimes children begin to understand a language even if they are not yet able to produce it. Production comes with time and the ability to understand a given language is already a step towards effective and fluent communication. Some multilingual children may experience a speech delay, but those who did have problems with this at the beginning caught on quickly and do not have further difficulties because of their multilingualism.

The last question, about possible changes if there were a chance to go back in time, made it clear that in general the parents are satisfied with their methods and their children's progress. 26 mothers (70.3%) answered confidently that they would not have changed anything at all in the process. One mother claimed she is not sure about the answer, and two mothers did not answer the question. The

138   Michał B. Paradowski et al.

remaining eight mothers had two main ideas. Three admitted that they should have put more emphasis on their native tongues, either by more frequent exposure, or stronger encouragement to learn the language. Three mothers underlined that they would definitely have introduced the third language earlier on. One declared that she should have applied a tighter schedule and a "more structural approach." Finally, one mother highlighted that she found the introduction of three languages very effective, but that if given a second chance, she would have been more patient about her son's speaking skills.

Conclusion

Even though multilingualism is a widespread phenomenon, its advantage are most easily accessible to people whose parents are of different nationalities. Nonetheless, the process of multilingual upbringing is complex and demanding, and its success greatly depends on parents' persistence and dedication.

This article aimed at presenting, discussing and assessing the effectiveness of the methods which parents may choose if they wish to raise their children multilingually. It focused on families in which the parents are of two different nationalities. Taken into consideration were examples of both simultaneous and sequential multilingualism. All of the concerned children are simultaneous bilinguals, but some acquired a third or latter languages sequentially. The analysis of the results showed that neither simultaneous nor sequential multilingualism leads to confusion or further problems with communication. The multilingual upbringing by parents of different nationalities turned out to be efficient and beneficial.

The survey was warmly welcomed by the parents and evaluated as interesting. They willingly filled in the questionnaires, answered the questions thoroughly, and provided information about the everyday life of a multilingual family.

References

Abdelilah-Bauer, B. 2008. *Zweisprachigaufwachsen: Herausforderung und Chance für Kinder, Eltern und Erzieher.* Munich: C. H. Beck.

Alladi, A., Mortimer, J. A., Bak, T. H., Duggirala, V., Surampudi, B., Shailaja, M., Shukla, A. K., Chaudhuri, J. R. and Kaul, S. 2014. Bilingualism delays age at onset of dementia, independent of education and immigration status. In: *Neurology* 81(22). 1938–1944.

Armon-Lotem, S., De Jong, J. and Meir, N. (Eds.). 2015. *Assessing Multilingual Children. Disentangling Bilingualism from Language Impairment.* Bristol: Multilingual Matters.

Armon-Lotem, S., Gordishevsky, G. and Walters J., 2010. Instructive bilingualism: Prepositions in the Hebrew of bilingual children with SLI. In: Costa, J., A. Castro, M. Lobo and F. Pratas (Eds.), *Proceedings of GALA 2009: Language Acquisition and Development*. Newcastle upon Tyne: Cambridge Scholars. 1–12.

Arnberg, L. 1987. *Raising Children Bilingually: The Pre-School Years*. Clevedon: Multilingual Matters.

Auer, P. and Li, W. 2007. *Handbook of Multilingualism and Multilingual Communication*. Göttingen: Hubert and Co.

Bagga-Gupta, S. 2013. The boundary-turn: (Re)locating culture, identity and language through the epistemological lenses of time, space and social interactions. In: Hasnain, S. I., S. Bagga-Gupta and S. Mohan (Eds.), *Alternative Voices: (Re)searching Language, Culture, Identity...* Newcastle upon Tyne: Cambridge Scholars. 28–49.

Baker, C. 1988. *Key Issues in Bilingualism and Bilingual Education*. Clevedon: Multilingual Matters.

Baker, C. 2011. *Foundations of Bilingual Education and Bilingualism* [5ᵗʰ ed.]. Bristol: Multilingual Matters.

Bedore, L. M. and Peña, E. D. 2008. Assessment of bilingual children for identification of language impairment: Current findings and implications for practice. In: *International Journal of Bilingual Education and Bilingualism* 11(1). 1–29.

Bialystok, E., Craik, F. I. and Freedman, M. 2007. Bilingualism as a protection against the onset of symptoms of dementia. In: *Neuropsychologia* 45(2). 459–464.

Bialystok, E., Luk, G., Peets, K. F. and Yang, S. 2010. Receptive vocabulary differences in monolingual and bilingual children. In: *Bilingualism: Language and Cognition* 13(4). 525–531.

Bloomfield, L. 1933. *Language*. New York: Holt, Rinehart, and Winston.

Canagarajah, S. 2004. Subversive identities, pedagogical safe houses, and critical learning. In: Norton, B. and K. Toohey (Eds.), *Critical Pedagogies and Language Learning*. New York: Cambridge University Press. 116–137.

Chilla, S. 2008a. *Erstsprache, Zweitsprache, Spezifische Sprachentwicklungsstörung? Eine Untersuchung des Erwerbs der deutschen Hauptsatzstruktur durch sukzessiv-bilinguale Kinder mit türkischer Erstsprache*. Hamburg: Verlag Dr. Kovač.

Chilla, S. 2008b. Störungen im Erwerb des Deutschen als Zweitsprache im Kindesalter–eine Herausforderung an die sprachpädagogische Diagnostik. In: *Diskurs Kindheits- und Jugendforschung* 3(3). 277–290.

Consonni, M., Cafiero, R., Marin, D., Tettamanti, M., Iadanza, A., Fabbro, F. and Perani, D. 2013. Neural convergence for language comprehension and grammatical class production in highly proficient bilinguals is independent of age of acquisition. In: *Cortex* 49(5). 1252–1258.

Cook, V. 1991. The poverty-of-the-stimulus argument and multicompetence. In: *Second Language Research* 7(2). 103–117.

Cook, V. 1999. Going beyond the native speaker in language teaching. In: *TESOL Quarterly* 33(2). 185–209.

Cook, V. 2002. Background to the L2 user. In: Cook, V. (Ed.), *Portraits of the L2 User.* Clevedon: Multilingual Matters. 1–28.

Cook, V. 2008. Multi-competence: Black hole or wormhole for second language acquisition research? In: Han, Z. H. (Ed.), *Understanding Second Language Process.* Clevedon: Multilingual Matters. 16–26.

Crystal, D. 1987. *The Cambridge Encyclopaedia of Language.* Cambridge: CUP.

De Carli, F., Dessi, B., Mariani, M., Girtler, N., Greco, A., Rodriguez, G., Salmon, L. and Morelli, M. 2014. Language use affects proficiency in Italian–Spanish bilinguals irrespective of age of second language acquisition. In: *Bilingualism: Language and Cognition* 18(2). 324–339.

De Houwer, A. 2003. Home languages spoken in officially monolingual Flanders: A survey. In: *Plurilingua* 24. 71–87.

De Houwer, A. 2007. Parental language input patterns and children's bilingual use. In: *Applied Psycholinguistics* 28(3). 411–424.

De Houwer, A. 2009. *Bilingual First Language Acquisition.* Bristol: Multilingual Matters.

De Houwer, A. 2015. Harmonious bilingual development: Young families' well-being in language contact situations. In: *International Journal of Bilingualism* 19(2). 169–184.

Gawinkowska, M., Paradowski, M. B. and Bilewicz, M. 2013. Second language as an exemptor from sociocultural norms. Emotion-Related Language Choice revisited. In: *PLoS ONE* 8(12): e81225. doi: 10.1371/journal.pone.0081225.

Gibson, T. A., Peña, E. D. and Bedore, L. M. 2014. The relation between language experience and receptive-expressive semantic gaps in bilingual children. In: *International Journal of Bilingual Education and Bilingualism* 17(1). 90–110.

Gollan, T. H. and Acenas, L.-A. R. 2004. What is a TOT? Cognate and translation effects on tip-of-the-tongue states in Spanish-English and Tagalog-English bilinguals. In: *Journal of Experimental Psychology: Learning, Memory and Cognition* 33(7). 246–269.

Gollan, T. H. and Silverberg, N. 2001. Tip-of-the-tongue states in Hebrew-English bilinguals. In: *Bilingualism: Language and Cognition* 4(1). 63–83.

González, J. M. (Ed.). 2008. *Encyclopaedia of Bilingual Education.* Thousand Oaks, CA: Sage.

Grosjean, F. 1982. *Life with Two Languages: An Introduction to Bilingualism.* Cambridge, MA.: Harvard University Press.

Grosjean, F. 2008. *Studying Bilinguals*. Oxford: Oxford University Press.

Grosjean, F. 2010. *Bilingual: Life and Reality*. Cambridge, MA: Harvard University Press.

Grosjean, F. and P. Li. 2012. *The Psycholinguistics of Bilingualism*. Oxford: Wiley-Blackwell.

Gupta, A. F. 1994. *The Step-Tongue: Children's English in Singapore*. Clevedon: Multilingual Matters.

Haman, E., Otwinowska-Kasztelanic, A. and Wodniecka, Z. 2015. Dwujęzyczność w warunkach naturalnych: Psycholingwistyczny rachunek zysków i strat. Plenary lecture, Konferencja Naukowa Polskiego Towarzystwa Neofilologicznego "Wielojęzyczność i międzykulturowość w glottodydaktyce", Warsaw. 9.9.2015.

Herdina, P. and Jessner, U. 2002. *A Dynamic Model of Multilingualism: Perspectives of Change in Psycholinguistics*. Clevedon: Multilingual Matters.

Ivanova, I. and Costa, A. 2008. Does bilingualism hamper lexical access in speech production? In: *Acta Psychologica* 127(2). 277–288.

Jarvis, S. and Pavlenko, A. 2007. *Cross-linguistic Influence in Language and Cognition*. New York: Routledge.

Jenkins, J. 2006. Points of view and blind spots: ELF and SLA. In: *International Journal of Applied Linguistics* 16(2). 137–162.

Jensen de López, K. and A. E. Baker. 2015. Executive functions in the assessment of bilingual children with language impairment. In: Armon-Lotem, S., J. de Jong and N. Meir (Eds.), *Assessing Multilingual Children. Disentangling Bilingualism from Language Impairment*. Bristol: Multilingual Matters. 275–298.

Jessner, U. 2006. *Linguistic Awareness in Multilinguals: English as a Third Language*. Edinburgh: Edinburgh University Press.

Jessner, U. 2008. Teaching third languages: findings, trends and challenges. In: *Language Teaching* 41(1). 15–56.

Komorowska, H. 2014. Analyzing linguistic landscapes. A diachronic study of multilingualism in Poland. In: Otwinowska, A. and G. De Angelis (Eds.), *Teaching and Learning in Multilingual Contexts: Sociolinguistic and Educational Perspectives*. Bristol: Multilingual Matters. 19–31.

Li, W. and Moyer, M. G. (Eds.). 2008. *The Blackwell Guide to Research Methods in Bilingualism and Multilingualism*. Malden, MA: Blackwell.

Luk, G. and Bialystok, E. 2013. Bilingualism is not a categorical variable: Interaction between language proficiency and usage. In: *Journal of Cognitive Psychology* 25(5). 605–621.

Luk, G., De Sa, E. and Bialystok, E. 2011. Is there a relation between onset age of bilingualism and enhancement of cognitive control? In: *Bilingualism: Language and Cognition* 14(4). 588–595.

Macaro, E. 2009. Teacher use of code-switching in the second language classroom: Exploring optimal use. In: Turnbull, M. and J. Dailey O'Cain (Eds.), *First Language Use in Second and Foreign Language Learning*. Bristol: Multilingual Matters. 35–49.

Mesthrie, R. 2010. Sociolinguistics and Sociology of Language. In: Spolsky, B. and F. M. Hult (Eds.), *The Handbook of Educational Linguistics*. Malden, MA: Blackwell. 66–82.

Nicoladis, E. 2006. Cross-linguistic transfer in adjective-noun strings by preschool bilingual children. In: *Bilingualism: Language and Cognition* 9(1). 15–32.

Oller, D. K. and Eilers, R. E. (Eds.). 2002. *Language and Literacy in Bilingual Children*. Clevedon: Multilingual Matters.

Ortega, L. 2010. The bilingual turn in SLA. Plenary address, 2010 AAAL Conference. Atlanta, GA. 8.3.2010.

Ortega, L. 2014. Experience and success in late bilingualism. Plenary address, 17th AILA World Congress "One World, Many Languages". Brisbane. 11.8.2014.

Otwinowska, A. 2015. *Cognate Vocabulary in Language Acquisition and Use: Attitudes, Awareness, Activation*. Bristol: Multilingual Matters.

Paradis, J. 2010. The interface between bilingual development and specific language impairment. In: *Applied Psycholinguistics* 31(2). 227–252.

Paradis, J., Crago, M. and Genesee, F. 2006. Domain-general versus domain-specific accounts of specific language impairment: Evidence from bilingual children's acquisition of object pronouns. In: *Language Acquisition* 13(1). 33–62.

Paradis, J., Genesee, F. and Crago, M. 2011. *Dual Language Development & Disorders: A Handbook on Bilingualism & Second Language Learning* [2nd ed]. Baltimore: Brookes.

Paradowski, M. B. 2008, Apr. Winds of change in the English language – Air of peril for native speakers? In: *Novitas-ROYAL (Research on Youth and Language)* 2(1). 92–119.

Paradowski, M. B. 2011. Multilingualism – assessing benefits. In: Komorowska, H. (Ed.), *Issues in Promoting Multilingualism. Teaching – Learning – Assessment*. Warsaw: Foundation for the Development of the Education System. 335–354.

Paradowski, M. B. 2013. *Understanding English as a Lingua Franca: A Complete Introduction to the Theoretical Nature and Practical Implications of English used as a Lingua Franca*. Barbara Seidlhofer [review article] *The Interpreter and Translator Trainer* 7(2) [*Special Issue: English as a Lingua Franca. Implications for Translator and Interpreter Education*]. 312–320.

Paradowski, M. B. and Michałowska, M. (in press). Establishing a bilingual home: Parents' perspective on the effectiveness of the adopted communication strategies. In: *Lingwistyka Stosowana*.

Pearson, B. Z. 2008. *Raising a Bilingual Child.* New York: Living Language.

Pearson, B. Z., Fernández, S. C. and Oller, D. K. 1993. Lexical development in bilingual infants and toddlers: Comparison to monolingual norms. In: *Language Learning* 43(1). 93–120.

Peets, K. F. and Bialystok, E. 2010. An integrated approach to the study of specific language impairment and bilingualism. In: *Applied Psycholinguistics* 31(2). 315–319.

Ramjoue, B. 1980. *Guidelines for Children's Bilingualism.* Paris: Association for American Wives of Europeans.

Roeper, T. 2012. Minimalism and bilingualism: How and why bilingualism could benefit children with SLI. In: *Bilingualism: Language and Cognition* 15(1). 88–101.

Rosenback, R. 2015. Time and place – T & P as a family language strategy. In: *Multilingual Parenting.* Available at: <http://multilingualparenting.com/2015/04/29/time-and-place-as-a-family-language-strategy/>.

Sauer, E. and Saudan, V. 2008. Aspects of a didactic of plurilingualism. Terminological proposals. Available at: < http://www.passepartout-sprachen.ch/services/downloads/download/664/>.

Schramm, E. 2008. *Dzieje nauki języka angielskiego i innych języków nowożytnych w Polsce w okresie zaborów.* Warsaw: Fraszka Edukacyjna.

Sheng, L., Bedore, L. M., Peña, E. D. and Fiestas, C. 2013. Semantic development in Spanish – English bilingual children: Effects of age and language experience. In: *Child Development* 84(3). 1034–1045.

Silverstein, M. 1996. Monoglot 'standard' in America: Standardization and metaphors of linguistic hegemony. In: Brennels, D. and R. Macaulay (Eds.), *The Matrix of Language.* Boulder, CO: Westview. 284–306.

Silverstein, M. 1998. Contemporary transformations of local linguistic communities. In: *Annual Review of Anthropology* 27. 401–426.

Singleton, D. and Aronin, L. 2007. Multiple language learning in the light of the theory of affordances. In: *International Journal of Innovation in Language Learning and Teaching* 1(1). 83–96.

Unsworth, S., Argyri, F., Cornips, L., Hulk, A., Sorace, A. and Tsimpli, I. 2014. On the role of age of onset and input in early child bilingualism in Greek and Dutch. In: *Applied Psycholinguistics* 35(4). 765–805.

Widła, H. 2015. Zmierzch bilingwizmu i jego skutki. Plenary talk, Konferencja Naukowa Polskiego Towarzystwa Neofilologicznego "Wielojęzyczność i międzykulturowość w glottodydaktyce". Warsaw. 8.9.2015.

Stefania Scaglione
(Università per Stranieri, Perugia, Italy)
Sandro Caruana
(University of Malta)

Bridging the Gap between Policies and Practices Related to Multilingualism in Schools in Southern European States[1]

Introduction

For the last twenty years at least, the promotion of plurilingualism and the fostering of linguistic diversity, which characterizes the European Union, have constituted an important priority on the agenda of European institutions: language has acquired an obvious strategic role in mapping out the European model of citizenship, democratic participation and competitiveness in the knowledge society[2].

The detachment from the *monolingual habitus* (I. Gogolin 1994), which relegates individual plurilingualism to the level of an elitist phenomenon and presents linguistic diversity ("multilingualism", as intended by the Council of Europe) as an obstacle to mutual cooperation and understanding within and among State communities, has become increasingly necessary in the face of demographic, political, cultural and economic conditions, irreversibly marked by internationalization, mobility and international migration. In this respect, the impact of some of the actions promoted by European institutions and geared to foster individual bilingualism has been remarkable: to provide just an example, from 2004/05 to 2009/10, in EU the percentage of pupils enrolled in primary education not learning a foreign language dropped from 32.5% to 21.8% (Eurydice 2012: 58)

However, a more analytical consideration of the progress achieved so far is required, in order to understand how the exhortations of the European institutions in favour of pluri- and multilingualism have been implemented by central

---

1   This contribution is the result of collaboration between the authors, and the contents are conjointly shared by both. The different sections have been drafted as follows: S. Caruana wrote the general introduction, the introduction to section 1 and conclusions; S. Scaglione wrote sub-sections 1.2, 1.3, and the section 2.

2   See: Commission of European Communities (1995, 2003, 2005, 2008); Council of the European Union (2008, 2014); Civil Society Platform (2011); Business Platform (2011).

and educational authorities of individual States and also to better understand the impact of these actions on citizens of different countries.

In particular, it is worth asking whether national policies are really fostering both plurilingualism and multilingualism *per se*, or whether they are oriented towards a more limited goal, privileging individual plurilingualism, often as a short-term attainable goal, over a more long-term and socially productive model of multi-lingualism, which may be conducive to an effective "integration" of the linguistic diversity brought about by so-called "immigrant languages". It seems, indeed, that the European Commission's exhortations to pursue the objective of "mother tongue plus two languages" is still intended as if "mother tongue" were merely the official language of each State, or an officially recognized minority language within spe-cific regions, and the other "two languages" were two "major" European foreign languages, to the exclusive advantage of EU-*internal* socio-professional mobility. Much less emphasis, on the contrary, has been placed on the intercultural potential of the linguistic diversity which is increasingly characterizing European societies involved in transnational and extra-EU migration movements.

Such an interpretation is reinforced, in particular, by the direction that some European national educational systems are choosing as far as the linguistic inte-gration of pupils with a migrant background is concerned. This is the case of five Southern European countries – Portugal, Spain, Italy, Slovenia, Malta – which are facing today very particular conditions, insofar as they have recently become immigration destinations, whilst, in the past, they experienced significant mass migration. This sudden change has implied a remarkable increase in linguistic diversity, to which these States have to respond by providing adequate models of linguistic and cultural integration, also through their educational policies.

In the light of the above, in this paper we discuss whether, at a macro-level, educational policies promote plurilingualism and linguistic diversity efficiently in these countries, and whether teachers' attention is drawn to such phenomena brought about by migration. At a micro-level we then consider if plurilingualism and linguistic diversity are part of everyday classroom activities in order to create a learning environment which fosters interlinguistic and intercultural awareness.

The MERIDIUM project (S. Caruana, L. Coposescu and S. Scaglione 2013), an EU-funded Life Long Learning project, conducted from 2009 to 2011, was aimed at addressing these issues, among others, in the aforementioned countries[3].

---

3   Besides Portugal, Spain, Italy, Slovenia and Malta, the MERIDIUM project included
     also Romania, as a country of origin of several immigrants in Portugal, Spain and Italy.
     Although Romania, in the last few years, is increasingly becoming itself an immigration
     destination (IOM: 2008), its situation from this point of view is currently not comparable

Research carried out through the project therefore included an investigation of both educational policies and practices, aimed particularly at observing how the diverse socio-linguistic background of primary school children and their parents is taken into account in the school context, and is eventually exploited as an enriching resource:

In the first part of this paper we will be discussing the macro-level question (1.1–1.3). The data on educational practices will be discussed in the second part of this paper (2), where some remarks about the micro-level question will be provided on the grounds of a survey carried out with 5ᵗʰ grade children (10 year-old) and their parents in 42 primary schools during the school year 2009/2010.

1. MERIDIUM countries' educational-linguistic policies on regional/minority languages and foreign languages

The MERIDIUM countries are all officially monolingual, except for Malta, where Maltese and English are both official languages. No regional or minority language is reported for Malta, whilst in Portugal the only officially recognized regional language is Mirandês; although Portugal has not signed the *European Charter for Regional or Minority Languages* (ECRML), a Law has been approved in 1999 which gives the inhabitants of the villages located within the Concelho de Miranda de Douro the right to have their language taught in primary and secondary educational establishments.

Italy has a remarkable internal linguistic diversity, represented by several dialects with no official status, together with regional and minority languages categorised as languages spoken by "historical linguistic minorities" by the Law 482/99. The languages of these minorities may be used beside Italian as languages of instruction, or taught as a subject (where applicable), in pre-primary, primary and lower-secondary schools, in municipalities where an adequate proportion of inhabitants (15%) so requests. Italy has signed, but not ratified, the ECRML.

A far more articulated situation characterizes Slovenia and Spain: having ratified the *Charter*, these countries apply a wide range of measures within the field of education, intended to promote the learning and the use of the languages traditionally spoken by members of two national minorities in the former case (Italian and Hungarian), and by members of some autonomous communities in the latter

to the situation of the other MERIDIUM countries; for this reason, the Romanian case will be not discussed here in detail.

(Basque, Catalan, Galician, Valencian). These languages are used as languages of instruction (or as other language of instruction in the case of Hungarian in Slovenia) in pre-primary, primary, secondary, technical and vocational education (ECRML art. 8, 1, a-d). In Spain, facilities are provided at university and at higher education level for the study of these languages as subjects, whereas this is just encouraged in Slovenia (art. 8, 1, e). Within the field of adult and continuing education, Basque, Catalan, Galician, Valencian are languages of instruction, whilst in Slovenia the study of Italian and Hungarian as subjects is encouraged (art. 8, 1, f). Finally, both States adopt arrangements to ensure that the teaching of the history and the culture which is reflected by these languages (art. 8, 1, g), provide basic and further training of teachers (art. 8, 1, h) and establish a supervisory body responsible for monitoring the measures taken and progress achieved (art. 8, 1, i).

On the basis of the above, broadly speaking, we note that MERIDIUM countries, to one extent or another, have measures that offer pupils and families from traditional minorities the possibility to learn their mother tongue at school, although such measures vary considerably from one community to another[4].

These countries have also taken on the EU initiative to offer the teaching of two foreign/modern languages (F/ML) within the general compulsory education system[5]. Generally, the first F/ML is a compulsory subject from ISCED 1 onwards, while a second F/ML is introduced later in the curriculum (see Table1), except for Spain, where learning a second FL is not compulsory.

---

4   For more information on the implementation of the Law 482/99 in Italy, see G. Iannàc-caro (2010); for Slovenia and Spain, see the "Reports and Recommendations" section on the ECRML website.
5   The term 'modern language' refers in particular to English in Malta, where defining this language as "foreign", due to the bilingual nature of the country, is inappropriate. Nonetheless, it must be taken into account that Maltese is widely attested as the L1 of the large majority of the population, with English having a status of L2 in most cases.

Table 1: *Starting age, duration and hours per notional year[6] for first and second foreign/ modern languages(F/ML) as compulsory subjects in general compulsory education: MERIDIUM countries, reference year 2011 (Eurydice 2012: 27 ff.; 120)*

Country	Duration of compulsory FIRST F/ML learning			Duration of compulsory SECOND F/ML learning			Ending age for compulsory education
	Age range	Years	Hours per notional year	Age range	Years	Hours per notional year	
SPAIN	6–18	12	81	--	--	--	16
ITALY	6–18	12	89	11–14	3	20	16
MALTA	5–16	11	120/126	11–16	5	34/40	16
SLOVENIA	9–19	10	55	15–19	4	17	15
PORTUGAL	10–17	7	48	12–15	3	18	18

From the table above one notes that the time dedicated to the teaching of a second F/ML in these countries is considerably less than the time allocated to the teaching of the first F/ML. It must be added that, although reforms have been implemented between 2005 and 2010 in order to target the "1+2 language" EU objective, percentages of students learning two F/ML at ISCED level 3 remain quite low in some cases (Italy, Spain, Portugal), if compared to percentages at ISCED level 2 (Eurydice 2012: 67; 71).

English is the only F/ML which, except in Spain, is explicitly mentioned by central education authorities as a language students must learn during their school years (Malta, Italy), or, in any case, as a language that schools must provide in the curriculum (Slovenia, Portugal); in fact, not surprisingly, it is the most widely chosen first F/ML, even when this is not mandatory, at all ISCED levels (Figure 1).

Notwithstanding remarkable progress in the last years, it is clear that current measures concerning F/ML teaching in MERIDIUM countries strongly privilege the primacy of English over the other "major" EU languages; on the other hand, the learning of a second F/ML is promoted limitedly during the compulsory education years, to the extent that doubts can be raised as to whether the allotted time allows students to build their communicative competence.

---

6   To obtain a notional year, the total teaching load in hours for primary and full-time compulsory secondary education has been divided by the number of years corresponding to the duration of each education level.

Figure 1: Percentage of students learning English at ISCED levels 1, 2, 3: MERIDIUM countries, reference year 2010 (Eurydice 2012: 62; 73)

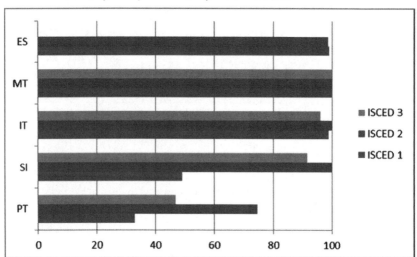

If we consider languages in which people declare to be competent as an additional language, we observe that English outdistances significantly other major EU languages (Eurobarometer 2012: Annex, D48T1). Moreover, figures of bi-/plurilingualism characterizing nationals aged 15 years and over in 2012 do not show any significant progress in comparison with the situation observed in 2005 (Eurobarometer 2012: Annex, D48T2): the percentage of bilinguals in Malta and Slovenia (92% in both cases) – well above the EU average (54%) – remain substantially stable, while in Spain, Portugal and Italy – where foreign language competence is traditionally below the EU average (ranging from 46% in Spain to 38% in Italy) – a modest increase or decrease is registered (from +2 percentage points, to –3 percentage points). On the other hand, trilingual and quadrilingual speakers' rates clearly decrease, with the remarkable exception of Italy (+6 percentage points for trilinguals, and +9 percentage points for quadrilinguals), probably partly due to a "second generation immigrants' effect", which will be elaborated upon further in the next section of this paper.

All in all, these data seem to suggest that in these MERIDIUM countries the EU "target" of an increase of individual "trilingualism" is not any closer than it was in the past.

1.1 Changes in MERIDIUM countries' demo-linguistic profiles

In the last fifteen years the demo-linguistic profiles of MERIDIUM countries have become more complex, due to the ingoing transnational migration (Eurostat 2013): in Table 2 we provide Eurostat Population Censusdata regarding the presence of foreign citizens in 2011; in Figure 2 these foreign citizens are classified according to when they arrived to their host country.

Table 2: *Composition of MERIDIUM countries' population in 2011: citizenship (Eurostat, Population Census 2011)*

Country	Total population (N)	Citizens of the country (N)	Foreign citizens (N)	Foreign citizens (%)
SPAIN	46 815 910	41 562 780	5 242 120	11.2
ITALY	59 433 744	55 406 117	4 027 210	6.8
MALTA	417 432	397 143	20 289	4.9
SLOVENIA	2 050 189	1 967 443	82 746	4.0
PORTUGAL	10 562 178	10 167 129	394 479	3.7

Figure 2: *Foreign citizens in MERIDIUM countries in 2011: time of arrival (%) (Eurostat, Population Census 2011)*

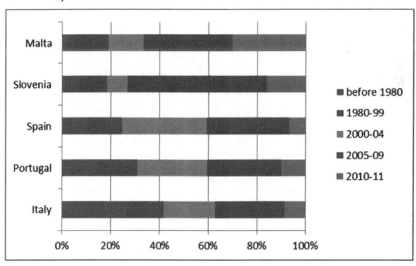

As one may see, with the exception of Italy – where over 1 in 4 foreign citizens had arrived before 1980 – mass immigration in MERIDIUM countries started in the Noughties, in particular from 2005 onwards.

In 2011, the six most represented foreign nationalities were Morocco, Romania, Ecuador, Colombia, the United Kingdom and Bolivia in Spain (51.4% of the total of foreign residents); Romania, Albania, Morocco, China, Ukraine, Moldova in Italy (54.3% of the total); the United Kingdom, Somalia, Italy, Bulgaria, Germany and the Russian Federation in Malta (53.4% of the total); Bosnia-Herzegovina, Macedonia, Croatia, Serbia, Ukraine and Bulgaria in Slovenia (78.9% of the total); Brazil, Cape Verde, Ukraine, Angola, Romania and Guinea-Bissau in Portugal (63.4% of the total). On the basis of these data, we observe that, while in Portugal and Slovenia the six most represented countries of origin sum up to over 60% of the total foreign residents, in three cases – Spain, Italy and Malta – they only reach the half of foreign resident population; in other words, in these three countries, nationalities are much more numerous. However, in Portugal, as well as in Spain and Malta, there are a number of foreign citizens who are (presumably) native speakers of (varieties of) the official languages of these countries; on the contrary, Italy and Slovenia receive migrants who, basing on their citizenship, are not native speakers of Italian or Slovene.

This drastic and qualitatively complex influx of foreign population has had an impact on the linguistic profile of these countries, bringing about native speakers of new languages and causing an increase in the number of speakers of official languages as L2 or, in the case of Italy – where immigration is one generation ahead with respect to the other MERIDIUM countries – also as L1 (ISTAT – Ministry of Internal Affairs 2014). Unfortunately, extensive and systematic language surveys have not yet been conducted in order to analyze this new situation of linguistic diversity[7]. Nonetheless, some relevant, though approximate indications can be obtained from the Eurobarometer (2012) survey. This, as mentioned earlier, was carried out among nationals of the EU Member States and naturalized citizens and citizens born from mixed marriages are therefore included in the sample[8]. On the basis of Eurobarometer data, we observe that native speakers of official languages are on the decline in most of the above contexts, while non-native speakers of these languages are on the increase (Eurobarometer 2012: Annexes, D48a and D48b): this suggests a link with changes induced by transnational immigration. On the other hand, the fact that, in Italy, Italian as L1 gains 2 percentage points

7   To date, as far as MERIDIUM countries are concerned, the report by ISTAT and the Ministry of Internal Affairs (2014) represents, to our knowledge, the only attempt to describe the language use of foreign residents in details.
8   As in MERIDIUM countries citizenship is assigned mainly on the basis of "ius sanguinis", children born from "mixed" marriages between a national and a foreign citizen also acquire the citizenship of the State.

reflects the increase of children born from mixed marriages and of the so called "second generation immigrants", i.e. children born in Italy from foreign parents and naturalized upon request at their coming of age.

The "new linguistic diversity" brought about by immigration in MERIDIUM countries could represent an opportunity to increase, both quantitatively and qualitatively, the linguistic repertoire of the whole society. This potentially positive impact, however, could be capitalized upon if attention is given to two possible side effects:

- the natural tendency of migrant groups to linguistic assimilation, which induces language shift. In this respect, it is important to keep in mind that language skills need to be exercised and cultivated, and that this is feasible only if the socio-cultural context offers opportunities and motivation to this end;
- the disadvantage caused by an abrupt immersion in educational contexts where the language of instruction is different from the language spoken at home. As the OECD-PISA 2009 and 2012 assessments have demonstrated (OECD-PISA 2010; 2014), speaking a language at home which is different from the language(s) of instruction at school represents an obstacle for a good performance, much more so if this factor is accompanied by a migrant family background.

Against this background, we will now review educational policies adopted in MERIDIUM countries in order to favour linguistic and educational integration of students with a migrant background.

1.2 Approaches to "new" linguistic diversity within the educational context

Since large-scale statistical studies based on students' mother-tongues have not yet been implemented by national authorities at all compulsory ISCED levels, the impact of linguistic diversity brought about by migrants on the educational systems of MERIDIUM countries can be only measured indirectly, by means of Eurostat and OECD-PISA data, respectively on age/citizenship and on the mother-tongue/s of 15-years old students.

According to the Eurostat database, in 2010 (which is the year when the MERIDIUM research was carried out), the percentages of foreign population among the total population of age groups 5–9, 10–14 and 15–19 years were as follows (Figure 3):

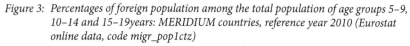

Figure 3: *Percentages of foreign population among the total population of age groups 5–9, 10–14 and 15–19 years: MERIDIUM countries, reference year 2010 (Eurostat online data, code migr_pop1ctz)*

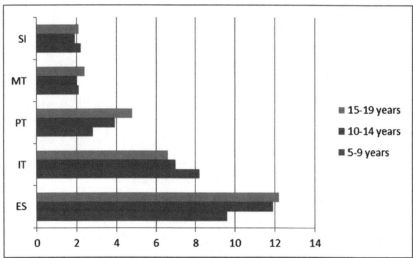

The OECD-PISA 2012 assessment reveals that, in 2012, the percentages of 15-year old students with an immigrant background who, at home, did not speak the language through which the assessment was carried out ranged from 4.7% (Spain) and 1.8% (Portugal), as shown in Table 3:

Table 3: *Percentages of 15-years old students who do not speak the language of PISA 2012 assessment at home: MERIDIUM countries (OECD-PISA (2013: 232)*

Country	Percentage of 15-years old students who did not speak the language of assessment at home		
	Students without an immigrant background	Students with an immigrant background	Total
SPAIN	13.7	4.7	18.6
ITALY	9.8	4.4	14.3
PORTUGAL	0.8	1.8	2.6
MALTA	--	--	--
SLOVENIA	1.3	4.6	5.9

According to the Eurydice report (2009: 20), in Italy and Spain there are "central-level regulations/recommendations on the provision of mother tongue tuition for immigrant pupils", whereas in Malta and in Portugal educational measures for teaching the language of origin of migrant pupils are based on mainly voluntary and private initiatives. In Slovenia there are both central-level regulations as well as specific measures to ensure that the range of foreign languages taught corresponds more closely to the mother tongues of migrant pupils. In particular, for their last three years of compulsory education, migrant students may choose their mother tongue as their foreign language option, provided that there is a sufficient number of pupils interested in attending such classes (Eurydice 2009: 26).

The provision of mother tongue tuition for migrant pupils is, in most cases, organised and funded by the host country's educational system, as in Italy, but this system heavily depends on demand for it and, above all, on availability of resources; furthermore, courses are generally extracurricular. In Spain and Slovenia, mother-tongue tuition can be organised by means of bilateral agreements: in these cases, lessons may be included during normal school hours.

Information provided in the same report indicates quite clearly that, in MERIDIUM states, obtaining financial and human resources depends on a largely centralized system. This, by and large, differs from the situation found in a number of other EU states, where determining access to such resources is more systematic, with decisions taken at a local, rather than at a national, level.

As we will show in the next section, as of 2010, the afore mentioned measures remained by and large unexploited by schools involved in the MERIDIUM survey, which seemed focused, instead, on the intensive teaching of the language of instruction to pupils with foreign background and, eventually, on intercultural education, interpreted mainly as the teaching of traditions and folktales of other peoples. Moreover, as remarked by the MIPEX 2010 report, in all these States a number of fundamental measures was lacking, such as central regulations regarding the assessment of learning and language qualifications obtained by migrant pupils prior to their arrival in the host country; provisions directed towards learning immigrant languages; possibilities to modify school curricula and teaching materials to reflect changes in the diversity of the school population; measures to support bringing persons of migrant origin into the teacher workforce[9].

2. The MERIDIUM survey on languages at school

In Spain, Italy, Portugal, Malta and Slovenia, the MERIDIUM survey was conducted in 42 Primary schools, located in small to middle-sized municipalities,

---

9   For details, see MIPEX 2010 website: <http://old.mipex.eu/>.

chosen specifically in each one of the countries because of the presence of a large number of foreign-born children in the school population[10]. Our initial hypothesis was that in these geographical areas, possibly even more than in others, one might expect to find measures directed towards a pedagogy within a multilingual context, together with a strong degree of awareness and sensitivity towards issues related to plurilingualism.

Two instruments were used for the data collection, carried out in the school year 2009–10: interviews with school principals and teachers, and questionnaires, distributed to 1,762 ten to eleven year-old students, of whom 574 (32.6%) had a partially or totally foreign background[11]. In addition, 1,514 parents/guardians of these students were also involved in the research, also via questionnaires: 402 of them (26.5%) were foreign citizens born abroad.

In all the Primary school systems of the countries included in our research, the language of instruction was the official language of the country (Maltese and English in Malta); in some provinces of Spain and Slovenia, a regional or minority language was taught as a first modern language. Moreover, English was taught in all schools: it was the only compulsory modern language in Italian schools, while, in Portuguese and Spanish schools, pupils had the opportunity to choose a second foreign language, which was, in most cases, French.

When considering pupils' language use at home, among the 1,685 subjects who provided valid answers, 1,408 (83.6%) declared to use the official State language/s with their parents/guardians, possibly in addition with other languages, dialects or varieties. The language of instruction was therefore a familiar code for these students. On the other hand, the remaining 277 pupils (16.4%) never used the language of instruction at home: in 13 cases they used a non-autochtonous variety of the language of instruction (e.g. Columbians or Argentinians in Spain); in 73 cases they used a regional language or a dialect; in 191 cases (11.3% of the total) at home they used exclusively non-autochtonous languages (NAL; see Table 4a for details on these cases)[12].

---

10 As mentioned before, the survey was also carried out in Romania (15 schools), but these data will be not discussed here.

11 Children with a "totally foreign background" are those whose parents are not born in the country of residence, nor have the citizenship of it; children with "partially foreign background" are those who have just one parent who was born in the country and is a citizen of it.

12 By the term "autochtonous languages" (AL), we refer to the national language(s) and/or minority or regional languages traditionally spoken in the survey country;

Table 4a.: Pupils who use exclusively non-autochtonous languages (NAL) at home (N and %) (MERIDIUM survey)

Country	N of pupils who use exclusively NAL at home	N of total respondents	% on total respondents
ITALY	120	689	17.4
SPAIN	39	372	10.5
PORTUGAL	19	308	6.2
MALTA	7	164	4.3
SLOVENIA	6	152	3.9
Total	191	1685	11.3

The NAL that students speak at home is taught as a school subject only in the case of 31 pupils: for 17 of them this language is English, for 8 it is French, for 6 it is Portuguese. In all other 160 cases, pupils attend schools where they cannot exploit and cultivate any linguistic resource from their family repertoire. Only in some cases (e.g. Italy), and depending on the availability of resources, linguistic mediators are employed for brief periods of time in order to facilitate the students' transition to the language of instruction.

Such a situation presents obvious pedagogical problems, much more so if we consider that among the schools involved in our research school principals and teachers were generally not trained on issues such as bilingual development in migration contexts. As a consequence, usually the sole objective of teachers was that students with a foreign linguistic background were to acquire the language of instruction used in school, while didactic activities aimed at stimulating metalinguistic reflection and fostering "translanguaging" abilities (O. García and W. Li 2013) of the students were totally absent. *A fortiori*, teachers seemed to ignore the situation and the language needs of children born from linguistically "mixed" parents, or of "second generation" immigrant students (which represented 48.6% of all foreign pupils attending primary school in Italy at the time of the survey), as they "sound like natives", while, on the contrary, their family linguistic background may be quite complex, dominated by a language which is different from the one used at school.

One may assume that this state of affairs is due to the fact that pupils who speak non-autochtonous languages at home constitute a negligible amount of

---

"non-autochtonous languages" (NAL) are languages which are not traditionally spoken within the survey country.

the students enrolled in the classes where the survey was carried out, but this is not the case.

If we integrate data in Table 4a with those regarding pupils who, at home, speak NAL beside AL, the linguistic diversity which characterizes the locations chosen for our survey becomes evident. This is represented in Table 4b, where the NAL which were mentioned most frequently by our informants are listed:

Table 4b: Pupils who use non-autochtonous languages (exclusively, or beside autochtonous languages) at home (N and %) and languages which were mentioned (MERIDIUM survey)

Country	N of pupils who use NAL at home	N of total respondents	% on total respondents	Languages
Italy	228	689	33.1	Albanian, Arabic, English, Romanian, Hindi, Serbian, Croatian, Macedonian, Bengali, Urdu, Spanish, Chinese, French, Bulgarian, Portuguese, Tagalog, Western African languages…
Spain	71	372	19.1	Portuguese, Romanian, English, French, German, Polish, Chinese, Korean, Guaraní…
Portugal	59	308	19.1	English, Portuguese-based creoles, French, Russian, Ukrainian, Moldavian…
Malta	24	164	14.6	Italian, Arabic, Serbian, Bulgarian…
Slovenia	19	152	12.5	Bosnian, Croatian, Serbian…
Total	401	1685	23.8	

Taking into account the number of classes involved in the survey in each country, and calculating how many pupils who speak non-autochtonous languages are, on average, enrolled in a class, the results obtained are far from negligible, mainly in countries such as Italy and Spain (Table 5).

Table 5: *Distribution across classes of pupils who use non-autochtonous languages (exclusively, or beside autochtonous languages) at home (average N, min/max N) and average size of classes attended by these pupils (MERIDIUM survey)*

Country	Total N of classes	N of classes with pupils who speak NAL at home	Average N per class of pupils who speak NAL at home	Min./max. N per class of pupils who speak NAL at home	Average size (total N of pupils) of classes attended by these pupils
ITALY	37	36	6.3	2/11	21.4
SPAIN	23	21	3.4	1/9	20.7
PORTUGAL	18	17	3.5	2/11	23.8
MALTA	11	10	2.4	1/5	20.1
SLOVENIA	9	6	3.2	2/4	20.5

The presence of non-autochtonous languages in the local contexts involved in the MERIDIUM survey cannot therefore simply be ignored or marginalized, and the substantial indifference to the languages of origin of children with a foreign background shown by teachers and school principals interviewed within the MERIDIUM project unveils, at least at a local level, a clear gap between policies and practices concerning the respect and promotion of multilingualism and plurilingualism.

2.1 On costs and lost opportunities

The consequences of this gap are severe. In the first place, this indifference hinders from adopting structural and research-grounded measures in order to improve the educational attainment of pupils with foreign background. If one takes reading abilities as an example, according to the OECD-PISA survey held in 2009, one will note that "second generation immigrant students" – who generally show a good oral command of the language of schooling – are at a disadvantage when compared to native speakers (OECD-PISA 2010: Tab. II.4.1). Although these students have generally been schooled in the host country, their reading skills have not developed as fully as they possibly could have been, and the results do not change even after accounting for socio-economic status, which in many cases explains part of the performance disadvantage among students with a migrant background. What is the problem with them? Till now, no attempts have been made, by central educational authorities in MERIDIUM countries, to pose this question seriously, or to conduct systematic research on the impact of different teaching methods, especially at ISCED level 1.

Furthermore, indifference to the languages of origin of children with a foreign background is in contrast with the proclaimed principles of intercultural education: how is it possible to foster, teach and learn intercultural understanding, if NAL spoken by school-children are "invisibilized", if not negated outright?

A closely related consequence regards the negation of benefits which could result from exploiting linguistic diversity positively. Making linguistic diversity "visible" in schools could help to promote plurilingualism and language awareness for all pupils, and could lead to innovations in school systems which so far have proved scarcely efficacious from the point of view of linguistic education, not only with pupils with a foreign linguistic background, but also with pupils speaking mainly dialects or minority languages. Here again, we may refer to the OECD-PISA results concerning reading performance. As widely known, one of the strategic targets of Europe 2020 is reducing the rate of low achievers in reading to below 15%: MERIDIUM countries fall short of this target, and this is not due exclusively to the poor performance of students with a migrant background, as Table 6 demonstrates.

Table 6: Percentages of 15-years-old students below the proficiency level 2 on the reading scale: students by background and birthplace in 2009, and comparison on total students between 2009 and 2012 (OECD-PISA (2010: 155; 172 and 2014: 376)

Country	% of 15-years-old students below the proficiency level 2 on the reading scale				
	Native students (2009)	2nd gen. immigrant students (2009)	1st gen. immigrant students (2009)	All students (2009)	All students (2012)
SLOVENIA	19.5	32.8	45	21.2	21.1
ITALY	19.2	34.1	50.5	21.0	19.5
PORTUGAL	16.7	18	31.6	17.6	18.7
SPAIN	17.1	25.6	40.1	19.5	18.3

This effectively means that structural measures have to be taken to improve reading skills of all students, regardless of the presence of non-native speakers in order to help learners develop competences through teaching methodologies which are directed to improve metalinguistic awareness, to broaden their lexicon, to understand the structure of a text, to learn how to make inferences etc. These abilities can also be developed by encouraging, for example, comparisons between the home language (be it a dialect, a regional or minority language, or whatever other language) and the language of instruction, and taking into account the transferability of languages skills from one language to the other (J. Cummins 2007; A. Y.

Durgunoğlu and L. Verhoeven 2013; O. García and W. Li 2013; D. Rodríguez, A. Carrasquillo and K. S. Lee 2014).

Finally, neglecting the plurilingual resources of pupils with a migrant background has a negative impact also on the very heart of the EU strategy concerning multi- and plurilingualism as key-factors in increasing the competitiveness of the economies of member countries. The global linguistic market is rapidly changing, hand in hand with the emergence of new economic powers: while the perception of the usefulness of English is unquestioned, other languages, including those spoken by large communities of migrants are gaining value. A remarkable example is represented by Chinese in Italy, where learning this language is deemed to be important for the future of young persons by 12% of citizens, with an increase of 9 percent points compared to 2005 (Eurobarometer 2012: Annex, QE1b). Moreover, as it happens in other multiethnic societies (V. Edwards 2011), the labour market in these MERIDIUM countries is increasingly seeking personnel with knowledge of immigrant languages, especially within the sectors of health, legal assistance, social or banking services, security and commerce. This potentially favourable situation, however, is heavily conditioned by intrinsic contradictions: on the one hand, in order to obtain such jobs, youngsters with a migrant background are required to have adequate qualifications and a good command of the official language, whereas the educational system does little to contrast early school leaving and drop-out from their part; on the other hand, their multilingual competences – which could represent a central qualification for employment – are not valued[13], insofar as they are not "certified" through any formal learning and, in fact, often remain under-developed with regard to fundamental skills such as writing.

Conclusion

Our MERIDIUM research, as well as data from various sources presented in this study, clearly outlines the need to bridge the gap between policies and practices in order to render school systems more sensitive to issues of a social nature and more aware of the richness and potential of multilingualism. The rapid transition of Southern European states to immigration-receptor countries necessitates both a number of adjustments in the area of educational policy as well as coherent practical initiatives to raise awareness and towards issues related to multilingualism in schools.

---

13 See A. Duchêne, M. Moyer and C. Roberts (2013).

One of the first steps that can be taken is to make non-autochtonous linguistic diversity more "visible" in schools: the dominant "homoglottic ideology" (G. Lüdi 2011) creates negative perceptions (and self-perceptions) in pupils and families towards alloglossia; this is confirmed by the answers that we obtained to one of the questions we formulated to the parents of the pupils who participated in the MERIDIUM research. In fact, parents, when asked whether children of migrants should be given the opportunity to learn their family language/s in the schools of their host country, generally took a negative or undecided stance, be they nationals or foreign citizens, except in Portugal, where a majority of positive responses was registered. This confirms, yet again, that the general trend is to render linguistic diversity "invisible" and to conform to the language of instruction: hence, the necessity of exposing students to the languages that all learners bring with them to the classroom, and to exploit their linguistic resources, including those that the teacher is unfamiliar with. Language learning thereby becomes a process of discovery, also involving teachers in the development of positive language attitudes that, in turn, could enhance competence.

As far as policy makers are concerned, there should be awareness that homoglottic and selective strategies in language education are costly, in all senses, in contexts with a high degree of language diversity: plurilingualism as a cognitive attitude, and not only the knowledge of specific languages, is the real educational resource which is worth investing in, with flexibility and open-mindedness. Exposing the assets of alloglossia could enhance confidence, generate curiosity and emulation, demystify ethnocentric myths.

Finally it is necessary to share good practices. Our MERIDIUM research showed us that these are neither few nor isolated. Yet, they depend largely on personal inventiveness or, at best, on school-based initiatives. Although every country has a different reality and there are no "one-size-fits-all" recipes to imbue teachers with, useful instruments are in place and they deserve further dissemination: these include the Council of Europe's *Platform of Resources and References for Plurilingual and Intercultural Education,* "translanguaging theory and practice" (O. García and W. Li 2013), and many other methods which researchers and practitioners are experimenting in many European countries. In order to spread the knowledge and the use of these instruments, however, a more effective intervention by central education authorities is needed, by means of targeted regulations, as well as through adequate funding policies. Unfortunately, from this point of view, little has changed in MERIDIUM countries since 2010: apart from measures of minor importance, and further cuts in funding policies, the situation depicted by the latest MIPEX integration policy index

(MIPEX 2015)[14] concerning education still displays all the weaknesses that our research has revealed.

References

Business Platform for Multilingualism. 2011. *Report for the period September 2009–June 2011.* Bruxelles: European Commission – DG EAC.

Caruana, S., Coposescu, L. and Scaglione, S. 2013. *Migration, Multilingualism and Schooling in Southern Europe.* Newcastle-upon-Tyne: Cambridge Scholars Publishing.

Civil Society Platform on Multilingualism. 2011. *Policy Recommendations for the Promotion of Multilingualism in the European Union,* Bruxelles: European Commission – DG EAC.

Commission of European Communities. 1995. *White paper on education and training: Teaching and Learning. Towards the learning society.* 11.1995. COM/95/590.

Commission of European Communities. 2003. *Promoting Language Learning and Linguistic Diversity: an Action Plan 2004–2006.* 24.7.2003. COM/2003/449 final.

Commission of European Communities. 2005. *A New Framework Strategy for Multilingualism.* 22.11.2005. COM/2005/596 final.

Commission of European Communities. 2008. *Multilingualism: an asset for Europe and a shared commitment {SEC(2008) 2443} {SEC(2008) 2444} {SEC(2008)2445}.* 18.9.2008. COM/2008/566 final.

Council of the European Union. 2008. Council Resolution of 21 November 2008 on a European strategy for multilingualism. In: *Official Journal of the European Union C 320.* 16.1.2008.

Council of the European Union. 2014. Conclusions of 20 May 2014 on multilingualism and the development of language competences. In: *Official Journal of the European Union C 183.* 14.6.2014.

Cummins, J. 2007. Rethinking monolingual instructional strategies in multilingual classrooms. In: *Canadian Journal of Applied Linguistics* 10(2). 221–240.

Duchêne, A., Moyer, M. and Roberts, C. 2013. *Language, Migration and Social Inequalities.* Clevedon: Multilingual Matters.

Durgunoğlu, A. Y. and Verhoeven L. (Eds.) 2013. *Literacy Development in a Multilingual Context. Cross-Cultural Perspectives.* London and NY: Routledge (I ed. 1998, NJ: Lawrence Erlbaum Associates).

---

14   See MIPEX 2015 website: <http://www.mipex.eu/>.

Edwards, V. 2011. Globalization and Multilingualism: the case of the U.K. In: *Intercultural Communication Studies* 20(1). 27–35.

Eurobarometer. 2012. *Europeans and their Languages*. Special Eurobarometer 386. Bruxelles: European Commission – DG COMM.

Eurostat. 2013. *European Social Statistics (2013 Edition)*. Luxembourg: Publications Office of the European Union.

Eurydice. 2009. *Integrating Immigrant Children into Schools in Europe*. Bruxelles: EACEA.

Eurydice. 2012. *Key data on Teaching Languages at School in Europe*. Bruxelles: EACEA.

García, O. and Li, W. 2013. *Translanguaging. Language, Bilingualism and Education*. New York: Palgrave MacMillan.

Iannàccaro, G. 2010. *Lingue di minoranza e scuola. A dieci anni dalla Legge 482/99*. Roma: MIUR.

IOM. 2008. *Migration in Romania: A Country Profile 2008*. Geneva: International Organization for Migration.

ISTAT – Ministry of Internal Affairs. 2014. *Diversità linguistiche tra i cittadini stranieri. Anno 2011–2012*. Roma: ISTAT.

Lüdi, G. 2011. Quale integrazione per i parlanti delle lingue di immigrazione? In: Giannini, S. and S. Scaglione (Eds.), *Lingue e diritti umani*. Roma: Carocci. 81–113.

OECD-PISA. 2010. *PISA 2009 Results: Overcoming Social Background. Equity in Learning Opportunities and Outcomes* (Vol. II). Paris: PISA-OECD Publishing.

OECD-PISA. 2013. *PISA 2012 Results: Excellence through Equity: Giving Every Student the Chance to Succeed* (Vol. II). Paris: PISA-OECD Publishing.

OECD-PISA. 2014. *PISA 2012 Results: What Students Know and Can Do. Students Performance in Mathematics, Reading and Science* (Vol. I). Revised edition. Paris: PISA-OECD Publishing.

Rodríguez, D., Carrasquillo, A. and Lee, K. S. 2014. *The Bilingual Advantage. Promoting Academic Development, Biliteracy and Native Language in the Classroom*. New York: Teachers College Press.

Kutlay Yağmur
(Tilburg University, The Netherlands)

Policies of Multilingualism in the European Union: How Compatible is the Policy with Actual Practice?

Introduction

Multilingualism is one of the core components of European identity. Unity in diversity describes European Union's philosophy of social cohesion, harmony and multiculturalism. In 2008, the European Commission (EC) reported that the European Union (EU) had about 500 million citizens, 27 Member States, 3 alphabets, 23 official national languages, around 60 regional and minority (R/M) languages as well as many immigrant languages (European Commission, 2008). As of July 2013, the number of Member States rose to 28 and the number official languages increased to 24 with the accession of Croatia. The Council of Europe (CoE) and the European Union (EU) are two of the major supranational organizations that safeguard linguistic diversity, and actively promote language learning and multilingualism in Europe with official conventions. In several recommendations from the CoE and the EU, multilingualism is identified as an asset for Europe. Ever since the formation of the European Economic Community, multilingualism has been at the heart of the European project, although not always in an explicit sense. Indeed for some years the European Community refrained from developing an overt language policy at Community level or from intervening in areas of language learning or teaching, which were considered to be exclusively the responsibility of the member states. The EU took a neutral stand in formulating policies promoting multilingualism because the balance between the EU policies and sovereign national applications is a highly sensitive matter. On the whole, the EU adopted institutional multilingualism by granting equal status to its official languages, and by developing specific policy formulations on languages that are deemed to be equal in linguistic and cultural terms. The aim was promoting unity in diversity, social cohesion and better understanding between peoples. Believing in freedom of language use and language choice in the national and international European context, the EU promoted cultural and linguistic diversity.

The European Union took some measures and issued a number of legislations to promote multilingualism. In the 1980s, the focus was on the provisions for lesser used minority languages. With the introduction of mobility programmes in the European Union, programs like *Erasmus* for Higher Education in 1987 and *Lingua* in the area of foreign language education in 1989 were implemented. Since then, the EU has taken highly progressive steps to develop multilingualism policies. The implementation has not always been successful but at least on the policy level the right measures were taken. While the European Union and the Council of Europe provide guidance and point out the value of multilingualism, the national policy and practice might diverge because of the national and local conditions. It is important to distinguish between what stake holders in the society think, regarding what is good for the society, and what types of policy decisions they make.

1. Investigating European policies on multilingualism

The findings reported in this paper are derived from Language Rich Europe project, which was carried out in 24 countries and regions in Europe. The investigation of multilingual practices in 24 different countries and regions is not an easy task because multilingualism is a very complex topic. Each community is organized in different ways and institutional culture in each society is different. We had 24 different countries/regions in LRE project. Each of these countries has their unique historical characteristics and societal conditions. Developing a common yardstick to measure multilingualism in these 24 different countries/ regions is a huge challenge in itself. Our point of reference had to be the same across all the national contexts. In this project, rather than focusing on value judgments, opinions or individual political views, we took European documents on multilingualism as our point of reference. In various language use domains, we identified the benchmarks as highlighted in the European recommendations. Our yardstick is derived from the European documents and recommendations on multilingualism. In spite of the challenges involved in the comparison of policies and practices for multi/plurilingualism in different national or regional contexts, comparative data presented in the Language Rich Europe (LRE) study provides a rich source of cross-national insights. Leaving aside the degree of recognition of multi/plurilingualism, there are multi/plurilingual policies and practices in all 24 countries/regions surveyed, with many European Union (EU) and Council of Europe's (CoE) recommendations being followed.

Linguistic diversity is a key property of Europe's identity, and both the EU Institutions based in Brussels and the Council of Europe based in Strasbourg have been active in promoting language learning and multilingualism/plurilingualism. The major language policy agencies in these two institutions are the Unit for Multilingualism Policy within the Directorate-General of Education and Culture in the

European Commission and the Language Policy Unit of the Directorate of Education in the Council of Europe. The work done by these agencies underpins the important resolutions, charters and conventions produced by the respective bodies.

Within the EU, language policy is the responsibility of individual Member States. EU institutions play a supporting role in this field, based on the 'principle of subsidiarity'. Their role is to promote co-operation between the Member States and to promote the European dimension in national language policies. Within the three constituent bodies of the EU, that is the Council of the European Union, the European Commission (EC), and the European Parliament, multilingualism has been a key area of focus for a number of years. The EU language policies aim to protect linguistic diversity and promote knowledge of languages, for reasons of cultural identity and social integration, but also because multilingual citizens are better placed to take advantage of the educational, professional and economic opportunities created by the integrated Europe. Multilingualism policy is guided by the objective set by the Council of the EU in Barcelona in 2002 to improve the mastery of basic skills, in particular by teaching at least two additional languages from a very early age. This in turn had built on the seminal 1995 *White Paper* on Teaching and Learning, which advocated that everyone should learn two European languages. 'European' was removed in later documents. In addition, Barcelona called for the establishment of a language competence indicator.

The Council of Europe's (CoE) mission is to promote human rights, parliamentary democracy and the rule of law. These core values underpin its actions in all areas, including language policy which draws on three distinct but complementary dimensions of the organisation's work: conventions, recommendations, and technical instruments. The European Cultural Convention encourages states to support the study of each other's languages, history and civilisation. The European Social Charter ensures the right of migrant workers and their families to learn the language(s) of the receiving state and supports the teaching of the migrant worker's mother tongue to the children of the migrant worker. Two CoE conventions are directly concerned with European standards to promote and safeguard linguistic diversity and language rights – the *European Charter for Regional or Minority Languages* and the *Framework Convention for the Protection of National Minorities*. The Charter is a cultural instrument designed to protect and promote regional or minority languages as a threatened aspect of Europe's cultural heritage. It provides for specific measures to support the use of this category of languages in education and the media, and to permit their use in judicial and administrative settings, economic and social life and cultural activities. The Framework Convention specifies the conditions necessary for persons belonging to national minorities to maintain and develop their culture, and to preserve the essential elements of their identity, namely their religion, language, traditions and cultural heritage. The states which have ratified these conventions are monitored with regard to their fulfilment of the commitments they have undertaken.

In spite of the ideology and the policy, what happens in real life is always very complex. The gap between European legislations and the Member State policies might be too large. In order to find out the extent of convergence and/or divergence between EU recommendations and the Member State policies, a large-scale European project has been conducted. In this section, some of the aims, methodology and results of Language Rich Europe project are presented.

2. Language Rich Europe Project

The findings reported in this article are derived from Language Rich Europe project, which is co-financed by the British Council and the European Commission to promote knowledge sharing about good policy and practice in language learning and teaching across Europe. The project evolved as a result of the (1) need to exchange good practices in enhancing intercultural dialogue and social inclusion through language learning and teaching; (2) the need for greater European cooperation on improving language policies and practices; and (3) the lack of awareness of Council of Europe and European Commission recommendations on language policies and practices for promoting language learning and linguistic diversity and the member states' performance against them. Through a large network of experts and partners from 24 different countries and regions, we have conducted an analysis of language policies and practices in Europe, comparing them against selected European Commission and Council of Europe recommendations. The project is co-financed by the European Commission under its Lifelong Learning Programme. It is managed by the British Council with supervision from a steering group made up of partner organisations. Over 30 partners from across Europe are involved in the project, contributing both funding and expertise. The research has been led by the Babylon Centre for the Study of Superdiversity at Tilburg University. The survey covers 15 EU member states: Austria, Bulgaria, Denmark, Estonia, France, Greece, Hungary, Italy, Lithuania, the Netherlands, Poland, Portugal, Romania, Spain and the United Kingdom – plus Bosnia and Herzegovina, Switzerland and Ukraine. In Spain, additional research was done for Catalonia and the Basque Country. In the UK, research was done separately for England, Scotland, Wales and Northern Ireland. In the Netherlands additional research was conducted in Friesland. The results are published as an official project report, *Trends in Policies and Practices for Multilingualism in Europe*, edited by Guus Extra and Kutlay Yagmur and published in 18 European national and regional languages plus in Turkish and Arabic as major immigrant languages in Europe by Cambridge University Press. (G. Extra and K. Yagmur 2012). Given the space limitations, only the findings related to 'languages in official documents and databases' and 'languages in pre-primary, primary and secondary education' are addressed in this paper.

2.1 Design of the investigation

In designing the LRE questionnaire for our survey, we drew on the key EU and CoE resolutions, conventions, recommendations and communications that have contributed to the development of policies and practices for multi/plurilingualism. In the project our ambition is to reflect the richness of languages present in European society and the extent to which all of these languages are included in policies and practices for multilingualism. Our challenge was to distinguish the language types and categorise them appropriately. In its 2008 Communication, the EC refers to the many 'national, regional, minority and migrant' languages spoken in Europe 'adding a facet to our common background' and also 'foreign languages', used to refer principally to both European and non-European languages with a worldwide coverage. The value of learning the national language well in order to function successfully in society and benefit fully from education is widely recognised. The learning of foreign languages has also been common in Europe. The language types which have been less emphasised are regional/minority and immigrant languages, but their value across the European Member States has been acknowledged and supported by both the CoE and the EU, which have emphasised that both types of languages need to be supported as they are an important means of intragroup communication and are a part of the personal, cultural and social identity of many EU citizens. In the context of the LRE project, we therefore explore and use the following language types and definitions.

National languages: Official languages of a nation-state.

Foreign languages: Languages that are not learnt or used at home but learnt and taught at school or used as languages of wider communication in non-educational sectors.

Regional or minority languages: Languages that are traditionally used within a given territory of a state by nationals of that state who form a group numerically smaller than the rest of the state's population.

Immigrant languages: Languages spoken by immigrants and their descendants in the country of residence, originating from a range of (former) source countries.

In the context of the Language Rich Europe project, we consider regional/minority languages as 'officially recognised' if such recognition derives from the nation-state under consideration. In addition to this, such recognition may also derive from the Council of Europe's European Charter for Regional or Minority Languages. The Charter came into operation in March 1998. It functions as a European benchmark for the comparison of legal measures and facilities of the Member States in this policy domain (M. NicCraith 2003), and is aimed at the protection and promotion of 'the historical regional or minority languages of Europe.' The concepts of 'regional' and 'minority' languages are not specified in the Charter ('States decide on the definition') and immigrant languages are explicitly excluded from it. The states are free in their choice of which regional/minority languages to include. Also, the degree of protection is not prescribed; thus, a state can choose loose or tight policies. The result is a wide variety of provisions across the EU Member States (F. Grin 2003).

2.2 Language domains addressed in the survey

Eight language domains are covered by the LRE survey. As the first domain, we include a meta-domain which looks at the availability of official national/regional documents and databases on language diversity. Given the key role of language learning in education, four domains focus on the main stages of publicly funded education from pre-school to university. In addition, three language domains outside and beyond education are addressed, in order to capture levels of multilingual services in society and business. All in all, the eight domains of the questionnaire are covered by a total of 260 questions, distributed across these domains as outlined in Table 1. The questions on language domains 2–8 are based on the European documents.

Table 1: Distribution of questions across language domains

	Language domains	N questions
1	Languages in official documents and databases	15
2	Languages in pre-primary education	34
3	Languages in primary education	58
4	Languages in secondary education	60
5	Languages in further and higher education	30
6	Languages in audiovisual media and press	14
7	Languages in public services and spaces	31
8	Languages in business	18
Total number of questions		260

The first domain explores the availability of nationwide or regional official documents and databases on language diversity in each of the participating countries/regions. The availability of such documents and databases may contribute significantly to the awareness of multilingualism in a given country/region and can inform language education policy. The division of this domain into official documents and databases is closely related to the common distinction in studies on language planning between status planning and corpus planning. In our study, the section on documents refers to efforts undertaken to regulate the use and function of different languages in a given society, and the section on databases refers to efforts undertaken to map the distribution and vitality of the spectrum of languages in a given society. Domains 2–4 of the survey focus on education for non-adult learners provided by the state. These domains include primary, lower and upper secondary education which may refer to age-related differences and/or differences related to type of schooling. In each of these domains, the organisation of language teaching is addressed in addition to the qualifications and training of teachers, for each of the four language varieties. The key distinction between organisations versus teachers is widely used in the European context (see, for example, Eurydice 2008). The responses in these sections are based on publicly available data as well as they come from official sources.

3. Research methodology

Various research methodologies can be chosen to investigate language policies and practices in a given society. In line with their research interests, researchers can take a micro-sociolinguistic or a macro-sociolinguistic perspective to document relevant policies and practices (J. Fishman and O. Garcia 2010). If the research is limited to case studies with few informants, researchers mostly opt for ethnographic observation and discourse-analytic approaches. Linguistic ethnography (M. Heller 2007) is one common methodology to investigate how and in which language people interact with each other. Linguistic ethnographers try to understand how people make use of their available linguistic resources in interacting with other individuals.

However, ethnographic methods cannot always be optimal in the investigation of language policies and practices at the societal level. The main focus of the LRE project is on societal multilingualism and in particular on institutional policies and practices promoting (or limiting) multilingualism. The methodology adopted for the LRE project was therefore to gather survey data on common language policies and practices in a variety of language domains in given national or regional contexts across Europe. The questionnaire for the survey was compiled by studying the main EU and CoE documents on language policies and practices described above and pulling out the key recommendations. However, given the fact that language policies and practices across Europe are a very complex phenomenon, it is not always possible to identify all the relevant variables, operationalise them and turn them into measurable constructs.

In terms of questionnaire construction, the following prerequisites for constructing questions were followed:

- each question should yield rateable data
- rateable data should be weighted, leading to differentiation of reported policies and practices
- yes/no-questions where one of the answers would predictably lead to 100% scores should be avoided
- the questions should be robust enough for repeated measurement over time.

Most commonly, each question had three response options and researchers had to select the option which was the closest to reality in terms of common policy or practice in their country/region. Each choice was given a score. The highest score for each question corresponds to the policy or practice which is most closely aligned with EU/CoE recommendations. Accumulated scores for each domain and sub-domain were turned into percentages so that countries could be compared to each other.

4. Key findings of LRE Project

In spite of the challenges involved in the comparison of policies and practices for multilingualism in different national or regional contexts, the comparative data presented in this study provide a rich source of cross-national insights. Leaving aside the degree of recognition of multi/plurilingualism, there are multi/plurilingual policies and practices in all 24 countries/regions surveyed, with many EU and CoE recommendations being followed. Below, due to space limitations, only the key findings for multilingualism in the educational domain have been summarized.

4.1 Languages in official documents and databases

Legislation on national and R/M languages is provided in almost all countries/regions, on foreign languages in 14 countries/regions, and on immigrant languages in only six countries/regions. Official language policy documents on the promotion of national and foreign languages are available in almost all countries/regions, on R/M languages in 18 countries/regions and on immigrant languages in only four countries/regions. The European Charter for Regional or Minority Languages (ECRML) has been ratified by Parliament in 11 out of the 18 countries surveyed, and signed by governments in France and Italy. It has been neither signed nor ratified by Bulgaria, Estonia, Greece, Lithuania and Portugal.

The largest numbers of officially offered R/M languages in education emerge in South-Eastern and Central European countries. In Western Europe, Italy and France are the clearest exceptions to this general rule, as they offer a wide variety of languages. The concepts of "regional" or "minority" languages are not specified in the ECRML but immigrant languages are explicitly excluded from it. In Western European countries, immigrant languages often have a more prominent appearance than R/M languages but enjoy less recognition, protection and/or promotion.

4.2 Languages in pre-primary education

Many EU and CoE documents underline the importance of early language learning. At pre-primary level, 14 of the 24 countries/regions surveyed provide additional support in the national language for all children funded by the state. The Netherlands and Ukraine devote the most time to this. Foreign-language provision at this level is offered by nine countries or regions: Bosnia and Herzegovina, the Basque Country, Bulgaria, Catalonia, Estonia, Spain and Ukraine, although it may be partly or fully funded by parents/guardians. English, French and German are the most common languages offered.

R/M languages are offered by 17 countries/regions, and are mainly funded by the state/region. In some countries there are minimum group size requirements to form a group. The widest variety of languages is offered in Austria, Hungary, Italy, Romania and Ukraine. Provision in immigrant languages in pre-primary education is not yet very common. However, in spite of the difficulties involved in identifying appropriate teachers and learning materials, three countries (Denmark, Spain and Switzerland) do offer support to very young children for the maintenance and development of their languages and cultures of origin. In Denmark national, regional and local funds cover all costs for these programmes, while in Spain and Switzerland source-country-related funds partly cover the costs through bilateral agreements. The only country offering early language learning across all language types is Spain.

4.3 Languages in primary education

According to both the EU and CoE, all young European children should learn two languages in addition to the national language(s) of the country in which they reside. In primary education, apart from Italy and Ukraine, all countries/regions offer extra support for newcomers in learning the national language. Apart from Wales, all countries/regions have foreign-language provision in primary education. Denmark and Greece make two foreign languages compulsory, while 18 countries/regions have one compulsory foreign language. In England, Northern Ireland and Scotland, foreign languages are optional. Foreign languages are taught from the first year of primary phase in 12 of the countries surveyed, from the mid-phase in seven, and from the final phase only in the Netherlands, Scotland and Switzerland.

English, French and German emerge as the most commonly taught foreign languages. In many cases, one of these languages is the compulsory subject to be studied by all pupils. Italian, Russian and Spanish are other languages offered either as compulsory or optional foreign languages. Content and Language Integrated Learning (CLIL) is widespread for foreign languages only in Spain, while this approach is being used in 13 other countries or regions, although not systematically. Seven countries/regions report using the Common European Framework of Reference for Languages (CEFR) explicitly in foreign-language learning, although more may base their national standards on its principles and approaches. A1/A2 is the CEFR target for this age group of foreign-language learning.

Apart from Denmark and Estonia, R/M languages are offered in 22 countries/regions. R/M-language classes and lessons in other subjects taught through R/M languages are open to all pupils irrespective of language background in 20 countries/regions, although Bulgaria and Greece only target native speakers of these languages. The offer is rich in a number of countries/regions, with Austria, Bulgaria, Hungary, Italy, Lithuania, Romania and Ukraine offering four or more R/M languages either as subjects or in the majority of cases as a medium of instruction. Twelve countries/regions report widespread CLIL, with another six saying that is used locally.

Only five countries/regions report offering immigrant languages at primary level. These are Austria, Denmark, France, Spain and Switzerland (in the canton of Zurich). In France and Switzerland, immigrant-language classes are open to all pupils, while in Austria, Denmark and Spain they are reserved for native speakers of immigrant languages. France, Spain and Switzerland offer lessons partly in school hours, whereas in the other countries they are offered as extra-curricular activities. Achievement in immigrant languages is not linked to any national, regional or school-based standards, although the development of language skills is monitored in all countries except Austria. Lessons in immigrant languages are fully funded by the state in Austria and Denmark, whereas in France, Spain and Switzerland they are mainly supported by the country of origin. In primary education qualified language teachers are employed to teach languages as follows in the countries/regions surveyed: 16 out of 24 in the national language, 17 out of 22 in R/M languages, 14 out of 23 in foreign languages, and 2 out of 5 in immigrant languages. In Austria, England, France, Italy, the Netherlands, Northern Ireland, Scotland and Switzerland, foreign languages are taught by generally qualified classroom teachers.

Pre-service and in-service training is widespread in most countries/regions except for immigrant languages. A clear area for development in foreign-language teaching is teacher mobility: 9 countries/regions out of 24 report having no support at all in this area, and only Catalonia reports structured teacher mobility programmes. More should be done to stimulate language teachers to spend more time in the country of the language they are teaching to acquire higher-level linguistic and cultural competencies.

4.4 Languages in secondary education

Additional support in the national language is provided for newcomers either before or during mainstream education in 21 countries/regions, with Denmark, Italy and Ukraine reporting no provision. As expected, all countries/regions surveyed offer foreign languages at both lower and upper secondary education. Significant differences emerge, however, in the number of compulsory languages offered, the range of languages, monitoring of language skills, the use of CLIL, and the extent to which the CEFR is used to evaluate the level achieved.

The only countries/regions to make two languages compulsory at both lower and upper secondary level are Austria, Estonia, France, Poland, Portugal and Romania. As expected, attainment targets in line with the CEFR for foreign languages are much better established in secondary schools than primary schools in the participating countries/regions, with 13 of them explicitly stating a level to be achieved. B2 seems to be the commonly agreed level for proficiency in the first foreign language, with B1 for the second. Nineteen countries/regions offer R/M languages within secondary education. The countries/regions not offering R/M language education are Denmark, England, Estonia, Greece and Poland. Seventeen countries/regions monitor the language skills acquired either through national/regional or school-based tests, with only Austria and Italy reporting no monitoring. Austria and Wales set no targets for the standard to be achieved, but all other countries/regions do. All countries/regions offer the languages free of charge to all pupils.

Few countries/regions are making immigrant-language provision available systematically (three in pre-primary and five in primary), and in secondary 8 countries/regions out of the 24 responded positively. These are Austria, Denmark, England, Estonia, France, the Netherlands, Scotland and Switzerland. Full state funding is available for immigrant languages in Austria, Denmark, England, the Netherlands and Scotland. In France and Switzerland funding is provided by the countries of origin of immigrant pupils and in Estonia parents meet the costs. The only countries/regions offering immigrant languages in both primary and secondary education are Austria, Denmark, France and Switzerland.

The most commonly offered foreign languages are English, German and French, although other European languages such as Spanish and Italian are also offered. Some immigrant languages such as Arabic, Croatian, Polish, Russian and Turkish are offered as optional foreign languages, and Arabic and Turkish have a firm status as examination subjects in secondary schools in France and the Netherlands. Russian is offered widely in Eastern European countries either as an R/M language or as a foreign language. As in primary education, CLIL is widespread in the teaching of R/M languages, but much less so in foreign languages, with only France reporting widespread practice, and 14 other countries/regions reporting localised examples.

Foreign-language teachers are well qualified, and only in Estonia and Northern Ireland general classroom teachers teach foreign languages. There is a little more structured support for mobility at secondary level than at primary, with Austria as well as Catalonia reporting that teachers spend a semester abroad as part of their pre-service or in-service development. Another 17 countries/regions encourage and support the mobility of teachers financially, leaving Estonia, France, Italy, Portugal and Romania as countries where teachers are less likely to spend time in a target-language country. In line with the EU and CoE recommendations, foreign-language teachers in most countries are required to have attained a certain proficiency level in the foreign language and this is measured against CEFR levels in eight countries/regions. C1 appears to be the most common level required, although B2 is considered appropriate in the Basque Country.

4.5 Languages in further and higher education

New/primary data was collected directly from the largest 69 Vocational and Education Training (VET) centres in our 67 participating cities: the national language is quite well supported, with 30 out of the 69 VET institutions surveyed offering a wide variety of support programmes in the national language, ranging from basic communication to advanced skills. Twenty-four institutions offer a limited variety of programmes, while 15 of the institutions surveyed offer no support.

Sixty-two of the 69 institutions surveyed offer foreign languages, with 15 reporting that more than four languages are taught, 22 offering three to four languages, and 25 one to two languages. Forty-one institutions offer a wide variety of programmes, from basic language skills to advanced, while 18 offer basic language skills only. Twenty-six institutions align their programmes with the CEFR. Twenty-five institutions offer R/M languages, with 13 fully covering the costs. The countries/regions offering R/M language courses in all three of the VET institutions surveyed are the Basque Country, Catalonia, Hungary, Northern Ireland and Wales. Immigrant languages are only offered in four of the institutions surveyed – one each in Austria, England, Italy and Wales. As expected, English, French, German and Spanish are prominent among foreign languages, with some Russian offered as an R/M language in some countries/regions and a foreign language in others. Arabic is also offered in a number of VET institutions. The main offer for R/M languages is from countries/regions where there is more than one official language. New/primary data was gathered on 65 general/public universities across countries/regions. As is to be expected, all of the targeted European universities in our sample cities provide instruction in the national language because in most cases it is the main language of their student population and it is the official state language. However, in the majority of institutions surveyed other languages can also be used.

The international mobility of students and staff, and the desire to attract a global and diverse student body, appear to be making English the second language of many European universities and many textbooks are also being written in English. A very high number of universities offer language courses to non-language students, as recommended by the European institutions. The offer is wide, with 31 institutions (almost half) giving students the choice of more than four languages. Only eight universities from our sample do not offer non-language students the opportunity to learn other languages. The actual take-up of the courses was beyond the scope of the research. Almost all universities make special efforts to attract international students. A half also report conscious efforts to attract students with an immigrant background at home. Student mobility is supported financially by European universities but only ten of the universities surveyed make mobility programmes compulsory for language students.

Conclusion

The comparative findings presented above highlight some interesting trends in policies and practices for multi/plurilingualism in the European context. While some countries/regions have highly developed policies and practices in specific domains, others need to develop further if they wish to align themselves more closely with European recommendations and create more language-rich societies. Of all the language domains researched, it is in primary and secondary education where most efforts are being made to promote multi/plurilingualism. However, in early language learning, and in the sectors of further and higher education, the media, public services and business, our LRE research findings suggest that the officially declared commitment of European countries/regions to support multi/ plurilingualism still needs to be turned into action plans and practices at the local and institutional level.

Of all the non-national language varieties researched, immigrant languages are the least recognised, protected and/or promoted, in spite of all of the affirmative action at the European level. More attention to languages other than national ones would allow European cities and enterprises to become more inclusive in the context of increasing mobility and migration in Europe. We believe that the findings presented here go beyond the current state of our knowledge with regard to language policies and practices in Europe from three different perspectives: (1) the high number of participating European countries and regions; (2) the broad spectrum of chosen language varieties in the constellation of languages in Europe; and (3) the range of chosen language domains within and beyond education.

While some countries/regions have highly developed policies and practices in specific domains, others need to develop further if they wish to align themselves more closely with European recommendations and create more language-rich societies. Of all the language domains researched, it is in primary and secondary education where most efforts are being made to promote multilingualism. Of all the non-national language varieties researched, immigrant languages are the least recognised, protected and/or promoted, in spite of all affirmative action at the European level. The largest numbers of officially offered R/M languages in education emerge in South-Eastern and Central European countries. In Western Europe, Italy and France are the clearest exceptions to this general rule, as they offer a wide variety of languages. The concepts of 'regional' or 'minority' languages are not specified in the ECRML but immigrant languages are explicitly excluded from it. In Western European countries, immigrant languages often have a more prominent appearance than R/M languages but enjoy less recognition, protection and/or promotion.

Many EU and CoE documents underline the importance of early language learning. At pre-primary level, 14 of the 24 countries/regions surveyed provide additional support in the national language for all children funded by the state. The Netherlands and Ukraine devote the most time to this. According to both the EU and CoE, all young European children should learn two languages in addition to the national language(s) of the country in which they reside. In primary education, apart from Italy and Ukraine, all countries/regions offer extra support for newcomers or minority groups in learning the national language. Apart from Wales, all countries/regions report foreign language provision in primary education.

Denmark and Greece make two foreign languages compulsory, while 18 countries/ regions have one compulsory foreign language. In England, Northern Ireland and Scotland, foreign languages are optional. English, French and German emerge as the most commonly taught foreign languages. In many cases, one of these languages is the compulsory subject to be studied by all pupils. Italian, Russian and Spanish are other languages offered either as compulsory or optional foreign languages. Finally, the European Union and the Council of Europe have the right policies for promoting linguistic diversity but most member states need to do much more to keep up with the European recommendations.

References

European Commission. 2008. *Communication from the Commission to the European Parliament, the Council, the European Economic and Social Committee, and the Committee of the Regions. Multilingualism: An Asset for Europe and a Shared Commitment.* Brussels: European Communities.

Eurydice/Eurostat. 2008. *Key Data on Teaching Languages at School in Europe.* Brussels-Luxembourg: Eurydice/Eurostat.

Extra, G. and K. Yagmur (Eds.) 2012. *Language Rich Europe: Trends in Policies and Practices for Multilingualism in Europe.* Cambridge: Cambridge University Press.

Fishman, J. and O. Garcia (Eds.) 2010. *Handbook of Language and Ethnic Identity. Disciplinary and Regional Perspectives.* Oxford and New York: Oxford University Press.

Grin, F. 2003. *Language Policy Evaluation and the European Charter for Regional or Minority Languages.* Hampshire: Palgrave Macmillan.

Heller, M. 2007. Bilingualism as ideology and practice. In: M. Heller (Ed.), *Bilingualism: A Social Approach.* Basingstoke: Palgrave. 1–24.

NicCraith, M. 2003. Facilitating or generating linguistic diversity. The European Charter for Regional or Minority Languages. In: Hogan-Brun G. and S. Wolff (Eds.), *Minority Languages in Europe. Frameworks, Status, Prospects.* Hampshire: Palgrave Macmillan. 56–72.

Eugen Zaretsky
(University Hospital of Frankfurt/Main, Germany)
Benjamin P. Lange
(Julius Maximilian University of Würzburg, Germany)

The Geography of Language Skills and Language(-Related) Disorders: A Case of Frankfurt/Main

Introduction

Children's language skills have been shown to be influenced by or at least correlated with numerous social and sociolinguistic variables (e.g. E. A. Cartmill *et al.* 2013; C. Letts *et al.* 2013; M. S. Schmid and E. Dusseldorp 2010; C. L. Taylor *et al.* 2013; M. S. C. Thomas *et al.* 2013). For instance, socioeconomic status (SES) is associated with language development in such a way that a low SES is correlated with worse language skills (C. Letts *et al.* 2013; M. S. C. Thomas *et al.* 2013).

Such social factors are not equally distributed among residential areas or districts in (big) cities. Accordingly, it is documented that the respective districts as well as related variables, such as the so-called residential segregation, are correlated with, for instance, income and education (L. Sager 2012).

It may thus not surprise that also the residential area or district in which a child grows up is associated with its development (E. Sellström and S. Bremberg 2006) and thus possibly its language skills as well. Indeed, children growing up in troubled areas demonstrate lower language skills than children from other areas. For instance, it was found that immigrant children growing up in neighbourhoods with fewer co-ethnics have more advanced language skills than those living in other districts (V. Rydland, V. Grøver, J. Lawrence 2014). In accordance, as was shown in E. Zaretsky and B. P. Lange (2015a), the distribution of the following sociolinguistic characteristics in Frankfurt/Main districts (Germany) was not a matter of chance for one of the samples of preschoolers used in this study (sample S2, see Methods): immigration background, whether the child attends a daycare centre for half a day or a full day, whether the child attended a nursery school in the first two years of life, whether the child has relatives with "problems with reading and writing" in the family, how much German is spoken at home (only German, German and (an)other language(s), only (an)other language(s)), stuttering, hoarseness, parents' educational level and German skills, whether the child needs additional educational or medical help in acquiring German, and length of daycare centre attendance in months.

The current study aimed at an examination of associations between demographic characteristics of Frankfurt districts and sociolinguistic characteristics of children who lived there. It was hypothesized that both favourable and unfavourable conditions of the language acquisition tend to cluster but that they cannot pre-determine completely the language competence. Therefore, moderate or weak correlation coefficients between total scores of language tests and characteristics of districts were expected. District-related variables might only be correlates of language skills, that is, not necessarily causally related to them. As such, districts are correlated with social variables, such as SES, with these variables being the ones actually associated with or even influencing language development.

1. Methods

Two samples of German preschoolers were analyzed retrospectively for this study (see Table 1). The samples differed in terms of age and tests used. Also, in the first test sample (S1) only children attending daycare centres were tested, whereas in the second test sample (S2) all children participated who were invited to pass the school enrolment examination in the local public health department. In both cases, written informed consent had to be signed by parents prior to the study participation, which means that the samples were not totally unselected. The same linguistic domains were assessed in both samples.

Table 1: Samples used in the study

	Sample 1 (S1)	Sample 2 (S2)
N	1100	802
Age range (months)	36–89	60–99
Average age (months)	53	71
Boys	605 (55%)	422 (53%)
Girls	495 (45%)	380 (47%)
Monolingual Germans	435 (39%)	287 (36%)
Bi-/multilingual children	631 (57%)	507 (64%)

	Sample 1 (S1)	Sample 2 (S2)
Tests	Modified, validated version of the "Marburger Sprachscreening" (MSSb; H. A. Euler *et al.* 2010, K. Neumann *et al.* 2011): speech comprehension, vocabulary, grammar, articulation, phonological short-term memory: repetition of sentences and nonce words	AWST-R (vocabulary; C. Kiese-Himmel 2005), ETS 4–8 (grammar, speech comprehension; M. J. W. Angermaier 2007), S-ENS (articulation, phonological short-term memory: repetition of words and sentences; M. Döpfner *et al.* 2005)
Questionnaires	For parents and daycare center teachers	For parents

In S1, languages spoken at home could not be identified for 34 children, in S2 for 11 children. The questionnaire items in S1 and S2 were not identical but comparable. The data originate in studies on language assessment and were taken "as it is", without additional data collection. No exclusion criteria were applied in the original studies except inappropriate age.

Most children were classified by a group of university language experts (researchers in clinical linguistics, speech and language pathologists, professors) as needing (ED) or not needing (NED) additional educational help (language courses) in acquiring/learning German and as needing (CLIN) or not needing (NCLIN) medical help (speech-, language-, language-related therapies) in acquiring/learning German. In S1, 382 out of 956 children were classified as ED (40%) and 159 as CLIN (17%). In S2, 174 out of 555 children were classified as ED (31%) and 51 as CLIN (9%). The respective percentages in the target population cannot exactly correspond to those in the samples because both S1 and S2 were not completely unselected. The classification was carried out on the basis of test batteries and audio records of test sessions. Children who were classified as ED usually belonged to the lowest 16% in at least one linguistic domain, children who were classified as CLIN to the lowest 5%.

A total of 47 characteristics of 45 Frankfurt districts were obtained from the official internet page of the city <http://www.frankfurt.de>. The districts were ranked according to their characteristics such as population density, percentage of immigrants, and percentage of unemployed inhabitants. These rankings were correlated (Spearman correlations) with the total scores of correct answers in the language tests and, in one case, with the error patterns of an MSSb plural item to exemplify the associations of error patterns with demographic characteristics of districts. Associations of the error patterns with children's sociolinguistic characteristics have already been discussed for test subjects from S1 in another study (E. Zaretsky and B. P. Lange 2014).

Next, differences in total scores of correct answers in Frankfurt districts were compared for both samples. In comparisons of more than two independent variables such as Frankfurt districts, Kruskal-Wallis H test was utilized. Only districts with at least 20 study participants were considered. Five districts where the best German was spoken were identified both for S1 and S2 by a simple ranking of averaged language test total scores.

Sociolinguistic characteristics of children who lived in the best five districts, that is, districts with the highest language test scores, were compared to those of children in all other districts (with Ns ≥ 20) by means of cross-tables (Chi-square and linear-by-linear association *lbl*) and Mann-Whitney U tests. The sample sizes varied both in S1 and S2 depending on how many parents answered the questions and on how many children were able to complete the test.

2. Results

Spearman correlations between demographic characteristics of Frankfurt districts and children's total scores of correct answers in the language tests can be found in Table 2. Because some researchers consider correlations below |.1| negligible (J. Cohen 1988), correlations of $r_s \geq |.1|$ were marked bold.

The distribution of error patterns in the answers of children from different districts was exemplified for S1 by the plural item *Ball-Bälle* 'ball-balls'. Error patterns were subdivided into comparatively simple (repetition of singular form, addition of the most frequent plural marker *-(e)n*, see E. Zaretsky *et al.* 2011.) and comparatively advanced ones (addition of other wrong plural markers). The former received label "1", the latter label "2". Point-biserial correlations between this error classification and the demographic characteristics of the Frankfurt districts yielded a number of significant results, see last column in Table 2.

Also, total scores of correct answers in the language tests differed significantly according to the Kruskal-Wallis H test: $\chi_{(25)} \geq 42.94$ (Sample 1, Ns between 764 and 851), $\chi_{(15)} \geq 25.95$ (Sample 2, Ns between 382 and 497), ps < .05. In S1, the highest total scores of the language tests were registered in the districts Bergen-Enkheim, Eschersheim, Nordend-West, Dornbusch, and Bornheim. In S2, the best German skills were identified for the districts Sachsenhausen Süd, Ostend, Nordend-West, Bergen-Enkheim, and Eschersheim. In both cases, five best districts were chosen according to the highest rankings in the language test scores. As can be seen in the listing of the districts, there are three ones (Bergen-Enkheim, Eschersheim, and Nordend-West) that are constantly among the ones where the best German language skills could be found. The characteristics of children who lived in the best five districts were analyzed in the next step.

Table 2: Correlations between rankings of Frankfurt districts according to their demographic characteristics and (a) total scores of correct answers in the language tests MSSb, AWST-R, S-ENS, ETS 4–8 (Ns between 554 and 1031), (b) simple and advanced error patterns with the plural item Ball-Bälle (Ns between 283 and 317). Correlations ≥ |.1| marked bold

Frankfurt district characteristics	Vocabulary (r_s)		Grammar		Speech comprehension		Repetition of nonce words		Repetition of sentences		Articulation		Ball-Bälle (r_{pb})
	S1	S2	S1	S2	S1	S2	S1	S2	S1	S2	S1	S2	S1
% of the employed	.17#	.19#	.20#	.18#	.09‡	.19#	.11‡	n. s.	.19#	.18#	n. s.	n. s.	n. s.
% of the unemployed	-.18#	-.28#	-.22#	-.24#	-.10‡	-.27#	-.09‡	n. s.	-.19#	-.23#	-.08*	n. s.	-.12*
% of the unemployed (SGB III)	-.07*	-.23#	-.10‡	-.18#	n. s.	-.20#	n. s.	n. s.	-.11‡	-.17#	-.08*	n. s.	n. s.
% of the unemployed (SGB II)	-.18#	-.28#	-.22#	-.23#	-.10‡	-.26#	-.09‡	n. s.	-.19#	-.23#	-.08*	n. s.	-.12*
% of the unemployed men	-.16#	-.28#	-.20#	-.24#	-.09‡	-.26#	-.07*	n. s.	-.17#	-.23#	-.07*	n. s.	-.13*
% of the unemployed women	-.20#	-.27#	-.25#	-.23#	-.11*	-.27#	-.10‡	n. s.	-.22#	-.23#	-.09‡	n. s.	n. s.
% of the unemployed Germans	-.19#	-.29#	-.23#	-.24#	-.12*	-.27#	-.10‡	n. s.	-.21#	-.24#	-.08*	n. s.	-.14*
% of the unemployed foreigners	-.15*	-.22#	-.18#	-.18#	-.06*	-.22#	-.07*	n. s.	-.14*	-.19#	-.07*	n. s.	n. s.
% of recipients of basic social help for the unemployed	-.21#	-.28#	-.26#	-.23#	-.11#	-.28#	-.10‡	n. s.	-.22#	-.25#	-.09‡	n. s.	n. s.
% of recipients of basic social help for poor senior citizens	-.10‡	-.26#	-.12*	-.18#	-.09‡	-.20#	n. s.	n. s.	-.10‡	-.17#	-.07*	n. s.	n. s.
% of recipients of subsistence grants	-.11‡	-.26#	-.14*	-.20#	-.09‡	-.20#	n. s.	n. s.	-.11‡	-.18#	-.07*	n. s.	-.12*
% of recipients of subsistence grants for senior and disabled citizens	-.09‡	-.25*	-.11‡	-.18#	-.09‡	-.21*	n. s.	-.07*	-.10‡	-.17#	-.07*	n. s.	n. s.
living area per person (m$_2$)	.22#	.26#	.26#	.20#	.13*	.26#	.10‡	n. s.	.23#	.21#	.09‡	n. s.	.13*
average gross salary	.18#	.23#	.23#	.19#	.09‡	.23#	.10‡	n. s.	.21#	.21#	.07*	n. s.	n. s.
% of minijobbers	-.19#	-.20#	-.23#	-.16#	-.11*	-.22#	-.12*	n. s.	-.22#	-.20#	-.09‡	n. s.	n. s.
% of the employed in the service sector	n. s.	n. s.	n. s.	n. s.	n. s.	n. s.	n. s.	n. s.	n. s.	n. s.	n. s.	n. s.	n. s.

Frankfurt district characteristics	Vocabulary (r_s)		Grammar		Speech comprehension		Repetition of nonce words		Repetition of sentences		Articulation		Ball-Bälle (r_{pb})
	S1	S2	S1	S2	S1	S2	S1	S2	S1	S2	S1	S2	S1
private cars per inhabitant	n. s.	.11‡	n. s.	n. s.	n. s.	n. s.	n. s.	n. s.	n. s.	n. s.	n. s.	n. s.	n. s.
% of inhabitants under 18	n. s.	n. s.	n. s.	n. s.	n. s.	-.10*	-.12#	n. s.	-.12#	-.11‡	-.10‡	n. s.	n. s.
average age	.14#	.14‡	.17#	.10*	-.09‡	.10*	n. s.	n. s.	.16#	.13#	n. s.	n. s.	.14*
% of people living alone	n. s.	n. s.	n. s.	n. s.	n. s.	n. s.	n. s.	n. s.	.08*	n. s.	-.07*	n. s.	-.12
% of lone parents	-.12#	-.13‡	-.13#	n. s.	n. s.	-.14‡	n. s.	n. s.	-.12#	-.16#	n. s.	n. s.	n. s.
number of people per household	-.09‡	n. s.	-.10‡	n. s.	n. s.	n. s.	-.08*	n. s.	-.11‡	n. s.	n. s.	n. s.	n. s.
population density per hectare	n. s.	n. s.	n. s.	n. s.	n. s.	n. s.	.08*	n. s.	.08*	n. s.	n. s.	.08*	-.16‡
% of families with children	-.09‡	n. s.	-.10‡	n. s.	-.08*	-.08*	-.07*	n. s.	-.11‡	-.08*	n. s.	n. s.	n. s.
% of families with 3+ children	-.18#	-.13‡	-.19#	-.10*	-.08*	-.18#	-.10‡	n. s.	-.19#	-.15#	-.08*	n. s.	n. s.
% of daycare center children who attend daycare centers for 7+ hours	.13#	n. s.	.11‡	n. s.	.06*	.12‡	.07*	n. s.	.12#	n. s.	n. s.	n. s.	n. s.
% of children who spoke German age-appropriately in the school enrolment test	.07*	n. s.	n. s.	.18#	n. s.	.09*	n. s.	.09*	n. s.	.11‡	n. s.	n. s.	n. s.
% of children who attended grammar schools	.13#	.23#	.16#	.18#	.07*	.24#	n. s.	n. s.	.15#	.23#	n. s.	n. s.	n. s.
% of foreigners	-.19#	-.27#	-.23#	-.24#	-.12‡	-.23#	-.09‡	n. s.	-.21#	-.20#	-.08*	-.09*	-.19‡
% of Germans with immigration background	-.19#	-.22#	-.22#	-.16#	-.11*	-.23#	-.12#	n. s.	-.20#	-.17#	-.08*	n. s.	n. s.
% of daycare center children with immigration background of at least one parent	-.19#	-.29#	-.23#	-.25#	-.12#	-.27#	-.09‡	n. s.	-.22#	-.23#	-.08*	n. s.	-.14*
% of daycare center children who speak predominantly foreign language(s)	-.17#	-.28#	-.22#	-.24#	-.13#	-.26#	-.10‡	n. s.	-.22#	-.24#	-.07*	n. s.	-.15‡

Frankfurt district characteristics	Vocabulary		Grammar		Speech comprehension		Repetition of nonce words		Repetition of sentences		Articulation		Ball-Bälle
	S1 (r_s)	S2	S1	S2	S1	S2	S1	S2	S1	S2	S1	S2	S1 (r_{pb})
% of native Germans from all children under the age of 5	.19#	.30#	.23#	.27#	.12#	.29#	.11‡	n. s.	.24#	.25#	.08‡	n. s.	.16‡
% of native Germans among primary pupils	.16#	.31‡	.20#	.24#	.09‡	.28#	n. s.	n. s.	.18#	.25#	n. s.	n. s.	.17‡
% of Greeks among immigrants	n. s.	n. s.	n. s.	-.11*	n. s.	n. s.	n. s.	n. s.	n. s.	n. s.	n. s.	n. s.	-.14‡
% of Turks among immigrants	-.13#	-.21#	-.18#	-.15#	n. s.	-.23#	-.10‡	n. s.	-.17#	-.20#	-.07*	n. s.	n. s.
% of inhabitants from Turkey among foreigners	-.08*	-.09*	-.10‡	n. s.	n. s.	-.15#	-.08*	n. s.	-.11‡	-.11‡	n. s.	n. s.	n. s.
% of Turkish citizens among foreigners	-.12#	-.21#	-.17#	-.15#	n. s.	-.23#	-.09*	n. s.	-.16#	-.20#	-.06#	n. s.	n. s.
% of inhabitants from Russia among foreigners	n. s.	n. s.	n. s.	.09*	n. s.	n. s.	n. s.	n. s.	.07*	n. s.	n. s.	n. s.	.13*
% of EU-foreigners among all foreigners	.10‡	.16#	.11‡	.09*	n. s.	.17#	n. s.	.08*	.09‡	.14#	.06#	n. s.	n. s.
% of Europeans among foreigners	n. s.	.11‡	n. s.	.09*	n. s.	.10*	n. s.	n. s.	n. s.	n. s.	n. s.	n. s.	n. s.
% of Italians among foreigners	.12*	.17#	.15#	.14‡	.11‡	.12‡	.09‡	n. s.	.11‡	.08*	.09‡	n. s.	n. s.
% of Africans among foreigners	-.18#	-.25#	-.21#	-.19#	-.10‡	-.26#	-.078*	n. s.	-.19#	-.21#	-.11‡	n. s.	n. s.
% of Asians and Australians among foreigners	n. s.	n. s.	n. s.	n. s.	n. s.	n. s.	n. s.	n. s.	n. s.	n. s.	n. s.	n. s.	n. s.
% of Americans among foreigners	.18#	.21#	.22#	.18#	.09‡	.22#	.10‡	n. s.	.21#	.19#	n. s.	n. s.	n. s.
number of foreign citizenships	n. s.	n. s.	n. s.	-.19#	n. s.	n. s.	n. s.	n. s.	n. s.	n. s.	n. s.	n. s.	n. s.
total number of significant results	36	34	35	33	27	37	28	3	39	35	26	2	16

#p < .001, ‡p < .01, *p < .05, n. s. = not significant, S1 = Sample 1, S2 = Sample 2, r_s = Spearman correlation, r_{pb} = point-biserial correlation, SGB II and SGB III = different kinds of unemployment and corresponding financial aids from the state.

In S1, children from the best five districts had the following characteristics in comparison with children from other districts according to cross-tables and Mann-Whitney U test:

- They were more often monolingual Germans than bi-/multilingual children: $\chi^2_{(1)}$ = 26.35, p < .001, N = 875,
- They spoke out more often during group activities: lbl = 13.01, p < .001, N = 333,
- They liked more often to play with other children: lbl = 5.66, p = .017, N = 335,
- They were less often classified by university language experts as ED ($\chi^2_{(1)}$ = 22.07, p < .001, N = 786) or CLIN ($\chi^2_{(1)}$ = 6.36, p = .012, N = 786),
- They began earlier to learn/acquire German: lbl = 14.22, p < .001, N = 369,
- They suffered less often from language-related diseases, impairments or illnesses: $\chi^2_{(1)}$ = 7.90, p = .005, N = 520.

Also, German skills of children from the best five districts were judged higher by daycare center teachers. According to their questionnaires, children from these districts had the following characteristics:

- They understood more often complicated action instructions: lbl = 8.37, p = .004, N = 371,
- They had more often age-appropriate German skills: lbl = 10.05, p = .002, N = 328,
- Their German could be more often well understood both by children and daycare center teachers: lbl = 10.29, p = .001, N = 333,
- Their articulation was more often age-appropriate: lbl = 13.08, p < .001, N = 331,
- They spoke more often in full sentences: lbl = 11.38, p = .001, N = 334,
- They used articles more often correctly: lbl = 10.81, p = .001, N = 373,
- They stuttered less often: lbl = 4.12, p = .043, N = 367,
- They received better school marks (given by daycare center teachers) for their German skills for the time point when they began to attend the daycare center (lbl = 9.56, p = .002, N = 136) and, marginally significantly, for the time point of testing (lbl = 3.46, p = .063, N = 135),
- Consequently, they participated less often in the language courses (usually offered by daycare centers): $\chi^2_{(1)}$ = 5.89, p = .015, N = 96.

Parents of the children from the best five districts also estimated the German skills of their children significantly higher than parents from other districts: $\chi^2_{(1)}$ = 5.68, p = .017, N = 162.

Children who lived in the five districts where the best German skills were documented in S2 had the following characteristics if compared to children from other districts:

- They were more often monolingual Germans: $\chi^2_{(1)} = 16.18$, $p < .001$, $N = 791$,
- They spoke more often only German at home: $lbl = 24.21$, $p < .001$, $N = 512$,
- They attended more often nursery schools in the first two years of life: $\chi^2_{(1)} = 27.96$, $p < .001$, $N = 496$,
- They had less often relatives with language disorders: $\chi^2_{(1)} = 5.26$, $p = .022$, $N = 519$,
- They spoke more often German age-appropriately according to their parents: $\chi^2_{(1)} = 7.02$, $p = .008$, $N = 474$,
- Their mothers ($lbl = 32.55$, $p < .001$, $N = 504$) and fathers' ($lbl = 25.93$, $p < .001$, $N = 493$) educational level was higher,
- Their mothers ($lbl = 14.45$, $p < .001$, $N = 315$) and fathers' ($lbl = 13.92$, $p < .001$, $N = 298$) German skills in reading and writing were better, estimated by the parents themselves,
- They were less often classified by university language experts as ED ($\chi^2_{(1)} = 21.27$, $p < .001$, $N = 555$) or CLIN ($\chi^2_{(1)} = 5.40$, $p = .020$, $N = 555$),
- Their fathers began earlier to learn/acquire German: $U = 3516$, $Z = -2.66$, $p = .008$, $N = 250$.

Unexpectedly, house numbers of children correlated with their total scores of language tests both in S1 ($r_s = -.09$, $p = .012$, $N = 830$, in MSSb) and S2 ($r_s = -.08$, $p = .049$, $N = 610$, in AWST-R). In other language tests (S-ENS, ETS 4–8) all correlations were also negative, but did not reach statistical significance. It should be mentioned in this respect that according to point-biserial correlations between immigration background and house numbers more immigrants lived in houses with high numbers both in S1 ($r_{pb} = .07$, $p = .035$, $N = 1060$) and S2 ($r_{pb} = .11$, $p = .002$, $N = 792$).

The distribution of children's sociolinguistic characteristics in the Frankfurt districts with Ns $\geq$ 20 in S2 has already been presented in E. Zaretsky and B. P. Lange (2015a) and described in the Introduction. Here, the distribution of sociolinguistic characteristics in Frankfurt districts was analyzed for S1 by means of cross-tables and Kruskal Wallis H tests.

The distribution of the following characteristics was not a matter of chance:

Whether the child speaks German age-appropriately according to the estimation of daycare center teachers ($\chi^2_{(25)} = 51.04$, $p = .002$, $N = 586$) and parents ($\chi^2_{(24)} = 53.27$, $p = .001$, $N = 162$),

- Whether the child attends an association or a study group: $\chi^2_{(25)} = 56.58$, $p < .001$, $N = 526$,

- Whether the child has a chronic hearing disorder according to parents ($\chi^2_{(17)}$ = 31.00, p = .020, N = 115) and does not hear well according to daycare center teachers ($\chi^2_{(25)}$ = 40.91, p = .023, N = 629),
- Whether the child suffers often from otitis media: $\chi^2_{(25)}$ = 32.83, p = .035, N = 154,
- Age when the child began to learn/acquire German: $\chi^2_{(125)}$ = 196.39, p < .001, N = 370,
- Language spoken predominantly at home (German, Turkish, Russian, Italian, Serbian/Croatian, Arabic, Greek, other): $\chi^2_{(175)}$ = 253.82, p < .001, N = 599,
- How much German is spoken at home (only German, German and (an)other language(s), only (an)other language(s)): $\chi^2_{(50)}$ = 114.46, p < .001, N = 727,
- Whether the child has some language-related illness, disorder or impairment both according to parents ($\chi^2_{(25)}$ = 47.19, p = .005, N = 520) and to daycare center teachers ($\chi^2_{(25)}$ = 40.71, p = .025, N = 292).

Compliance in the test situation (good, average, bad) differed significantly in the Frankfurt districts with Ns ≥ 20 in S1 ($\chi^2_{(50)}$ = 76.37, p = .010, N = 786), but not in S2 (p > .05).

3. Discussion

The distribution of German preschoolers' sociolinguistic characteristics in 45 Frankfurt districts was analyzed statistically in this study. To sum up, better German skills were found in the districts with two characteristics:

- Higher income: more employed, less unemployed, higher average gross salary, larger average living area (interestingly, it was a better indicator than the gross salary), less lone parents (possibly because they usually earn less than families with both parents, apart from other unfavorable factors such as less language input), less „minijobbers" (those earning only 450 EUR/month);
- less immigrants (except Italians, generally Europeans, Americans): e.g., a low percentage of foreigners, of Germans with immigration background, of children with immigration background in daycare centers (especially Turks and Africans), a higher average age and less inhabitants under 18 years of age (because Germans have fewer children than immigrants and, consequently, are on average older), less families with children, especially with 3 and more children (for the same reason).

Many of the variables from both categories mentioned above (income, immigration background) are interrelated. As was shown by E. Zaretsky and B. P. Lange (2015b), the percentage of foreigners in the Frankfurt districts yields significant correlations with the percentage of the employed and unemployed, average living area, gross salary, percentage of minijobbers and of people receiving various kinds of financial aid from the state, average age, number of inhabitants under 18 years of age, and families with 3 and more children. So, we are concerned here with a complex setup of numerous potential social factors affecting or being correlated with language development. The district might not directly causally influence language skills. Rather, the district in which people live merely correlates with other factors (e.g., income, percentage of people with immigration background, education, and the like), with these other factors being the ones that actually affect language skills. For instance, the residential segregation of immigrant people in poorer environments might go along with worse educational opportunities that subsequently affect language skills (P. R. Bennett 2011).

In Frankfurt, children with immigration background acquire German under double pressure: first, immigrants tend to cluster in certain areas where a high percentage of inhabitants have a limited command of German and, second, in the same areas the average income is limited. Because the income is related to many other variables associated with the language development (access to the high-quality language courses and therapies, books, sophisticated toys etc.), it demonstrated a statistically significant correlation with the language skills of our test subjects.

The factors being associated with language skills might not always be the same. For instance, we demonstrated here that children in districts with less immigrants have better language skills. This result, however, is not always found (J. M. Froiland *et al.* 2014). The study by J. E. V. Lloyd and C. Hertzman (2010) even suggests that living in a district with a high percentage of immigrant people is not necessarily associated with worse language development. This result might be explained by the fact that a high percentage of people with immigration background leads to the formation of strong social networks with enhanced interaction that is also beneficial for the language skills of the children growing up in these large social groups. So, there is potential here, too, that might be used to support immigrant children of poor language development. Still, our study might not be entirely comparable with those by J. M. Froiland *et al.* (2014) and by J. E. V. Lloyd and C. Hertzman (2010). These studies were carried out using English as the target language in English-speaking countries. But English, contrary to or much more than German, is, as the *lingua franca*, more often spoken by people of immigration background *per se*. For these people, English is not as much a foreign language as German is for many people with immigration background living in Germany. Therefore, one can hardly expect that clustering of immigrants in Germany would result in their better German skills, although clustering of (often English-speaking) immigrants in English-speaking countries sometimes does. On the contrary, a high geographical concentration of immigrants in Germany results in more advanced skills in their (non-German) mother tongue, as was shown by E. Zaretsky and B. P. Lange (2015b) for the Turkish speaking immigrants in Frankfurt.

The sums of significant correlations between demographic characteristics of Frankfurt districts and the total scores of correct answers in language tests/subtests varied considerably both in S1 (26–37) and S2 (2–37). The lowest sums – those for repetition of nonce words and articulation in S2 – indicate, in our opinion, not a weak link between demography and these two linguistic domains but, rather, certain problems with the validation of the language test S-ENS. This is also supported by the fact that, according to S-ENS results, 43% of children from S2 would have been linguistically too weak for the school enrolment, which is a far too high value. It should be also taken into account that the S-ENS subtests were very short in comparison with other language tasks used in this study and, consequently, delivered a less specific, comparatively short range of values. Therefore, the results of other language tests such as AWST-R should not be directly compared to those of S-ENS.

Also, some results were to a certain extent pre-determined by the available statistical information on Frankfurt districts. Among other things, unfortunately, it was not differentiated in the original data between North and South Americans (however, the number of North Americans might be much higher in Frankfurt), and, strangely, between Asians and Australians.

The distribution of German skills measured by total scores of language tests was also uneven between the districts. Children from the districts where the highest values were reached acquired German under comparatively favorable sociolinguistic conditions in respect to the immigration background, parents' educational level and German skills, age of the active contacts to the German language, but, interestingly, they also suffered less often from language-related impairments and stuttered less often. Obviously, due to stratification of test subjects according to the income and immigration background, stratification according to medical issues also took place, which might indicate, as has already been assumed above on the basis of correlation values, that not all German citizens have equal access to the healthcare system. Such factors as better compliance in the test situation, eagerness to play with other children and to speak out during group activities in the five districts where the best German was spoken might have resulted from the better German skills of the children living in these districts in comparison with children from other districts.

The fact that no correlation between demographic characteristics of districts and children's German skills surpassed the level of .4 demonstrates that advances in German are not completely pre-determined by the districts children live in. A somewhat unexpected finding that children's German skills were negatively (very weakly) associated with their house numbers found its explanation in the preference of immigrants to live on very long streets which are usually less prestigious and, consequently, comparatively cheap in respect to both rent costs and price sector of shops and services located there.

To conclude, German preschoolers' sociolinguistic characteristics are indeed associated with the demographic characteristics of the districts they live in, but these associations are predominantly not very strong and children from the comparatively poor districts do have a chance to speak German age-appropriately. Low correlation coefficients regarding such associations indicate that the identified tendencies have many exceptions and do not pre-determine completely children's German language skills. The relation between district characteristics and language skills might be mediated by many social and/or sociolinguistic factors that are the very ones that actually affect language skills after all. As these factors have been identified (see above), there is much potential for interventions in order to support children who demonstrate poor language skills.

References

Angermaier, M. J. W. 2007. *ETS 4–8. Entwicklungstest Sprache für Kinder von 4 bis 8 Jahren*. Frankfurt am Main: Harcourt Test Services GmbH.

Bennett, P. R. 2011. The Relationship between Neighborhood Racial Concentration and Verbal Ability: An Investigation Using the Institutional Resources Model. In: *Social Science Research* 40. 1124–1141.

Cartmill, E. A., B. F. Armstrong, L. R. Gleitman, S. Goldin-Meadow, T. N. Medina and J. C. Trueswell. 2013. Quality of Early Parent Input Predicts Child Vocabulary 3 Years Later. In: *Proceedings of the National Academy of Sciences* 110(28). 11278–11283.

Cohen, J. 1988. *Statistical Power Analysis for the Behavioral Sciences* (2nd ed.). Hillsdale: Erlbaum.

Döpfner, M., Dietmair, I., Mersmann, H., Simon, K. and Trost-Brinkhues G. 2005. *S-ENS. Screening des Entwicklungsstandes bei Einschulungsuntersuchungen*. Göttingen: Hogrefe.

Euler, H. A., Holler-Zittlau, I., Van Minnen, S., Sick, U., Dux, W., Zaretsky, Y. and Neumann, K. 2010. Psychometrische Gütekriterien eines Kurztests zur Erfassung des Sprachstandes vierjähriger Kinder. In: *HNO* 58. 1116–1123.

Froiland, J. M., Powell, D. R. and Diamond, K. E. 2014. Relations among Neighborhood Social Networks, Home Literacy Environments, and Children's Expressive Vocabulary in Suburban At-Risk Families. In: *School Psychology International* 35(4). 429–444.

Kiese-Himmel, C. 2005. AWST-R. Aktiver Wortschatztest für 3- bis 5-jährige Kinder – Revision. Göttingen: Hogrefe.

Letts, C., Edwards, S., Sinka, I., Schaefer, B. and Gibbons, W. 2013. Socio-Economic Status and Language Acquisition: Children's Performance on the New Reynell Developmental Language Scales. In: *International Journal of Language and Communication Disorders* 48(2). 131–143.

Lloyd, J. E. V. and Hertzman, C. 2010. How Neighborhoods Matter for Rural and Urban Children's Language and Cognitive Development at Kindergarten and Grade 4. In: *Journal of Community Psychology* 38(3). 293–313.

Neumann, K., Holler-Zittlau, I., Van Minnen, S., Sick, U., Zaretsky, Y. and Euler, H. A. 2011. Katzengoldstandards in der Sprachstandserfassung. Sensitivität und Spezifität des Kindersprachscreenings (KiSS). In: *HNO* 59. 97–109.

Rydland, V., Grøver, V. and Lawrence, J. 2014. The Second-Language Vocabulary Trajectories of Turkish Immigrant Children in Norway from Ages Five to Ten: The Role of Preschool Talk Exposure, Maternal Education, and Co-Ethnic Concentration in the Neighborhood. In: *Journal of Child Language* 41(2). 352–381.

Sager, L. 2012. Residential Segregation and Socioeconomic Neighbourhood Sorting: Evidence at the Micro-Neighbourhood Level for Migrant Groups in Germany. In: *Urban Studies* 49(12). 2617–2632.

Schmid, M. S. and Dusseldorp, E. 2010. Quantitative Analyses in a Multivariate Study of Language Attrition: The Impact of Extralinguistic Factors. In: *Second Language Research* 26(1). 125–160.

Sellström, E. and Bremberg, S. 2006. The Significance of Neighbourhood Context to Child and Adolescent Health and Well-Being: A Systematic Review of Multilevel Studies. In: *Scandinavian Journal of Public Health* 34. 544–554.

Taylor, C. L., Christensen, D., Lawrence, D., Mitrou, F. and Zubrick, S. R. 2013. Risk Factors for Children's Receptive Vocabulary Development from Four to Eight Years in the Longitudinal Study of Australian Children. In: *PlosOne* 8(9). e73046.

Thomas, M. S. C., Forrester, N. A. and Ronald, A. 2013. Modeling Socioeconomic Status Effects on Language Development. In: *Developmental Psychology* 49(12). 2325–2343.

Zaretsky, E. and Lange, B. P. 2014. Influence of Intra- and Extralinguistic Factors on the Distribution of Plural Allomorphs in German. In: *California Linguistic Notes* 39(1). 73–114.

Zaretsky, E. and Lange, B. P. 2015a. Geolinguistics of Language Competence: A Case of Frankfurt am Main, Germany. Presentation at the Sixth International Symposium on Linguistics. Bucharest. 29–30.5.2015.

Zaretsky, E. and Lange, B. P. 2015b. Soziolinguistische Porträts der größten Gruppen der Vorschulkinder mit Migrationshintergrund in Deutschland. Presentation at the 23. conference *Linguistik- und Literaturtage: „Die Sprachen Mitteleuropas und darüber hinaus".* St. Petersburg. 22–24.6.2015.

Zaretsky, E., Lange, B. P., Euler, H. A. and Neumann, K. 2011. Pizzas, Pizzen, Pizze: Frequency, Iconicity, Cue Validity, and Productivity in the Plural Acquisition of German Preschoolers. In: *ActaLinguistica* 5(2). 22–3.

Authors

Katarina Aladrovic Slovacek is a research fellow at the Faculty of Teacher Education, University of Zagreb, Croatia. Her research interests focus on Croatian as a first language, especially communicative competence in a mother tongue and linguistic creativity in children.

Katja Andersen is a member of the Faculty of Language and Literature, Humanities, Arts and Education at the University of Luxembourg. She is an Associate Professor in Primary Education and specializes in learning and teaching at primary school level with an emphasis on multilingualism and science education. She completed her PhD in 2000 and her postdoctoral degree in 2014. At the University of Luxembourg, she is a member of the research unit Education, Culture, Cognition and Society (ECCS) and a member of the Institute of Applied Educational Sciences (AES). Besides she shares her expertise being a member of editorial boards in international journals.

Aleksandra Bator obtained her Bachelor's degree from the Institute of Applied Linguistics, University of Warsaw. She is interested in multilingual upbringing and education. As part of her teacher training she finished an internship in a bilingual kindergarten, where she was working with children aged three to five. Currently living in London, where she works as a tutor to a three-and-a-half-year-old English boy, introducing him to French as a second language.

Sandro Caruana is a Professor of Italian Language Teaching Methodology. He is the Dean of the Faculty of Education and the Head of Department, Languages and Humanities in Education at the University of Malta. He holds courses in Italian language teaching and learning, Italian Linguistics, Sociolinguistics and intercultural communication. Besides language teaching and Sociolinguistics, his other areas of interest include multilingualism, language attitudes, second language acquisition and the Romance element in Maltese. He has participated in international projects on intercultural communication and language teaching, presented his works at several international conferences and was invited as keynote speaker on a number of occasions.

Wai Meng Chan is an Associate Professor and the Director of the Centre for Language Studies at the National University of Singapore. He earned his Master's degree as well as PhD in German Language and Literature from the German Universities of Würzburg and Kassel, respectively. His research currently focuses on bilingualism and multilingualism, learner autonomy, metacognition, language learning motivation, and the application of new technologies in language learning. He has published several books as well as numerous book chapters and journal articles in these fields. He is also Editor of the peer reviewed Electronic Journal of Foreign Language Teaching, e-FLT, available online at <http://e-flt.nus.edu.sg>, and sits on the editorial boards of two other international journals published in Japan and Germany. In addition, he is Editor of the book series "Studies on Second and Foreign Language Education" published by the international publishing house, De Gruyter Mouton.

Virag Csillagh earned a Master's degree in English Literature and Linguistics from Eotvos Lorand University, Budapest, Hungary where she specialized in Applied Linguistics. She is currently pursuing her PhD at the University of Geneva, Switzerland while working as an Assistant at the English Department. Her main fields of interest include language teaching methodology, research design and cognitive psychology. Her research focuses on the dynamics of language learning motivation as an element of successful acquisition, and its role in the broader framework of language teaching methodology and educational policy making.

Una Cunningham is originally from Northern Ireland and studied at the University of Nottingham in the UK, but came to New Zealand and the University of Canterbury in 2013 as Associate Professor in Learning and Teaching Languages after spending more than 30 years in Sweden as a language and linguistics teacher and lecturer. Her research interests are in technology-enhanced language learning and family bilingualism.

Lidija Cvikic is an Assistant Professor at the Faculty of Teacher Education, University of Zagreb, Croatia. Her research interest focuses on the acquisition of Croatian as a second language, language teaching methodology and e-learning of languages. She has been teaching Croatian as a second language at the University School of Croatian Language and Culture for many years. She also spent two years at the Indiana University, Bloomington, USA as a visiting instructor for the Croatian language.

Kyria Finardi completed her PhD in English and Applied Linguistics and is a Professor in the Department of Languages, Culture and Education and in the Postgraduate Programmes of Linguistics (PPGEL) and Education (PPGE) of the

Federal University of Espirito Santo (UFES) in Brazil. She is currently undertaking her postdoctoral research in the Department of English Language and Literature of the University of Geneva, Switzerland.

Jeanette King teaches Māori language and is an Associate Professor in the School of Māori and Indigenous Studies at the University of Canterbury, where she also leads the bilingualism theme of the New Zealand Institute of Language, Brain and Behaviour. Her research interests include language revitalization, non-verbal cues and sound change over time.

Benjamin P. Lange is a linguist and psychologist conducting his postdoctoral research at the Faculty of Human Sciences, Julius Maximilian University of Würzburg in Germany. Earlier, he worked at the Institute of Medical Psychology and Medical Sociology, University of Göttingen as well as at the Frankfurt University Hospital, Germany. His research interests are, among others, language evolution, language acquisition, and language-related sex differences.

Monika Michałowska got her Bachelor's degree at the Institute of Applied Linguistics, University of Warsaw. Her areas of interest include bilingualism, psycholinguistics and second language acquisition. As part of her teacher training she completed an internship in a secondary school in Germany, where she taught English to the local students. She is currently a student of the Master's interpreting programme at the University of Warsaw.

Jasna Novak Milić is a tenured professor at the Faculty of Social Sciences and Humanities, University of Zagreb. She has recently relocated to Sydney in order to pursue her further research. Her professional interests cover areas of applied linguistics (language acquisition, bilingualism) and aspectology, as well as intercultural education. She has published numerous scholarly articles and book chapters and has taught various courses in linguistics, including Croatian (as a second/foreign language) and Swedish in Croatia, USA (as a Fulbright fellow) and Sweden. She has been a member of the Governing Council since 2014.

Ana Cristina Neves completed her Bachelor's in Modern Languages and Literatures at New University of Lisbon in 1995 obtaining teaching qualifications. She has taught three languages on three different continents: Portuguese, English and German in Africa, Europe and Asia. She worked as a translator specialising in tourism and law and an intercultural mediator. She completed her Master's in Translation at the Johannes Gutenberg University of Mainz in Germany. In 2006 she received a grant from the University of Zurich to study for a PhD in Linguistics and participated in the Swiss National Research Programme *Linguistic Variety and Competence*. Currently she has been working as an Assistant Professor at the University of Saint Joseph in Macau, P. R. C., where she took on the position of coordinator of Studies in Linguistics, Languages and Literatures in 2012. She has been a member of the editorial board of JLSP, Journal of Languages for Specific Purposes since 2014. Her research interests focus on second language acquisition, diglossia, curriculum and teaching material development, language assessment, sociolinguistics and corpus linguistics.

Michał B. Paradowski is an Assistant Professor at the Institute of Applied Linguistics, University of Warsaw, Poland. His interests include issues relating to second and third language acquisition research, cross-linguistic influence, bi- and multilingualism, psycholinguistics, corpus linguistics, and complexity science. Author of numerous book chapters and journal articles including high-IF publications, editor, reviewer for journals and research councils, presenter at conferences, invited speaker in Europe, America, Africa, Eastern, Western and Southeast Asia, teacher and translator trainer, ELT consultant for television. His recent edited volumes are *Teaching Languages off the Beaten Track* (2014) and *Productive Foreign Language Skills for an Intercultural World* (2015).

Stefania Scaglione is an Associate Professor of Linguistics at Università per Stranieri, Perugia, Italy. She holds courses in Sociolinguistics, Language Policy and Planning. Her main areas of research include contact linguistics, language acquisition, language attrition in migration contexts, sociolinguistics of migration; language policies and education, language legislation and linguistic rights. She has coordinated *MERIDIUM* (*Multilingualism in Europe as a Resource for Immigration – Dialogue Initiative Among the Universities of the Mediterranean*), a three-year (2009–2011) network project financed by the European Commission as part of the Life-Long Learning Program (LLLP), key-action 2 (Languages), aimed at providing active support for the promotion of the European policy of pluri-/multilingualism in Southern European countries. Her recent publications include *Lingue e dirittiumani* (2011, edited with Stefania Giannini) and *Migration, Multilingualism and Schooling in Southern Europe* (2013, edited with S. Caruana and L. Coposescu).

Kutlay Yagmur is a Professor of Language, Identity and Education in the Department of Language and Culture Studies, University of Tilburg in the Netherlands. He obtained his Master's degree in Applied Linguistics from Macquarie

University (Australia) and PhD in Applied Linguistics from Radboud University (the Netherlands). In his ongoing project, he investigates the relationship between the integration ideology of the receiving society and the socio-cultural adaptation of immigrants in four national contexts. He has published extensively on language contact issues in Australia, Germany, France and the Netherlands. Next to his many research articles in various International Journals, his co-edited book *Urban Multilingualism. Immigrant Minority Languages at Home and School* (with Guus Extra, Multilingual Matters, 2004) has been a considerable conceptual and methodological contribution to the study of multilingualism. Most recently, he was involved in *Language Rich Europe* Project funded by European Commission and British Council, the findings of which were published by Cambridge University Press and British Council in 2012.

Eugen Zaretsky is currently a researcher (post-doc) at the Department of Phoniatrics and Pediatric Audiology, University of Frankfurt/Main, Germany, where he has been working for six years, with a break of several months which he spent at the University of Bochum, Germany. He graduated from the University of Erlangen-Nuremberg, Germany, in 2008 with a "doctor of philosophy" degree. In the University of Erlangen-Nuremberg, he studied English and German linguistics as well as British and American culture. His research interests are language acquisition, language contact, language and fluency disorders, multilingualism, grammar, and genderlects. He is a chief editor of the journal "Acta Linguistica" (Bulgaria) and an author of two books on language contact and typology.

Warschauer Studien zur Germanistik und zur Angewandten Linguistik

Herausgegeben von Sambor Grucza und Lech Kolago

Band 1   Sambor Grucza: Fachsprachenlinguistik. 2012.

Band 2   Paweł Bąk: Euphemismen des Wirtschaftsdeutschen aus Sicht der anthropozentrischen Linguistik. 2012.

Band 3   Der Mensch und seine Sprachen. Festschrift für Professor Franciszek Grucza. Herausgegeben von Magdalena Olpińska-Szkiełko, Sambor Grucza, Zofia Berdychowska und Jerzy Żmudzki. Unter Mitarbeit von Ewa Bartoszewicz, Monika Płużyczka und Justyna Zając. 2012.

Band 4   Urszula Topczewska: Konnotationen oder konventionelle Implikaturen? 2012.

Band 5   Agnieszka Szarkowska: Forms of Address in Polish-English Subtitling. 2013.

Band 6   Sambor Grucza / Monika Płużyczka / Justyna Zając (eds): Translation Studies and Eye-Tracking Analysis. 2013.

Band 7   Małgorzata Świderska: Theorie und Methode einer literaturwissenschaftlichen Imagologie. Dargestellt am Beispiel Russlands im literarischen Werk Heimito von Doderers. 2013.

Band 8   Justyna Zając: Communication in Global Corporations. Successful Project Management via Email. 2013.

Band 9   Lech Kolago: Die Dichterin Annette von Droste-Hülshoff als Komponistin. Zum Wort-Ton-Verhältnis in ihrem lyrisch-musikalischen Werk. 2013.

Band 10   Ewa Żebrowska: Text – Bild – Hypertext. 2013.

Band 11   Małgorzata Guławska-Gawkowska: Somatische und emotionale Konzepte in der deutschen und polnischen Phraseologie. Ein lexikografischer Ansatz zum phraseologischen Übersetzungswörterbuch. 2013.

Band 12   Martyna Szczygłowska: Übersetzungsfehler. Eine kritische Betrachtung aus der Sicht der anthropozentrischen Translatorik. 2013.

Band 13   Silvia Bonacchi: (Un)Höflichkeit. Eine kulturologische Analyse Deutsch – Italienisch – Polnisch. 2013.

Band 14   Justyna Haas: Erinnerungsliteratur von Jehovas Zeugen als NS-Opfern. 2013.

Band 15   Sambor Grucza / Mariola Wierzbicka / Justyna Alnajjar / Paweł Bąk (Hrsg.): Polnisch-deutsche Unternehmenskommunikation. Ansätze zu ihrer linguistischen Erforschung. 2014.

Band 16   Joanna Albin: The Reflective Translator. Strategies and Affects of Self-directed Professionals. 2014.

Band 17   Katarzyna Grzywka-Kolago: Verzauberte und unverzauberte Welten. Studien zum polnischen und deutschsprachigen Volksmärchen. 2014.

Band 18   Magdalena Olpińska-Szkiełko / Loretta Bertelle (Hrsg.): Zweisprachigkeit und bilingualer Unterricht. 2014.

Band 19   Agata Zofia Mirecka: Max Brods Frauenbilder. Im Kontext der Feminitätsdiskurse einiger anderer Prager deutscher Schriftsteller. 2014.

Band 20   Roman Laskowski: Language Maintenance – Language Attrition. The Case of Polish Children in Sweden. Translated by Łukasz Wiraszka. Edited by Anna Czelakowska. 2014.

Band 21   Maciej Ganczar: Romantische Künstlerfiguren in der Prosa von Peter Härtling. 2015.

Band 22   Sambor Grucza / Justyna Alnajjar (Hrsg.): Kommunikation in multikulturellen Projektteams. 2015.

Band 23   Justyna Alnajjar: Communication Audit in Globally Integrated R&D Project Teams. A Linguistic Perspective. 2016.

Band 24   Sambor Grucza / Magdalena Olpińska-Szkiełko / Piotr Romanowski (eds.): Advances in Understanding Multilingualism: A Global Perspective. 2016.

www.peterlang.com